F.V.

 St. Louis Community College

Forest Park
Florissant Valley
Meramec

Instructional Resources
St. Louis, Missouri

COMMUNISM'S COLLAPSE, DEMOCRACY'S DEMISE?

Communism's Collapse, Democracy's Demise?

The Cultural Context and Consequences of the East German Revolution

Laurence H. McFalls
Assistant Professor of Political Science
Université de Montréal, Canada

NEW YORK UNIVERSITY PRESS
Washington Square, New York

First published in the U.S.A. in 1995 by
NEW YORK UNIVERSITY PRESS
Washington Square
New York, N.Y. 10003

Library of Congress Cataloging-in-Publication Data
McFalls, Laurence H.
Communism's collapse, democracy's demise? : the cultural context
and consequences of the East German revolution / Laurence H.
McFalls.
p. cm.
Includes bibliographical references and index.
ISBN 0-8147-5521-6
1. Communism—Germany (East)—History. 2. Germany (East)-
-Politics and government. 3. Germany (East)—Politics and
government—1989-1990. I. Title.
HX280.5.A6M4 1995
306. 2'09431—dc20   94-20535
                                                      CIP

Printed in Great Britain

Contents

v

Preface

Few of us who watched the Berlin Wall crumble in 1989 would have suspected that within five years of communism's collapse in East Germany, democracy would be in danger in an enlarged Federal Republic of Germany. Yet, at the time of writing, reunited Germany's economy is descending into its worst crisis since 1933; its social order is riven with anomie and racist violence; and its political system is facing its greatest challenge in over forty years. Voters will be going to the polls on 19 different occasions at the local, regional, national and European levels in 1994. Culminating in the vote for a new Bundestag in October, these elections will reshape Germany's political landscape for the close of the century, and the prospects do not look good.

Although the contingencies and dynamics of an eight-month electoral campaign and voting cycle render the prediction of exact outcomes impossible, current trends nonetheless suggest that the new balance of political forces will threaten the survival of German democracy. Over the course of forty years the western Federal Republic had developed a stable and effective 'two-and-a-half' party system in which the small Free Democratic Party (FDP) coalesced in alternation with either the larger Christian Democratic Union parties (CDU and CSU) or the Social Democratic Party (SPD). Now, with voters increasingly abandoning – whether out of protest or conviction – the two-and-a-half traditional parties to support the Republikaner on the far right, the Greens on the left, the Statt Partei (the 'instead' party) in the centre, or most likely the so-called party of non-voters, it is unlikely that a stable, coherent majority will emerge from the 1994 elections. Instead, perhaps only a grand coalition of CDU and SPD will be numerically capable of governing. Unfortunately, such a government would probably lack the leadership and the programme to pull Germany out of its post-unification economic, social and political crisis and would thus further polarise and fragment the electorate.

The possible demise of German democracy so close on

the heels of communism's collapse comes as something of a surprise. In the triumphant mood of 1989 and 1990, some went so far as to proclaim the world-historic victory of liberal capitalist democracy: the failure of the only apparent alternative, socialist authoritarianism, left no choice. Yet today liberal capitalist democracy is not taking root in Eastern Europe and is in crisis not only in Germany but throughout much of the West. Of course, not everyone saw capitalist democracy as the only alternative for the future. Well before communism's final crisis, Vaclav Havel (1978) diagnosed a fatal illness common to communism and capitalism. Communism, however, would succumb first, because its modern, rationalist hubris was greater and its capacity to perpetuate consumerist productivism was less than that of the capitalist West. If liberal democracy finds itself in crisis, is it perhaps because capitalism today, like communism yesterday, cannot find rational solutions to the problem of economic growth that do not incur unsustainable social and ecological costs?

Germany's current social, economic and political problems are certainly not unique, but they do have some causes particular to Germany's recent history. In fact, the peculiarities of German history and geography mean that the country is once again a crucible for world-historic trends. For forty years, divided Germany was the focal point of the East–West conflict, the two states becoming model children of the opposing social systems that had adopted them. Thus, it is natural that the most powerful image from the momentous events of 1989 remains that of the German people emotionally rediscovering their kinship atop the Berlin Wall on the night of 9–10 November. With formal unification on 3 October 1990, Germany again became a test case: there alone one nation, one political system faced the task of reconciling forty years of divergent social, economic, and cultural development. If Germany did not succeed in this task of reconciliation, the rest of Europe and of the world could scarcely hope to mend the wounds of the Cold War.

Germany's experience with unification has not yet been a complete failure or success. The economic, social and political costs have been high, but the standard of living has risen in the East and remained high, though threatened, in the West; the outbursts of racist violence have spurred nearly universal indignation and constructive citizens' initiatives; and faith in democratic institutions has kept strong even as disapproval of particular politicians and parties has grown. In 1994, Germany thus stands at a turning-point. Whether the economy recovers or slips further into crisis, whether social tensions diminish or rise, and whether Germans turn against democracy depend largely on the outcome of the year's elections. Germany probably cannot afford to continue to muddle through its post-unification crisis without stable and effective leadership. A Bundestag in stalemate will win neither investors' nor voters' confidence, and liberal capitalist democracy in Germany may thus soon find itself on the rapid road to demise.

This book offers an explanation for Germany's present political problems. Specifically, it argues that the democratic crisis stems in large measure, though of course not exclusively, from conflicts within German political culture that have their roots in communism's collapse in the German Democratic Republic. While this book may not be the first or the last to link Germany's current crisis with reunification and the East German revolution, it presents the only empirically grounded cultural analysis of these political events. Based primarily on the qualitative and quantitative analysis of over 200 original survey interviews, this book shows how the undermining of a specific, regime-stabilising East German political culture contributed to the revolutionary mobilisation of 1989 and how the subsequent conflict between East and West German cultural values has exacerbated the problems of unification. In offering a cultural account of the East German revolution and of post-unification politics, this book does not pretend to substitute but rather to complement the necessary but insufficient economic, social and political structural analyses. I hope, however, that its readers will in the end agree that without a cultural counterpart, structural analyses have limited meaning.

Cultural interpretation is a very personal undertaking, but it can occur only within a particular context. Hence, while I must alone take responsibility for the quirks and foibles of my analysis, I owe great thanks to those who made them possible in the first place. I therefore wish first of all to thank the German Marshall Fund of the United States for funding my field research in what was still the German Democratic Republic when I arrived. I benefited from the generosity of their Younger Scholars Post-Doctoral Fellowship Programme designed to encourage those who studied other countries to study Germany as well. The German Marshall Fund launched the now-discontinued programme at a time shortly before anyone knew Germany was about to return to the centre of the world stage. Having just completed a dissertation on French politics, employing survey research, I entered the programme's first competition, proposing to interview those ordinary East Germans who were starting to make the headlines in the late summer of 1989.

It is to those ordinary East Germans, 202 of them in particular, to whom I owe special thanks. They opened their homes and their hearts to my wife and to me, complete strangers who had written them a letter seemingly out of the blue. The letter promised a short, painless interview. In fact, the interviews sometimes lasted up to four painful hours–not so much because of any misrepresentation or unduly prying questions on our part but because our interview partners wanted to share with us the sorrows, but also the joys, of life in the GDR and in reunited Germany. Since interviewing them in 1990 and 1991, I have maintained contact with a good number of the survey respondents, and in a follow-up project I hope to interview as many of them as possible, at least those who have not moved away in search of a better life or otherwise disappeared.

My wife and I did not arrive as complete strangers to the GDR. We both wish to thank for their repeated and generous hospitality my cousins the Berliner Schilferts and also my mother's numerous classmates and contacts in East Germany who helped us set up our research. A distant relative of a family friend turned out to be the newly-elected Neues Forum mayor of Freyburg an der Unstrut (Sachsen-Anhalt). We are very grateful to Martin Bertling and his family for their friendship and for finding us a comfortable place to live in their historic winegrowing town. I cannot name everyone in eastern Germany to whom we owe thanks for their hospitality and help, but Doris Trebitz, Klaus Marsiske, and Wolfgang and Gerda Quies deserve very special mention.

I also wish to thank a number of individuals and institutions who have given me intellectual or financial help with the completion of this book: Bernd Lindner, formerly of the Zentralinstitut für Jugendforschung in Leipzig; Thomas Koch and Rudolf Woderich, of the Berliner Institut für Sozialwissenschaftliche Studien; my colleagues at the Université de Montréal, Stéphane Dion, Pierre Martin, Claudia Mayer-Iswandy, and Brigitte Schroeder; my friends, colleagues, and teachers at Harvard University's Center for European Studies, especially Peter Hall; my friends and colleagues elsewhere, Andreas Pickel, Ghislaine Machabée, Volker Gransow, Melissa Williams, David Welch and Susan Solomon; my mother, Hannelies McFalls, for correcting my German; the Université de Montréal for internal research funding; and the Canadian government's Social Sciences and Humanities Research Council for follow-up research funding. I also thank the editors of *German Politics and Society* and of the *Revue canadienne de science politique* for allowing me to reproduce here materials I presented in articles in those journals (McFalls, 1992b and 1993).

Finally and above all, I wish to thank Marion Dove, my spouse, who gave up a year of her career to accompany me to East Germany, conducted numerous interviews with me and for me, helped me enter into the computer all my quantitative data, discussed my ideas, added her own insights, read and corrected my texts and, despite trying, unpaid working conditions, went on strike only once. It is to the memory of her parents, John and Lois Dove, admirers of German science and music, that I dedicate this book.

LHM
Outremont (Québec)
1 March 1994

1 Who Overthrew Honecker?

A little more than five years after welcoming him to Bonn as head of the East German state, the Federal Republic of Germany brought Erich Honecker to trial. The man whom Chancellor Helmut Kohl and the entire West German political class had honoured in September 1987 faced, along with five other tottering co-defendants, twelve charges of manslaughter as the result of an alleged shoot-to-kill order designed to guarantee the inviolability – from within – of the German Democratic Republic's borders. Honecker's lingering liver cancer and allegedly imminent death, however, prevented the trial's completion, and politicians in the West probably breathed a secret sigh of relief; for the trial would have become a political embarrassment. Although the prosecution would have argued, as it successfully did against the border guards who actually fired the shots, that fundamental human rights transcend sovereign authority, a healthy Honecker would not have hesitated to cite almost twenty years of public and secret dealings with Western politicians as evidence not only of his sovereign authority but of implicit Western complicity with his policies.

Of course, the Western politicians would have tried to hide their embarrassment, as they have in the retrospective public debate about the wisdom of their *Ostpolitik*, with justifiable claims that they had made the best of a bad situation; that they had acted in humanitarian concern for the East German population; that they had opened the door for change; that in any case they could not have known how long the imposed division of Germany would last. Indeed, no one who watched Erich Honecker arrive in Bonn in 1987 suspected that first his regime and then the entire communist bloc would collapse in 1989.

Politicians may today be held accountable for their past ignorance, but they derived their ignorance at least in part from unaccountable social science. While politicians must

1

live with their mistakes, political scientists live from them. Political science has thus greeted the collapse of communism not as a vindication of its predictive powers (how could it?) but as another occasion for *post hoc* theorisation. What had once been unimaginable – 'the likelihood of democratic development in Eastern Europe is virtually nil' [Huntington, 1984: 217] – has suddenly found a multitude of necessary causes. The new theories of communism's collapse in the GDR and elsewhere, though, are scarcely more convincing than the old ones of communism's stability. Hastily deduced, the new theories, like the old, too often lack an empirical base.

Fortunately, new possibilities for primary research in the former Eastern bloc now make possible the empirical (re)construction of valid theories of communism's stability and collapse. In this book I contribute to that inductive project, presenting the findings of field research in the former GDR. Specifically, on the basis of quantitative and qualitative analysis of original survey data, I call into question the common structural accounts of communism's collapse in East Germany. Instead, I argue that an understanding of political culture is necessary to explain the relative stability of East German state socialism until the 1980s, its decline and fall in the late 1980s, and the current crisis of German democracy.

A simple observation served as the point of departure for my analysis: Although crises in the East German economic, political, and social systems may have been necessary prerequisites, the form and the speed of communism's collapse in the GDR ultimately depended on the popular mobilisation against the party-state. Beginning with a relatively small number of demonstrators in Leipzig, Dresden and Berlin in late September and early October 1989, a rising tide of popular protest swept away first the Honecker government, then the Wall, and ultimately the East German state. In their rush to explain an event they had not foreseen, most scholars have tended to forget the ordinary men and women who actually brought it about and have identified the cause of East German communism's collapse in the systemic weaknesses of state socialism. A sufficient explanation of the GDR's demise must, however, account for the motives of the people who marched against the regime until the Wall came tumbling down. It must answer the questions: *who* overthrew Honecker? and then, more importantly, *why*?

To seek answers to these questions, I undertook an intensive survey of over 200 ordinary East Germans shortly after reunification. With such a relatively small random sample I could not hope to identify all the actors, motives, and events that in sequential combination brought down the SED regime, but I could hope to explain more generally the massive mobilisation of popular opinion against the regime that propelled the revolutionary process and also to uncover some of the specific motives for complacency or revolt of an indicative sample of East Germans. Before describing my survey research methodology and its explanatory strengths and weaknesses and offering an overview of my findings, however, I shall briefly review the theoretical considerations that informed my research, for although my approach to analysing the collapse of East German communism was essentially inductive, the various theories of totalitarianism and its evolutionary potential unavoidably shaped my research.

IT CAN'T HAPPEN HERE: FROM TOTALITARIANISM TO REVOLUTION

Like the regimes themselves, social scientific thought on communism in Eastern Europe was a product of the Second World War. The conflagration that left Stalin master of half of Europe had shown the frightening mobilisational capacity of a new form of political organisation that sought, and by-and-large attained, total control of society. The war had also driven some of the best minds of Central and Eastern Europe into exile in the West, where they reflected on the 'breakdown of our civilisation' (Polanyi, 1944: 5). The Soviets' imposition of new, repressive, single-party, ideological regimes in the lands they had liberated from Nazi rule left little doubt about the resemblance of the West's formal ally to its former foe. Thus, almost immediately, the Cold War became a continuation of the World War by other means.

Because the struggle against Nazi Germany had proved that only concerted force could defeat a regime that had remained internally united and strong until the bitter end, the assumption arose among scholars who had fled Hitler's Europe, as well as among policymakers, that the defeat of communism could come about only through sustained external pressure. The comparison of German Nazism and Soviet communism as expansive 'totalitarian' systems was not unfounded, of course, and although the methods and costs were often questionable, the democratic West, after having been too slow to oppose Nazi Germany, was correct quickly to adopt a policy of containment of the Soviet Union. The comparison has its limits, though. Central and Eastern European communism outlived Nazism by almost half a century, and when it finally collapsed, it did so from within. Despite the rhetoric and reality of the Cold War, communism succumbed more from internal contradictions than from external pressure.[1]

Although communism's crumbling from within contradicted the expectations of the original theorists of totalitarianism, the classic works of Hannah Arendt (1951) and of Carl Friedrich and Zbigniew Brzezinski (1956) contained the seeds of a differentiated analysis of communism's internal developmental potential. Arendt, like Friedrich and Brzezinski, saw totalitarianism as an expansionary system whose fate international competition and conflict would determine. Based on a philosophical critique of modernity and twentieth-century mass society, Arendt's analysis stressed the revolutionary ideology of totalitarianism, with its claims to absolute validity. Because the mere existence of other ideologies and ways of life threatened the claims to absolute legitimacy of revolutionary institutions and their leaders, Arendt argued, '[t]he struggle for the total domination of the total population of the earth, the elimination of every competing nontotalitarian reality is inherent in the totalitarian regimes . . .' (1951: 378). The frustration of a totalitarian regime's global ambitions would therefore spell the system's end even in the absence of military defeat, for the failure to eliminate competing ideologies and life forms would entail a relativisation, or 'normalisation', of totalitarian rule and undermine its absolute claim to power (Arendt, 1951: 377–8).

For Friedrich and Brzezinski, who saw totalitarianism as a product less of modern philosophy than of modern science and technology, normalisation posed no threat to the system. They considered chiliastic ideology to be but one of six features that allowed totalitarian regimes to break any societal resistance to the party-state's ambition of absolute control. Twentieth-century technology enabled a single ideological party and its leader to pulverise, if not always terrorise, society through the nearly total control of the means of communication, of production, and, not least, of violence (Friedrich and Brzezinski, 1956: 9–10). Thus, in the late 1960s, Friedrich could argue that as long as the organising principles and potentially violent techniques of totalitarianism remained intact, the apparent ritualisation and routinisation of ideology in the Soviet bloc did not signal an end to totalitarian rule, as some critics of the theory had contended, but rather its stabilisation (Friedrich, Curtis and Barber, 1969: 136, 154).

Although totalitarian parties and leaders had mastered the techniques to perpetuate their rule, Friedrich and Brzezinski recognised that these regimes could never perfect their system of control. As an ideal type, 'the totalitarian dictatorship seeks to divide and rule in the most radical and extreme way: each human being should, for best effects, have to face the monolith that is the totalitarian rule as an isolated "atom"' (Friedrich and Brzezinski, 1956: 281). In reality, 'islands of separateness', including the family, the church, the academic and scientific community and the military establishment survived and offered a basis of societal resistance to totalitarian rule. That resistance, however, had to remain hopeless in the absence of outside intervention, Friedrich and Brzezinski contended (1956: 283–4).

The Red Army's crushing of popular resistance to communist rule in June 1953 in East Germany, in October 1956 in Hungary, and in August 1968 in Czechoslovakia – each time without any substantial opposition from the West – confirmed Friedrich and Brzezinski's as well as Arendt's contentions that Eastern and Central European totalitarianism would not succumb from within. Still, their theories did point to potential internal weaknesses of totalitarian systems: normalisation of ideology and institutions threatened to delegitimate the regimes from above, while pockets of societal resistance threatened to undermine them from below.

Subsequent theories of communism's evolution and revolutionary end have, in fact, merely elaborated on one or more of the three possible sources of change that the classic theories of totalitarianism identified: international competition, ideological and institutional erosion and corruption, or societal resistance. The three approaches to change within communist societies are analogous, moreover, to the different contemporary theories of revolution. These emphasise either (1) the mobilisation of society from below on the basis of material interest (Marx and Engels, 1848) or of socio-cultural 'desynchronisation' resulting usually from rapid modernisation (Johnson, 1966); (2) the inadaptation or breakdown from above of existing institutions and their legitimating ideologies (Huntington, 1968); or (3) the world-historic context of international military and economic competition (Skocpol, 1979). I do not wish here to review the evolution of theoretical perspectives on communist regimes (cf. Janos, 1991) nor to explore their relationship to theories of revolution, but to identify the kinds of hypotheses the three general approaches have generated for explaining the collapse of communism in Eastern Europe in general and in East Germany in particular.

Communism did not end in military defeat, but the argument that international competition brought it to its knees is probably the most popular in the West. Policymakers as well as taxpayers, who footed the bill for the forty-year arms race, take comfort in the claim, 'We won the Cold War.' While the capitalist West never proved its military superiority, it does seem to have brought the communist East to its knees economically. The relative costs of the arms race and of the maintenance of empire were always much higher for the Soviet Union than for the United States and its allies, but as long as competition remained quantitative, repressive means had allowed the Soviet Union to extract the necessary resources.

A turning-point came in the late 1960s and early 1970s, however, when both the East and the West had exhausted the growth potential of extensive industrial development based on mass production and economies of scale (cf. Maier, 1991). Whereas the West weathered the crisis of the 1970s with a socially costly restructuring of the economy around special-ised production that new micro-electronic technologies facilitated, the East banked on a 'further perfection' of central planning through marginal reforms, on an improvement of worker productivity through increased consumption possibilities, and on an industrial renewal through the importing of Western technology.

The attempt to graft Western consumerism and technology on to a centrally planned economy failed: consumption subsidies and foreign debt loads grew untenable as economic growth stagnated. By the mid-1980s it was clear that the Soviet bloc could no longer compete with the qualitatively superior Western economies nor even meet the consumer desires of its population unless it underwent a radical restructuring (*perestroika*). Economically, the will to reform came too late. Although communism did not collapse from an acute economic crisis (in many respects its economic performance had been worse in the early 1980s than in the late 1980s [cf. Drach, 1990]), the chronic reality of international economic competition had disabused totalitarian leaders of their belief in ideological infallibility and had augmented opposition within a society that had begun to find an independent base in the more or less flourishing unofficial economy (cf. Poznanski, 1991). Thus, the relative, though by no means absolute, failure of the planned economy unleashed the forces (a leadership divided between reformers and conservatives and discontented societies) that in one combination or another brought down communism in the Soviet bloc in 1989 and in the Soviet Union in 1991.

The international economic competition explanation of communism's collapse thus points to and even subsumes institutional breakdown and societal mobilisation explanations. Communist ideology and institutions as well as the societies that survived totalitarianism's unperfected control, however, followed a developmental logic independent of the system's absolute or relative economic performance. Already in the 1960s, well before the Soviet bloc showed any obvious signs of economic stagnation, outside observers detected an evolution in totalitarian ideology and institutions. In fact, the rapid industrialisation of the Soviet bloc led some to predict a convergence of Eastern authoritarian and Western democratic regime types as the functionalist, Durkheimian

logic of social differentiation pushed the East towards West-
ern-style pluralism (or corporatism) or as the rationalist
Weberian logic of bureaucratisation pushed both types of
political and social organisation towards technocratic utopia
(or, in the pessimistic view, dystopia) (cf. Brzezinski and
Huntington, 1964; Janos, 1991; Pakulski, 1986).

Convergence did not come, though, for modernisation
and bureaucratisation never broke the force of single-party
rule. Nonetheless, it was clear in the post-Stalinist era, particularly in the post-1968 Brezhnevite age, that totalitarian
rulers had lost their charismatic claim to authority. Weberian
theory suggests that unsustainable charismatic authority can
undergo either ritualisation to assume the authority of tradition or bureaucratic routinisation to become legal-rational
authority (cf. Jowitt, 1983). In fact, to varying degrees in
the different countries of the Soviet bloc, both processes
seem to have occurred with dysfunctional consequences. On
the one hand, the ritualisation of revolutionary communist
ideology sapped the system of its voluntarist developmental
dynamic. Vaclav Havel in his now classic essay 'The Power
of the Powerless' (1978) describes how, in what he calls the
post-totalitarian phase of communism, ideology became a
meaningless communicative code providing access to power
and an alibi for mindless conformism. The loss of faith in a
goal-rational ideology left dispirited leaders' authority vulnerable to bureaucratic usurpation and societal resistance
(cf. Di Palma, 1991; Thaa, 1992). On the other hand, the
bureaucratisation and autonomisation of the leadership's
political staff, the *nomenklatura*, rendered any reform that
might violate bureaucratic interests impossible. All hopes of
overcoming the inefficiencies of the planned economy, from
the Libermanite reforms of the 1960s to Gorbachev's desperate efforts of the 1980s, were dashed on the rock of bureaucratic resistance. Thus, according to some observers (cf.
Thibaud, 1989), Gorbachev's latter-day steps towards democratisation were little more than a last-ditch effort to mobilise society against a *nomenklatura* only nominally at his service.

Not everywhere in the Soviet bloc did society have to wait
for mobilisation from above, though. For the case of Poland in particular, it was evident that totalitarianism had
only briefly held a war-ravaged society in its grip. The sur-

vival of the Catholic Church, the traditional keeper of the Polish nation, and the revival of an independent peasantry provided Polish society with 'islands of separateness' whose resistance was not futile. Repeatedly (1970, 1976, 1980), the peasantry's demands for higher agricultural prices provoked crises in which the Church mediated between a feeble party-state and a mobilised society until finally a civil society capable of challenging state authority emerged with the birth of the independent trade union Solidarity in 1980. The Polish experience thus suggested another model for change within communist societies.

According to the 'civil society' perspective, the post-Stalinist normalisation of communist ideology and institutions did not so much spur the system's erosion from above as offer space for the development of resistance from below. Since a defining characteristic of totalitarianism had been its ambition to eliminate the independent existence of society, the mere presence of independent thought among cultural dissidents or of independent economic or social activity, be it even informal or apolitical, signalled the rebirth of civil society (cf. Havel, 1978). As an analytic category, civil society came to refer to everything outside of official ideology and organisations. In some definitions, civil society included even pre-political activities beyond direct state control, such as family life and the informal economy; in others, only independent organisations capable of contesting state authority counted (cf. Ekiert, 1991; Keane, 1988). In general, though, the civil society perspective suggested a kind of hydraulic model of change within totalitarian regimes: every increment of dissidence or independent activity implied an equal decrement of totalitarian control. At some critical point, the relative strength of civil society would provoke the party-state to resort to force to reassert its authority, as occurred with the imposition of martial law in Poland in 1981, or force it to negotiate its own disappearance, as occurred in Poland and Hungary in 1989.

As this rapid review of the analyses of post-Stalinist communism has revealed, the possibilities for the devolution and demise of totalitarian authority were greater than the original postwar theorists had suspected. Communist totalitarianism incorporated economic, political and social dynamics that guaranteed its self-destruction, or so it would seem with the benefit of hindsight. The limited growth-potential of the centrally planned economy meant that the communist East would eventually fail to compete with the capitalist West in military spending and consumer satisfaction and lose faith in its goal-rational ideology. The political logic of bureaucratisation also spelt the death of revolutionary utopianism and rendered the *nomenklatura*'s resistance to reform insurmountable. Finally, post-terroristic totalitarianism's inability completely to control society rendered even the tiniest moral or organisational opposition paradoxically powerful since the very idea of autonomous societal activity (civil society) undermined the party-state's absolute claim to authority.

Thus, although the collapse of communism in Central and Eastern Europe and the Soviet Union in 1989–91 took the world by surprise, political scientists were not entirely unprepared to explain it. They quickly formulated theoretically informed hypotheses about the structural crisis of the socialist economy, about the incapacity of political institutions and the illegitimacy of ideology, and about the remobilisation of society. Common to the various explanations of communism's collapse was their systemic, or structural, character. That is, communism had proven unviable as an economic, political and/or social system. As the speed of its disappearance testifies, Soviet-style communism in the late 1980s found itself, without a doubt, in deep structural crisis, yet the manner in which Eastern and Central European communism dissolved did not clearly reveal how the crisis articulated itself nor which structural factors had causal primacy. Indeed, the sudden and dramatic events of 1989 probably raised more questions about communism's developmental logic than they answered. In the gradual process of the party-state's self-destruction that began in Hungary and Poland in early 1989, the various structural elements came at least fairly observably into play: a divided, self-doubting political leadership entered into negotiations with a more (Poland) or less (Hungary) developed and mobilised civil society against a background of more or less severe chronic economic crisis. By contrast, in the process that sealed communism's fate – the popular mobilisation that swept from

East Germany to Czechoslovakia, Rumania and even Bulgaria in the autumn of 1989 – the structural forces at play were far from obvious. The leadership had shown little sign of division or self-doubt, civil society little sign of strength, and, in East Germany and Czechoslovakia in particular, the economy little sign of impending calamity. What forces moved the tide of popular protest that swept away communist rule?

In 1989 Western pundits and politicians offered the somewhat naïve, ideological response that the innate human desire for freedom had motivated popular anti-communist protest. Such an idealistic answer entirely begs the question since something else, possibly some structural constellation, must explain the sudden possibility for this desire to express itself. Still, the idealistic emphasis on consciousness offers an important hint for answering this puzzling question. Although the structuralist explanation of human events denies the causal significance of individual consciousness, it recognises that structural forces impinge on consciousness and thus prompt social action. In fact, the proof of a structuralist argument depends on its demonstration of a causal link between social forces and individual behaviour even if, as the father of structuralism conceded, it is usually possible only logically to imply structural causality in individual cases (cf. Durkheim, 1930 [1897]:313). Since, in the absence of any other readily apparent immediate cause, it is safe to assume in the East German case in particular that popular mobilisation in the form of mass demonstrations was the social action that engendered the collapse of the communist regime, it would seem that an examination of the social characteristics, behaviour and motives – or consciousness – of individual demonstrators (in comparison to non-demonstrators) might provide access to the possible underlying structural causes.

RESEARCH METHODOLOGY: THE INTENSIVE SURVEY

Survey research, of course, provides a method for conducting such an examination. The aggregated answers of a large, randomised sample of individuals to questions about their economic, social, and political biography, behaviour and beliefs can permit the statistical inference of structural causality. A survey of the ordinary people who did or did not participate in the demonstrations that ultimately ended communist rule could therefore help establish the causal relevance of the economic, political and social structures that the various theoretical approaches to change within communist societies have identified. From December 1990 to May 1991, I undertook precisely such a survey to uncover the causes of the East German popular revolution of 1989 and the origins of communism's collapse.

The objective of my survey, however, was not merely the testing of a series of more or less simple hypotheses about the causal relationship between individuals' objective and subjective social, economic and political conditions and their likelihood of participating in anti-government protest in the fall of 1989, though such hypotheses are implicit in the majority of the survey's questions (see the Survey Questionnaire in the Appendix). Three other objectives – historical, methodological and politico-moral – influenced the form my survey took. First, because the fall of the Wall made unhampered survey research possible for the first time, I wanted my survey to capture as much of the detail of daily life under state socialism as possible before East Germans' memories began to discolour. Second, because only the qualitatively interpretable context in which individuals answer questions lends meaning to statistical findings, I wanted to conduct my survey in personal-interview format. Third, because a political system allegedly based on social scientific truths had for so long disenfranchised East Germans, I above all wanted to be certain to give my respondents the opportunity to respond freely and fully to open-ended questions and not merely to check-off preconceived categories and answers. In light of these multiple objectives, I chose to conduct an intensive survey.

By comparison to more typical extensive surveys, intensive surveys offer certain methodological advantages. In extensive surveys, researchers send either pre-printed questionnaires or professional interviewers to large and therefore potentially more representative samples of respondents. To avoid contextual ambiguities as well as resistance and confusion on the part of respondents and/or interviewers, however, researchers must limit their questionnaires to relatively small numbers of simple, almost exclusively closed-ended questions. A trade-off thus occurs between representativeness and richness of detail and context. In intensive surveys, by contrast, researchers personally conduct a smaller number of interviews in which they can ask a greater number of more nuanced closed- and open-ended questions as well as appropriate follow-up questions. Although the smaller sample sizes of intensive surveys entail a probable sacrifice of representativeness, they provide more detail, contextual accuracy, and opportunity for informed qualitative interpretation of findings. What is more, even if a small randomised sample is less likely to be fully representative of a target population, it can be large enough (depending on the number of sample subgroups under comparison) to allow statistical analysis suggestive of differences between major population categories. For example, an intensive survey's sample size may be too small to allow statistical conclusions about full-time working women's political preferences but big enough to be indicative of political differences between women and men.

In the case of my own intensive survey of ordinary East Germans, the sample included 202 randomly selected men and women, who responded to up to 235 questions (including all possible follow-ups) in personal interviews with me (or in 40 cases with my spouse) all conducted in the six months between December 1990 and May 1991. The questionnaire (see Appendix) included both open-ended and closed-ended questions, which I had developed on the basis of a reading of various scholarly, literary and journalistic works on daily life in the GDR (cf. Chapter 4) and had refined in the autumn of 1990 with the help of pre-test interviews with 15 non-randomly selected persons of different regional, social and political characters. I selected my 202 survey respondents in four very different regions of the former GDR (see Figure 1.1): East Berlin and its suburbs in Brandenburg (46 respondents); the south-central industrial region between and including the cities Halle, Leipzig and Jena (92 respondents including 27 from Leipzig); the agricultural region around the north-eastern university town of Greifswald (46 respondents); and mountainous southern Thuringia (15 respondents).[1] The remaining three respondents had lived

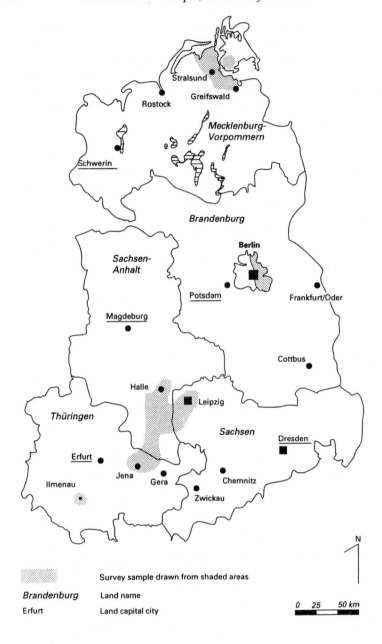

Figure 1.1   The German Democratic Republic, including boundaries of the reconstituted Länder

in different regions of the GDR before 1990. To maximise the representativeness of my sample, within each region I chose towns at random (except for East Berlin and Leipzig) and through on-site visits randomly picked out neighbourhoods, streets, and finally the mailboxes into which I inserted letters requesting participation in my survey. Because I was entirely dependent on the good will of my respondents to participate in a lengthy interview,[2] the sample necessarily suffered from a self-selection bias. Thus, as might be expected, the respondents tended to be better-educated and politically more active than the population at large: 22 per cent had a university-level education as compared to about 8 per cent of the total workforce, and 34 per cent had been members of a political party as opposed to 25 per cent of the total adult population (cf. Chapter 5 for further discussion of the sample's characteristics).

Despite the sample's self-selection bias, my survey interviews gave me personal access to women and men aged 17 to 83 from a broad range of East German social milieus: from artist-intellectuals in Berlin's Prenzlauer Berg to animal-tenders on collective farms; from university professors to kindergarten attendants; from enthusiastic border guards to discouraged emigration applicants; from loyal Socialist Unity Party (SED) members to religious dissidents; from dull bureaucrats to flamboyant private entrepreneurs; from social activists to personal retreatists; and, most importantly, from die-hard regime-supporters to active opponents during the fall of 1989. All these different types of survey participants gave me widely varying responses to questions about life in their communities, participation in social and political organisations, experiences with the state and its agents of social control, economic activities, attitudes towards socialism and the divided German nation, and experiences with and opinions about the revolution and reunification.

While the concrete answers to such questions made the testing of various hypotheses about the origins of East German communism's demise possible, my survey interviews offered me something even more useful for my analysis. Through hundreds of hours of structured conversations with scores of ordinary and extraordinary East Germans, I was able to construct in my mind a picture of what life had been like under state socialism. No doubt my mental image was distorted, but surely it was more accurate than any picture I could have pieced together on the basis of statistical description and second-hand accounts alone.[3] This picture provided me not only with the cultural context that allowed me to interpret my statistical findings but a framework for elaborating a qualitative cultural analysis of East German communism's collapse.

While the strengths of my analysis rest on the advantages of intensive survey research technique, (some of) its weaknesses must of course lie in the technique's disadvantages. Ideally, an intensive survey provides the representative breadth of opinion-polling and the psychological depth of oral history, but it might just as well offer the opposite: superficial insights into the lives of a narrow spectrum of a population. Needless to say, my intensive survey suffered from some of these disadvantages, which in turn limit the strength and scope of this book's argument. I have already mentioned the survey sample's self-selection bias. More limiting, however, is the relatively small sample size. The collapse of East German communism, like any other complex revolutionary process, involved numerous, differently motivated individual and collective actors ranging from hard-core reactionaries to revolutionaries of the first hour and silent bystanders, all playing their parts in a particular historical sequence. Although the survey sample counted among its number some of each of these types of actors, their quantities often did not suffice for generalisation or for a chronologically differentiated analysis. For example, the random sample included only a handful of those thousands of East Germans who had taken an active role in initiating the first decisive demonstrations against the regime. By contrast, 45 per cent of those surveyed had participated in at least one demonstration before the fall of the Wall, but those demonstrations occurred at different times and places with different risks and significances. For the purposes of quantitative analysis, I must often assume the equivalence of participation in various demonstrations. Although every demonstration before the fall of the Wall contributed to the regime's demise, it is clear that participating in a Leipzig demonstration early in October was qualitatively different from marching with a candle in Greifswald in late October or showing up on Berlin's Alexanderplatz for the great democratic socialist rally of 4 November.

Although I attempt a differentiated statistical analysis of my survey results (in Chapter 5), the relatively small sample size limits the nuance of my argument. As a result, this book (like any other single work) cannot fully explain the East German revolution. An adequate explanation would not only have to show how structural weaknesses rendered the East German communist system dysfunctional and how individuals subjectively appreciated (or culturally interpreted) that systemic dysfunction; it must also show how and when that subjective appreciation translated into specific actions (or historical events). My survey findings simply cannot provide the final step of historical explanation. They cannot explain precisely, for example, how and why opposition began to crystallise in response to the electoral fraud of 7 May 1989, and then coalesced around organisations such as the New Forum in early September; how and why individuals surmounted their fear to stand up to amassed repressive force at the decisive 9 October demonstration in Leipzig; nor how and why East Berliners and border guards came to interpret the Politburo's ambiguous 9 November statement on travel freedom as an order to open the border and thereby ultimately dissolve the state. Only precise historical and biographical research can provide answers to such questions, and even then only partial answers. The historian Dirk Philipsen (1993), for example, conducted revealing interviews with 106 well-known and little-known East German revolutionary activists, but even their testimonials cannot explain events they initiated but over which they lost control.

My personal interviews did offer some of the historical and biographical details prerequisite for understanding the events of 1989, and while trying to avoid sinking into anecdotal history, I have incorporated as many of those details as possible into my argument. Nonetheless the intensive survey technique provides both too few personal testimonials to furnish a complete picture of revolutionary events and too many testimonials to explore particular events or personal experiences in depth. While some of my survey interviews lasted over four hours, widely surpassed the framework of my questionnaire, and took on a therapeutic character for the respondent, they still lacked the richness of veritable oral histories, in which the researcher repeatedly interviews a respondent over the course of months or years and can discover deeper psychological motives (cf. Niethammer, 1991).

If my intensive survey yielded neither the societally representative breadth nor the psychological depth necessary for adequate historical explanation of the East German revolution, what can it offer in this book? My survey can help establish the cultural context if not the direct causes of the revolution. As I have already said, my intensive survey allowed me to develop an understanding of more than 200 East Germans' subjective appreciation of their lives under communist rule and during the revolution. These East Germans all played different parts in the revolutionary process: a few took leading, even heroic roles in toppling the regime; some joined in the demonstrations after the dangers were gone; the majority stood silently by. Common to all, however, was direct personal experience with life under the communist regime and during its demise. This common experience with communism was constitutive of a distinct East German culture, which gave meanings and motives to East Germans' different (in)actions during the revolution. The qualitative interpretation of my survey findings allows me to describe that common experience and consequently to develop a cultural analysis of East German communism's relative stability until the mid-1980s, its subsequent erosion, and its legacy for contemporary German politics. What is more, the statistical analysis of my survey permits me to test the explanatory limits not only of common structural accounts of East German communism's collapse but of the motives for protest that my cultural analysis suggests.

OVERVIEW

I develop my cultural account of the popular revolution in East Germany and of the political crisis of post-reunification Germany in the remaining five chapters. Before entering into my analysis, I outline in Chapter 2 the historical and institutional peculiarities of socialism in the GDR. Specifically,

I argue that East Germany was both typical and exceptional for the countries that came under Soviet and communist control after 1945. As the only state where communism could not easily appropriate nationalism, let alone anti-German sentiment, the GDR nonetheless became in many ways the showcase of communist Eastern and Central Europe. The relative success of the East German economy contributed to the coherence and orthodoxy of the party leadership there and to the weakness of societal opposition to 'real existing socialism'. At the same time, however, the constant West German political and economic challenge to the GDR's legitimacy rendered its apparent stability all the more remarkable. In Chapter 2, I contend that communist rule in Eastern Europe stood and fell with communist rule in East Germany: the success of communism in the artificial frontline state, whose very existence had given the Eastern bloc its original *raison d'être*, made its survival possible and plausible in the rest of the bloc. An explanation of communism's collapse in the critical East German case could therefore be highly suggestive of the causes of its demise elsewhere.

In Chapter 3, I consider the common existing explanations for communism's collapse in the GDR. On the basis of my own survey findings and other sources, I test and reject hypotheses drawn from the general theories (sketched above) of the weaknesses of totalitarian communist political, economic and social structures as well as hypotheses particular to the East German problem of national identity. Specifically, I argue that the origins of the popular revolution, or what the Germans call the *Wende* (turnabout), did not lie in nationalist revival, in political delegitimation of the regime, in economic crisis, in resurgent civil society and organised opposition, in altered international constraints, or in changing opportunity structures for individual rational actors. Instead, I suggest the need for a closer examination of the motivations of those actors who introduced sudden, drastic and irreversible political change: the ordinary people who took to the streets in the autumn of 1989.

In Chapter 4, I present a cultural model that can account for individual East Germans' motivation to risk their lives and careers by participating in anti-government demonstrations in the period before the fall of the Wall sealed the regime's fate. After discussing the interpretive method and its recognition of the necessity of identifying cultural values as the cause of human behaviour, I sketch the picture of daily life under East German real existing socialism that emerged from my survey interviews. This picture reveals the value system that allowed East German society and the individuals within it to function. I argue that the common values of modesty, solidarity and equality allowed ordinary East Germans to live respectively with consumer frustration, with dependence and public duplicity, and with monotony peppered with political privilege. Conjunctural circumstances (as opposed to a general structural crisis of state socialism), however, undermined the culture's positive values in the late 1980s, thus creating the motives for revolt. Although I maintain that the motives for revolt were essentially conservative, even socialist, the breakdown of the East German value system did not create a coherent set of revolutionary motives but rather made the expression of competing and conflicting values possible.

In Chapter 5, I turn to further quantitative analysis of my survey data in order to try to identify more specifically the motives for revolt of different categories of respondents. By distinguishing the attitudinal and social characteristics of demonstrators who were party members or non-partisans, young or old, churchgoers or atheists, men or women, northerners or southerners or Berliners, my analysis shows the East German revolution to have resulted from the confluence of diverse currents, often with opposite motives. The statistically evident diversity of motives, however, suggests an alternative model to the cultural account based on my qualitative analysis. According to the alternative model, it was the breakdown of state authority, and not the erosion of common values, that unleashed the competing motives that underlay the popular revolution.

In Chapter 6, I return to and argue in favour of my cultural analysis because it can explain more than the alternative state-authority model. It can account not only for the stability and apparent popular legitimacy of the GDR from the 1960s until the late 1980s but also for the current crisis afflicting democracy in reunited Germany. I contend that the conflict between surviving East German values and the liberal, consumerist values of the West has created the conditions for passive resignation in the East, for political disenchantment in the West, and for the sometimes violent deflection of mutual antipathy on to foreigners in both the East and West. Finally, in the concluding section of Chapter 6, I make an appeal for social scientific awareness of the cultural legacy of communism, for the subjective experience of forty years under communist rule will continue to shape political attitudes and behaviour in the reunited Germany and the struggling democracies of Central and Eastern Europe.

2 Behind the Wall: The East German *Sonderfall*

There was no more powerful symbol of communist rule than the Berlin Wall. A place of pilgrimage for presidents from Kennedy to Reagan, the Wall on its western face became a screen on to which defenders and critics of democracy quite literally projected their political images: by the end of its 28-year life, the Wall had become a politico-cultural artifact, if not artwork. On its eastern side the Wall remained a blank slate, empty like the white spaces on an ancient map where the known world came to an end. Although a shared symbol, the Wall clearly had different meanings on its two faces. For West Berliners, for Westerners, for everybody but East Germans, in fact, the Wall stood exterior to daily experience. For East Germans, the Wall defined life experience; it was constituent of a common identity. By a strange process of psychological inversion, East Germans internalised the Wall that enclosed them.

The Wall's different meanings grew obvious when it fell. In the West, where its symbolic externalisation was complete, the fall of the Wall quickly became a media event of almost pure entertainment value and a marketable experience. In stores and on street corners, vendors sold bits of brightly coloured concrete, alleged pieces of the Wall, to serve as talismans against totalitarianism and the tensions of the Cold War. In Eastern and Central Europe, the Wall had more real-life relevance. Its fall provided definitive proof that even the most hardline communist leadership had lost the will to rule and that the Soviet Union would not intervene to save its empire. A week after the fall of the Wall, popular revolution broke out in Czechoslovakia and soon thereafter in Rumania and Bulgaria. East Germans, however, responded to the fall of the Wall with strange ambivalence. Initially and understandably they greeted it with an unfathomable joy that for a time even infected their generally indifferent compatriots in the West. Then came the profound identity crisis that haunts East Germans to this day. An East Berlin artist whom I interviewed anticipated in her immediate reaction to the fall of the Wall the mixed emotions that have since torn East Germans. On the morning of 10 November 1989, she stood on her balcony with tears of confusion streaming down her face and screamed, 'Where have all our enemies gone?' She had not only lost the state she loved to hate but the necessary illusion that she was living an alternative to the capitalist evils of consumerism and inequality.

As a Westerner, for whom the Wall had been an unambiguous but impersonal symbol of evil, I was surprised to discover through my survey the East Germans' ambivalence towards the Wall. Although I never directly asked about the Wall, my interviews offered plenty of occasions for respondents to talk about it. Only one respondent complained about the Wall being a personal psychological burden, and I almost suspected that he told me that because he thought I wanted to hear that; all the other respondents who talked about the Wall did so with remarkable nonchalance. The Wall for them was simply a fact of life. Even a couple who had illegally emigrated in the 1950s and who had been trapped behind the Wall during a secret visit to a sick relative in August 1961 did not exhibit particular bitterness. They had learned to live with their fate. Everyone, including the most convinced communists, recognised that the regime's survival depended on the Wall, and those who wished to prosper or survive accepted enthusiastically or begrudgingly the necessity of the Wall. Indeed, the life-story of the GDR is little more than that of the rise and fall of the Wall. In this chapter, I shall review that history, illustrating it from time to time with the personal experiences of my survey respondents. In recounting the pre-history and history of the GDR, I shall argue that the particular difficulties of constructing state socialism before and behind the Wall made of the GDR a critical case for understanding the successes and failures of East and Central European communism.

FROM THE ANTI-FASCIST BLOC TO THE ANTI-FASCIST WALL

The GDR was not the only state in the Soviet bloc to assert its authority by restricting its citizens' freedom of movement. The construction of the Berlin Wall on 13 August 1961 merely dramatised – and rendered effective – a policy in place since the carving of Germany and Europe into two opposing armed camps. Cutting a nation's former capital in two, however, the Wall made glaringly obvious the particular difficulties the East German party-state faced in imposing its authority over society. In the absence of popular legitimacy, the regimes of Eastern Europe all had to resort to more or less naked force, but in East Germany the regime's legitimacy deficit coincided with a profound identity crisis partly of the regime's own making: even for several years after the Wall's construction, the regime continued to claim to speak in the interests and name of Germans living to its west. Despite the drastic sealing of its borders in 1961, the East German regime kept the 'German question' open until the early 1970s (cf. Naumann and Trümpler, 1991). Although the question of national identity exacerbated the East German regime's ongoing legitimacy crisis and hampered the construction of a stable polity, the East German communists had means at their disposal for gaining popular acquiescence if not support. Indeed, as we shall see, despite its birth-defect of national division, the GDR developed perhaps the most stable and effective regime in communist Eastern and Central Europe.

In none of the countries that Stalin's armies liberated did communists come to power with widespread popular support. Although the Communist Party was the largest popular force in Czechoslovakia in 1945, after the 1948 coup and subsequent Stalinisation, the party came under the control of a clique of Moscow's henchmen. Elsewhere Moscow installed its own handpicked leaders, initially in coalition with other 'democratic, anti-fascist' forces, after having allowed the Nazis to destroy indigenous popular communist forces, as in Poland, or after having created communist parties where none had existed, as in Rumania. The men who came from Moscow's party schools to take power had learned to fear

Stalin and to distrust everyone, particularly local communists who had stayed behind heroically to resist the Nazis and, even more, those who had emigrated to the West (cf. Leonhard, 1955). Thus, they had to build up their ruling parties and, if possible, popular support from scratch. Such was also the case in the Soviet-occupied zone of Germany (SBZ), where future party and state leader Walter Ulbricht and other Moscow-trained German Communist Party (KPD) members flew on the very day of Hitler's suicide, 30 April 1945, and immediately began taking over civilian administration from the Red Army.[1] As elsewhere, the war-weary population was hardly in a position to contest the power grab of an organised clique under the protection of a 'liberating' army. Within a few months the reconstituted KPD, aided by Soviet denazification of the public administration, had full control over civilian power.

While the Red Army's presence made the seizing of formal authority relatively easy for the communists in the Soviet occupation zone, winning popular support and thus preparing the ground for a new German state in the SBZ proved more challenging. Eastern Germany did include traditional strongholds of the left in Berlin and Saxony, and these seemed to revive quickly. Upon their refounding in June 1945, the Social Democrats (SPD) in the SBZ actually adopted social and economic positions well to the left of the KPD, which had embraced moderate, even bourgeois positions in line with the Stalinist tactic of the Popular Front of the late 1930s. In late 1945 the KPD leadership in the SBZ saw unification with the initially favourable but then hesitant SPD as a means for expanding its mass base of support. Under pressure from the Soviet occupation authorities and with misplaced confidence in its numerical superiority, the SPD agreed in April 1946 to merge with the KPD in a new Socialist Unity Party (SED), in which the two constituent parties enjoyed parity in all instances. The merger bore fruit: in October 1946 in the first and last contested elections in East Germany before 1990, the SED won a slim majority in the Landtag elections of the reconstituted federal states with the two other 'anti-fascist bloc' parties, the Christian Democrats (CDU) and Liberal Democrats (LDP), evenly dividing the remaining votes, though the newly-united party went down to defeat in the freer elections in Berlin.

Controlling half of a slim majority outside Berlin did not satisfy the communists for long, however, particularly as it grew clear that the Soviet military presence in East Germany was becoming permanent. With the outbreak of the Cold War and the Tito–Stalin split in 1948, the Soviet military administration did not hesitate to force the transformation of the SED into a Leninist party of the new type. As control commissions purged the SED of social democratic leaders and ideas, the Soviets and their German communist allies did not abolish the 'bourgeois' parties but replaced their leaders with communist sympathisers and diluted their support by creating two more parties, the Democratic Peasants (DBD) and National Democrats (NDPD). The SED then invited its mass organisations – the trade union (FDGB), youth (FDJ), intellectual (Kulturbund) and women's (DFD) movements – to join it and the other anti-fascist bloc parties in what under the SED's leading role was in 1950 to become the governing National Front of the GDR. Thus, in the three years between the Landtag elections and the founding of the GDR on 7 October 1949, the East German communists, with the help of the Soviet military administration, established the institutional mechanisms of their subsequent political control.

The anti-fascist, democratic fig-leaf over the communists' naked grab of power fooled few East Germans, yet the physical and moral exhaustion following Nazi Germany's defeat allowed the new regime to win a certain credibility if not legitimacy in the immediate postwar period. In the stereotypical (and perhaps not entirely false) interpretation of the founding of the SED regime, the East German population simply exchanged one form of totalitarianism for another: the Prussians, in their tradition of subordination to authority, had found their perfect master in Hitler, and upon his defeat it proved easier for them to change masters than to break the habit of obedience. In fact, Nazi totalitarianism prepared the ground for its communist counterpart in a morally more positive manner. After the horrors of Nazism, in which they had participated, many East Germans eagerly wanted to believe the communists' anti-fascist rhetoric and use it to conceal their own past responsibility. Behind the perversions of

Stalinism, moreover, they could catch at least a glimmer of the humanistic, universalistic idealism that underlay communism and contrasted it with Nazism's unmistakable barbarity. Several of my older survey respondents who had joined the SED in the late 1940s said they had done so to atone for the war or to prevent another war that would inevitably result from the survival of the capitalist system. One woman, who claimed to have lost her job and apartment in the late 1970s because of her anti-socialist attitudes, summarised her perhaps selectively nostalgic recollections of the immediate postwar period thus: 'We swallowed Marxism-Leninism hook, line, and sinker [Wir haben den Marxismus-Leninismus verschlungen].'

The SED regime not only satisfied some East Germans' hunger for new ideals in the horrible moral aftermath of the war; it won the allegiance of many more with its concrete efforts to reconstruct the war-ravaged economy and society. The task of reconstruction offers any new regime, whatever its ideological orientation, manifold opportunities for winning citizens' loyalty. The obvious need for authoritative allocation of scarce resources enhances the power, patronage and prestige of leaders, who starting from nothing can always claim great successes. In the SBZ, the process of denazification between 1945 and 1948 allowed the occupation authorities and the local communist authorities to replace over 520 000 public officials with communists or their sympathisers, including tens of thousands of young people quickly trained (and indoctrinated) to teach in the schools. As the party leaders and their new administrative staff addressed the most pressing needs of refugees, of rationing, and of rebuilding, they could not help but gain credibility and some approval. Several older survey respondents from Berlin recalled picking up rubble side-by-side with party-leader Walter Ulbricht or future president Wilhelm Pieck (whose participation featured in propaganda films at the time, thus reinforcing or perhaps creating the respondents' memories). Of course, for thousands of eastern Germans, the political repression and economic hardship grew so unbearable that they abandoned house and home and fled west. For at least some of the vast majority who remained behind, however, small victories in the struggle for daily existence could become great achievements (of socialism). As one not untypical respondent recounted: 'In 1949, a bread roll with jam was an accomplishment [*Errungenschaft*, the word commonly used to describe the regime's successes]. When we got something like that, we thought, "The system is good."'

Just exactly what the system was or would be, however, was not entirely clear until well after the GDR's founding on 7 October 1949. Already in 1945 the Soviet occupation authorities had introduced substantial socio-economic reforms, beginning with an expropriation of all landholdings over 100 hectares. Since the Soviets redistributed the land to over half-a-million smallholders including refugees from East Prussia, Silesia and Pomerania, this land reform was clearly not communising in intent. Similarly, the expropriation of all industry belonging to the state, the Nazi party, the military, or war criminals did not immediately imply the construction of a Soviet-style economy. Leaving 40 per cent of industry in private hands, the Soviets simply wanted to break German military–industrial power and to assure themselves of reparation payments. (These expropriations by the Soviet military administration between 1945 and 1949 are, incidentally, the only ones not subject to restitution today.) Although in the following years the Soviets established the institutional mechanisms for a state-led planned economy in the SBZ, the GDR in 1949 had a command economy still largely under private control. The Soviets tolerated and in fact encouraged such ambiguity in their newest satellite state, because as late as March 1952, Stalin may have nurtured a belief in the possibility of Germany's reunification at the cost of its neutrality in Cold War Europe.

Thus, only at its Second Congress of July 1952 did the SED announce its programme of 'the construction of socialism'. In laying its cards on the table, however, the party put itself on a collision-course with a society perhaps willing to live with the leadership of an anti-fascist, democratic bloc but certainly unready for the dictatorship of the proletariat. Following the Nineteenth Congress of the Soviet Communist Party (CPSU) of October 1952, at which the GDR had representation alongside the other people's democracies, the SED regime launched an aggressive campaign to catch up with its more fully socialised allies. With techniques ranging from tax policies to the withdrawal of private entrepreneurs' rationing cards, the regime sought to drive private artisans and farmers into cooperatives, and private industry into bankruptcy, while at the same time it reinforced Stakhanovite work norms in state enterprises (cf. Pickel, 1992: 31–8). Within a few months the GDR found itself falling short of plan targets and of tax receipts and haemorrhaging citizens in a wave of emigration that would become perennial. On 9 June 1953, the regime announced a New Course including a truce in the class struggle against private enterprise and a withdrawal of consumer price-hikes. The regime neglected to roll back work norms, though, and on 17 June workers in Berlin and then throughout the country rose up against the regime, demanding at first economic changes and then democratic political reforms as well. As the government, its police forces, and the Ministry for State Security (or Stasi, founded in 1950 with no formally enumerated tasks) proved incapable of quelling the rebellion, Soviet tanks restored order throughout the country on 18 June.

Although the announcement of the New Course failed to prevent the workers' uprising of June 1953, it did signal the beginning of a pattern of advances followed by slight retreats on the path towards socialism. These policy fluctuations in turn conditioned the population's antagonism towards or arrangement with the regime, as reflected in the number of emigrants leaving for West Germany. After purges and a hardening of the party line in the wake of the 1953 uprising, the partial ideological thaw following the Twentieth Congress of the CPSU in 1956 seemed to heighten acceptance if not support for the regime. While Ulbricht and his hardline allies drove oppositional revisionists (the so-called Schirdewan–Wollweber group) from the leadership, brought humanist socialists such as Walter Janka to trial for treason, and tightened legislation against any behaviour that could be construed as oppositional, the party softened its ideological tone with the population at large. Spectacular economic growth rates (including a doubling of industrial production between 1950 and 1955) seemed to win popular acceptance for the socialist economic system. Even workers who fled the GDR praised positive features of the social system, and a majority of them opposed the reprivatisation of industry. (Weber, 1990: 88). Indeed, in 1958 emigration from the GDR slowed down, reaching a ten-year low in 1959 (cf. Hirschmann, 1993: 179), and a few workers even returned to the GDR, as did, for example, a woman in my survey sample who quit her well-paid job in West Berlin to come back home when her mother wrote that things were looking up in the East.

Emboldened by its economic successes and apparent consolidation of popular consent, the SED at its Fifth Congress of July 1958 announced an intensification of the construction of socialism with the goal of surpassing West German per capita consumption in 1961. With 88 per cent of industrial production already in state, or rather 'people's' ownership (VEBs), agriculture, still 70 per cent private, became the chief target of the new campaign. In the first three months of 1960 alone, more than half a million farmers 'voluntarily' joined cooperative farms (LPGs) as the 14 Bezirke (created in 1952 to replace the federal Länder) competed to be the first to announce total collectivisation (Weber, 1990: 87). At the same time, private artisans faced somewhat less effective pressure to join or form cooperatives (PGHs) while much of remaining private industry and retail came under partial state ownership or other control arrangements (cf. Pickel, 1992: 47–54). In such a context of socio-economic disruption, East German production and productivity, needless to say, did not surpass West German levels but fell as tens of thousands of East Germans fled west each month. The government blamed the economic crisis on the 50 000 East Germans who commuted to work in West Berlin each day and exploited the differences between the systems, but in doing so, the regime was probably only preparing the ideological ground for the construction of the Wall.

THE *LEBENSLÜGE* OF THE WALL

In January 1961, I went to Berlin (East) for a training programme. I was surprised to observe how many East-Berliners went to work in West Berlin and how many West-Berliners came East to buy up subsidised goods. I realised the border had to be closed if socialism was to stand a chance. When the Wall went up on August 13, I drew the logical consequence: I joined the party.

Although few East Germans shared this survey respondent's immediate reaction to the construction of the Berlin Wall, his sentiment anticipated the long-term popular response to the Wall. By sealing its borders, the SED regime had conceded the loss of whatever legitimacy it may have garnered in the late 1950s, yet in a strange twist, the building of a Wall may have been the necessary condition for capturing popular consent. To be sure, the regime did not present the construction of the Wall as a concession of defeat but rather as an act of self-defence: the anti-fascist protective wall would shelter the worker-and-peasant state from saboteurs and kidnappers from the neighbouring monopoly capitalist NATO puppet-state. Such ideological justifications may have assuaged the consciences of a few true believers in the party but, for the bulk of the population, alleged anti-fascism and socialist idealism had lost any of the persuasive power they may have had in the immediate postwar period. Despite the repressive excesses of Stalinism, socialism was not yet a dead letter, but to be credible as a legitimating ideology, it had to deliver the material and symbolic goods. By permitting the perfection of the state socialist economy and forcing a resolution, albeit imperfect, of the German national identity crisis, the Wall provided the means for the regime to deliver.

As long as citizens could opt out of the East German economic and political systems, the SED regime had little chance of consolidating its hold over society. The relative facility with which East Germans before 1961 could move to the economically more prosperous and politically more liberal Federal Republic with instant, full citizenship rights posed a historically unique challenge to the survival of the East German state. Once the GDR had a captive citizenry, it found itself on an equal, if not superior footing to its Soviet bloc allies for developing legitimating socio-economic policies and a sense of national community. In fact, in the decades after 1961, the GDR's economic performance and quest for national identity were so successful that outside observers and maybe even most citizens until the late 1980s forgot about the *Lebenslüge* of the Wall.]

The positive economic effects of the Wall were more immediately evident than its contribution to the symbolic construction of an East German political community. The Wall provided the objective and, more importantly, subjective conditions for sustained economic growth. Although the radical severing of ties to West Germany required a costly decoupling of the economy from Western connections (achieved through the awkwardly named operation *Störfreimachung* [disruptionless-making]), the halt to skilled labour's westward flight and the full integration of women into the workforce helped quench the planned economy's chronic thirst for labour. Because workers no longer had the option of leaving, they had every incentive to make the best of their situation and to accept the existing social order. Thus, instead of provoking unrest as in 1953, the party's hard line in 1961 ushered in a period of social stability.

In fact, the Wall seems even to have made a general liberalisation of the regime possible. By late 1961 persecution of people who had tried or wanted to leave the country ceased, and in keeping with the second phase of de-Stalinisation announced at the Twenty-second Congress of the CPSU of October 1961, terroristic techniques as well as statues of Stalin disappeared from the GDR. Instead, the GDR began to develop a type of socialist Rechtsstaat, in which comprehensive legal texts replaced ideological injunctions as mechanisms for governing society (cf. Ludz, 1970: 13). Also parallel to developments in the Soviet Union, the SED leadership allowed a lively debate on the economic reforms necessary to restore the high growth rates of the 1950s, and in late 1962 the Politburo introduced a New Economic System in which price and profitability would play a role alongside planning. While pushing for the application of cybernetics and systems theories to increasingly automated production, the Party also encouraged individual professional and social advancement as a means of stimulating integration into and positive attitudes towards the economic system (Ludz, 1970: 29).

The economic and political liberalisation of the 1960s seems to have given the SED regime a boost in popular support and self-confidence. A German-American who conducted surreptitious surveys in the GDR between 1962 and 1966 thus reported a rise in popular loyalty to the regime from 37 per cent to 71 per cent during that period (Schweigler, 1975: 121). My own survey respondents recalled the 1960s positively as the decade during which rationing had ended and their standard of living had unambiguously improved. The party leadership was no doubt aware of its economic successes for, to the great annoyance of the Soviet Union, Walter Ulbricht began trumpeting the GDR in international forums as the model for socialist industrial development. At home, the regime announced the completion of socialism and the successful establishment of a 'socialist human community'. At the height of its confidence, the SED adopted the slogan 'Wirtschaftswunder DDR', thus directly inviting comparison to the economic performance of the FRG. To be sure, East Germans could be proud of their economic achievements, which gave them a standard of living significantly higher than most of their eastern and southern neighbours, but the comparison to the still richer FRG may have been premature, particularly since the GDR had not developed its symbolic basis of legitimacy as well as it had its material basis in the 1960s.

In retrospect it is surprising that the East German leadership did not attempt more quickly to create a separate national identity for the GDR after erecting the Wall. Indeed, the regime's hesitations probably testified to the strength of the ideal of German unity even among those whose power depended on division. In 1962 an SED spokesperson justified the Wall with a remarkable application of dialectical reasoning: '[B]efore we can unite ourselves, we must differentiate ourselves' (Schweigler, 1975: 97). Thus, reunification remained an official objective of the regime at least until 1966 when the West German SPD's entrance into a grand coalition with the 'revanchist' CDU provided the pretext for abandoning the goal of reunification for the foreseeable future. Only very slowly over the next five years, however, did SED leaders and ideologues develop a theory of a distinct socialist German nation. The 1967 citizenship law for the first time proclaimed the existence of separate German citizenships, but the new constitution of 1968 assigned East German citizens 'the responsibility of showing the entire

German people a way into the future of peace and socialism' (cited in Krisch, 1978: 109; for texts cf. Thomaneck
and Mellis, 1989). Following Willy Brandt's rise to the Chan-
cellorship in 1969, the GDR had to resort increasingly to a
policy of political and national *Abgrenzung* (isolation and
differentiation from the West). The improvement of East–
West relations that Brandt sought threatened to revive popular
aspirations for reunification at the expense of the SED leadership, as became evident in March 1970 when Brandt visited Erfurt to great popular acclamation. In response to
Brandt's overtures, SED ideologue Albert Norden, erstwhile
champion of the two-states-one-nation doctrine, at the June
1970 Central Committee meeting introduced the distinction
between the historically rooted, mutually exclusive and hostile bourgeois and proletarian nations, with the GDR of course
embodying the latter (cf. Naumann and Trümpler, 1991:
180–2). A year later, the Eighth Congress of the SED officially adopted the new class-based conception of the nation, and by 1974 the ethnic designation 'German' had
disappeared from everything from the henceforth unsung
national anthem to the amended constitution.

HONECKER AND THE SOCIAL CONTRACT

The Eighth Party Congress of June 1971 marked a turning-
point, not only for the East German concept of the nation
but also for the political and socio-economic systems. In
consecrating the new party-leader Erich Honecker, who had
replaced Ulbricht the previous month, the Eighth Congress
put the GDR on a new developmental path. Whereas Ulbricht
had to step down because his economic boasting and resistance to Brandt's *Ostpolitik* had made him a liability for his
Soviet patrons and Politburo colleagues alike, Honecker
seemed to recognise that an improvement of relations with
the FRG, coupled with a strengthening of *Abgrenzung*, could
actually help to consolidate East Germany's identity and
economic system. Despite the easing of contacts between
East and West Germans after 1971, the policy of *Abgrenzung*
and the continued, even heightened repression of dissent,
like the construction of the Wall ten years earlier, convinced

East Germans to give up hopes for reunification and to make the best of the system in place. At the same time, *rapprochement* with the FRG in a context of global *détente* brought the GDR a wave of international diplomatic recognition, which lent the regime not only prestige (as did the successful pursuit of excellence in international athletic competitions) but material payoffs in the form of international trade and cooperation.

Along with this shift in foreign policy, the Eighth Party Congress also brought a sea-change in socio-economic policy. The New Economic System of the 1960s, with its introduction of market mechanisms, had in fact never called into question the predominant roles of planning and the party. Nonetheless, as Ulbricht's boasting had suggested, East German economic policy had deviated from the Soviet model, and in the wake of the Prague Spring – during which reformers had been brazen enough to challenge the Party's leading role and thus to provoke the Warsaw Pact invasion of August 1968 – deviation was ill-advised. Even if only mildly deviationist, the New Economic System by encouraging individual achievement had generated social inequalities, which Ulbricht had tried to conceal with the notion of the socialist human community that denied class conflict. In announcing 'the unity of social and economic policy', the Eighth Congress signalled a break with Ulbricht's policies and a return to the principles of subordination to the Soviet model, of centralised planning, of egalitarianism and of class struggle.

To give the ideological shift proclaimed at the Eighth Congress some substance, the Central Committee, now under Honecker's leadership, decided late in 1971 to launch a new 'socialist offensive' against what remained of the private sector. In a few weeks in early 1972, the private sector shrank from 11.2 per cent to 0.1 per cent of industrial production and from 15 per cent to 7.6 per cent of total employment, with what survived almost exclusively in the handicraft and service sectors. This final onslaught on the vestiges of capitalism was by and large symbolic and subsequently partly reversed when shortages in the service sector arose (Pickel, 1992: 65–9). Substantively more important for the GDR's development after the Eighth Congress was the expansion of egalitarian social policy, including the introduction in 1972 of generous maternity leave and the right to abortion. In 1973 Honecker launched his most ambitious, visible and lasting social programme, when he promised to solve the GDR's chronic housing shortage by 1990. Although new building and particularly renovations fell short of the promise, the Honecker era gave virtually every East German city and town its characteristic suburb of prefabricated, concrete-slab apartment blocks with rusty, futuristic pipelines running through the countryside to feed them with heating steam. Just a year before his forced resignation, Honecker himself handed over the keys to the three-millionth housing unit built since 1971. A very large plurality of East Germans thus found themselves sharing remarkably uniform living conditions by 1989. My survey interviews allowed me to experience the levelling effects of Honecker's socialism first-hand. When I entered an apartment, I could predict the furniture arrangement since standard pieces fit only in standard spots, and I always knew where to find the bathroom.

Honecker's egalitarian social policies, which in the 1980s expanded to include massive subsidies for basic consumer goods, were in fact typical for the evolution of politics in the Soviet bloc in the 1970s. They represented the East German variant of what scholars have called the social contract that underpinned communist rule in the 1970s and 1980s. The crushing of the Prague Spring and its justification with the Brezhnev doctrine had left no doubt that the Soviet Union and its subordinated allied socialist regimes would abide no questioning of the governing parties' absolute authority. In exchange for societal submission and in order to prevent uprisings such as that of Polish workers in 1970, the party-state promised a modest but improving standard of living. *Détente* with the West allowed not only a redirection of spending from the military to consumption but, more importantly, access to Western credit and technology. Although *détente* came at the cost of the formal concession of human rights guarantees at the 1975 Helsinki Conference, the communist parties quickly demonstrated their continued intolerance of dissent, as the SED, for example, made clear in 1976 with its forced expatriation of singer Wolf Biermann during a tour in the West and its subsequent crackdown on his intellectual sympathisers.

Among the Eastern bloc states, the GDR was particularly well-placed to profit from the social contract. Already the best-performing economy in the communist world in 1971 – the SED liked to boast that the GDR was the world's ninth industrial power – the GDR could exploit its free access to the Western market through the FRG and continue to deliver its citizens an improving standard of living. In the late 1970s, however, a fundamental weakness of the social contract as the basis for regime legitimation became evident: consumer expectations began to outstrip economic growth rates. The relative slowing of growth in the GDR, as in the rest of Eastern Europe, stemmed in part from the greater integration into a world economy in crisis but also from the inherent limits to intensive growth under centralised planning. Whatever the objective causes of slower growth, though, its subjective consequences threatened popular acceptance of the regime. My survey interviews exposed this largely subjective nature of the economic crisis of late socialism. Virtually all respondents agreed that the economy's long and slow decline had begun some time in the mid-1970s, yet over the same period they reported considerable improvements in their personal living standards.

To restore confidence in the social contract, the SED regime, like the other communist bloc regimes in the early 1980s, could turn either to economic reform or to a new strategy for mobilising popular support, namely nationalism (cf. Rupnik, 1990: 182ff.). The Hungarian party leadership, for instance, opted for the introduction of market-based reforms, while in Bulgaria and especially Rumania, the leadership initiated a practically neo-fascist revival of nationalism. In Poland, the new military regime of General Jaruzelski played on nationalist sentiment and adopted some of Solidarity's reform proposals. By contrast, in Czechoslovakia and the GDR, the regimes banked primarily on a 'further perfection' of central planning. In the GDR, this perfection took the form of the organisation of industrial *Kombinate*, which had the task of vertically and horizontally integrating production for entire industrial branches. Such concentration was supposed to permit a decentralisation of planning and thus a more efficient distribution of resources. The modest success of this industrial restructuring later allowed

SED leaders to claim that they had already completed their *perestroika* in the early 1980s and that they therefore did not need to imitate Gorbachev's reforms. Indeed, between 1981 and 1986 the GDR was able to cut its foreign debt in half while actively promoting if not achieving a micro-electronic revolution in industrial production (Dennis, 1988: 136–47). The introduction of robotic production, for example, became an official plan objective, which enterprises often met by renaming ordinary machines as robots (cf. Scherzer, 1989: 46; Dennis, 1984).

Although the GDR in the 1980s was able to consolidate its position as the most developed industrial economy of the communist world, it did so at the expense of a stagnation in living standards, and its leadership had had to acknowledge openly the need to close the growing technological and productive gap with the West. Because relative economic success did not suffice to legitimate SED rule, the party in the late 1970s and 1980s also sought symbolic legitimation through a renewed effort to construct a GDR-specific national identity. The denial of German ethnicity of the early 1970s had proved ineffective and hence shortlived. At the Ninth Party Congress, in 1976, Erich Honecker for the first time in years spoke of the socialist *German* nation. Perhaps precisely because it declared the national question closed, the Ninth Congress called for the study of history to help the development of a GDR-specific national consciousness. In an article in the GDR's principal historical journal, a Central Committee member hailed the 1976 Congress as a landmark call for the re-examination of all periods of German history, thus leaving no doubt about the Party's intentions and prompting a flowering of East German historiography (cf. Ludz, 1977; Schulz, 1982; Neuhäußer-Wespy, 1983; Asmus, 1984).

The officially sanctioned expansion of East German historiography gradually to cover virtually all periods and subjects of German history suggested a new confidence *vis-à-vis* the problem of national identity on the part of the SED. Previously GDR historiography had selectively and self-servingly studied events such as the Bauernkrieg of 1525, the revolution of 1848, the rise of the working-class movement, and the founding of the SED. After 1976 it became possible and even necessary to study the 'reactionary' as well as 'progressive' sides of the dialectic of history, for the task of the historian of what henceforth was to be called the 'national history of the GDR' was to pick out the positive, progressive 'traditions' from the mixed, contradictory German 'heritage' (cf. Dittrich, 1982; Bensing, 1984). While the identification and promotion of traditions of national and local scope were supposed to foster pride in the GDR as the historical culmination of Germany's progressive heritage, East German historians began studying and celebrating many of the same eras and figures as their West German colleagues, though the historiography of the twentieth century in particular remained under tight ideological strictures. Thus, in 1983 the GDR organised huge celebrations including tens of thousands of West German visitors on the occasion of the 500th birthday of Martin Luther, the same man whom earlier SED historians had condemned as the spiritual ancestor of Hitler (cf. Asmus, 1984). Perhaps even more telling than the Luther Year (incidentally celebrated simultaneously with the centennial of Marx's death) was, however, the earlier rehabilitation of Frederick the Great and the Prussian generals Scharnhorst, Gneisenau, and Clausewitz. As territorial successor to Prussia, the GDR in the early 1980s seemed to want to assume the legalistic-authoritarian mantle of Hegel's ideal state, thus confirming Oswald Spengler's observation from 1919: 'The spirit of Old Prussia and the socialist attitude, at present driven by brotherly hatred to combat each other, are in fact one and the same.' (Spengler, 1967: 3).

The relative self–confidence the GDR exhibited in its relationship to the German past extended in the mid-1980s to its relationships with both the Soviet Union and the West. During the period of heightened East–West tensions in the first half of the 1980s, Honecker, whose regime had a material and symbolic interest in maintaining good relations with the FRG, distanced himself from the Soviet decision to instal new short-range nuclear missiles in Central Europe. Although Moscow could still order Honecker to cancel his September 1984 visit to the FRG, the SED leader gained international respect for his independence and even for his 'liberalism' when he ordered the dismantling of border minefields in 1983 and allowed 40 000 East Germans to emigrate in 1984. Honecker became a celebrated guest in

Western capitals, reaching the apogee of his personal prestige in September 1987 when he was greeted with full military honours in Bonn.

THE GDR: BEST OF A BAD SITUATION OR DOOMED FROM BIRTH?

In retrospect it appears that Honecker's heralded independence and liberalism were little more than desperate ploys to secure vital Western credits for the faltering East German economy and to build prestige at home for a regime that relied increasingly in the 1980s on Stasi repression to govern. In the mid- and even late 1980s, however, few Western observers had recognised the economic and political fragility of the GDR. To be sure, the stagnation of growth and the rise of small oppositional groups in the shelter of the Protestant Church had not gone unnoticed, but by and large a consensus reigned among experts: despite the economic problems of the 1980s and the lingering legitimation deficit, the GDR had made the best out of a bad situation. Thanks to the GDR's relative successes in economic performance, social policy, and international relations, no one suspected that the rapid unravelling of the communist world would begin there in late 1989. If anything, the GDR appeared to have the most stable and secure regime in the bloc.

The GDR owed its apparent stability and security to its historic success in mitigating if not entirely overcoming the adverse conditions of its birth. In fact, the construction of socialism in a relatively resourceless, artificially created state suggested proof of the system's viability. From a war-ravaged territory with few natural resources and an industrial plant the Soviets had picked clean for reparations, 'the SED regime had created the strongest industrial economy with the highest standard of living in the communist world.' At the same time, the SED had transformed a state that in its official pursuit of reunification had initially proclaimed its partial, provisional character into an internationally recognised and respected state that apparently commanded some loyalty on the part of its citizens.

Although they were never able empirically to measure the

degree of citizen loyalty to the East German state, some outside observers believed that the strength of the socialist economy and of social and political institutions had generated not only stability but a certain popular pride in the GDR and hence legitimacy for the regime. Already in 1964, for example, Theo Sommer, journalist for the liberal weekly *Die Zeit*, had reported a distinct 'state consciousness' among GDR citizens (Dönhoff, Leonhardt and Sommer, 1964: 102) while the American political scientist Jean Smith (1967: ii) called the GDR an 'awakening nation'. More cautiously, Peter Ludz (1968: 325) argued that, thanks to the development of 'consultative authoritarianism', East German society had become a 'self-stabilising system'. In the 1970s and 1980s, some West German and other scholars spoke of an emerging GDR national consciousness (Schweigler, 1975; Steele, 1977) and virtually all admitted to the regime's stability, its leaders' self-assurance, and its people's 'passive acceptance', 'functional loyalty' and 'pride in East German accomplishments' (Starrels and Mallinckrodt, 1975: 384–6; Dennis, 1988: 197; Legters, 1978: 13). These scholars recognised, of course, that the GDR's successes in building its economy, in stabilising its political system, and in forging a national identity ultimately depended, as we have seen, on the existence of the Wall, yet precisely the apparently permanent division of Europe and Germany into two armed camps guaranteed the conditions for the GDR's continued success.

Since the fall of the Wall exposed the GDR's economic weakness, its reliance on Stasi repression, and its citizens' apparent desire for rapid reunification, former GDR experts have had to suffer, perhaps unjustly, much criticism and self-flagellation. Their subject of inquiry seems to have seduced them, or perhaps they simply had too much self-interest in its survival. Experts on East Germany were not alone, though, in discerning stability and a certain legitimacy in a state socialist regime (cf. Rigby, Brown and Reddaway, 1980; Rigby and Feher, 1982; Lewis, 1984). As Jan Pakulski argues, however, scholars who in the 1970s and 1980s applied the term legitimacy to Soviet-style regimes tended to confuse normatively accepted domination with non-legitimate domination based on fear, expediency or fatalism. A regime that gains citizen compliance and even popularity still does not enjoy legitimacy unless citizens accept its authority as unconditionally and morally binding. Legitimacy is what allows a regime to weather crises and to impose unpopular measures without recourse to force (Pakulski, 1990: 271–5). The rapidity of communism's collapse in the crisis of 1989 is therefore 'the best proof of the absence of mass legitimacy'. (ibid.: 284)

In light of communism's rapid collapse, scholars have had to revise their assessment of East German history. Before 1989 they had naturally tended to emphasise the GDR's stability and success because the underlying and apparently permanent reality of Soviet military and political domination of the GDR and East-Central Europe seemed to render the East German state's fundamental birth defects inoperative or irrelevant. Since 1989, scholars have reversed their emphases and argued that the GDR was doomed from birth. Thus, in the contemporary revised view, the GDR's economic growth and attempts to forge a national identity had never won over anything more than the citizens' instrumental obedience to the regime. The construction of the Wall in 1961 convinced citizens that their only choice was to make the best of their lot or face repression. Fatalism, expedience, and fear thus became the basis for fundamentally illegitimate Party rule. The ultimate proof of that illegitimacy came on the night of 9 November 1989 when, in a last-ditch effort to preserve power, the party flung aside the Wall. Almost immediately, the demonstrators, who had until then only requested the democratisation of socialism, demanded its dismantling and ultimately the dissolution of the GDR.

Just as the construction of the Wall had provided the objective conditions for the GDR's survival in 1961, its fall in 1989 within a year engendered the GDR's dissolution. Yet subjectively the Wall has outlived the GDR. The Wall endures not only as a psychological barrier between East and West Germans but as a common symbol, though once again with different meanings. East and West Germans alike today joke about rebuilding the Wall, only this time higher and from both sides. It is understandable, if reprehensible, that West Germans long for the good old days of the smaller Federal Republic with its lower taxes, social stability, and minor international role. By contrast, the East Germans' widespread, sincere nostalgia for the modest comfort and security they enjoyed behind the Wall is less comprehensible unless we recognise that the Wall was simultaneously an instrument of repression and a material condition for the construction of some form of popular consent. East Germans' nostalgia for the Wall, which (as we shall see in Chapter 6) is not purely reactive to the difficulties of reunification, suggests that behind the Wall the GDR had succeeded in forging a sense of identity and loyalty among its citizens after all. The SED regime's rapid demise may have proved that it was not legitimate, but the survival of a certain pride and loyalty towards the GDR today proves that something more than force and fatalism kept the state afloat. The East Germans' relationship to their state before the popular revolution of 1989, it would thus seem, was one ambiguously located somewhere between the normative loyalty constituent of popular legitimacy and the expedient obedience of illegitimate domination.

Whatever the nature of the authority relationship between East German citizens and their state, that relationship clearly underwent a fundamental transformation over the course of 1989, as hundreds of thousands of citizens, by taking to the streets, called the authority of the party-state into question. In the following chapters, I shall try to discover the reasons why so many East Germans suddenly and openly turned against their state. By identifying the demonstrators' motives for revolt, I should also be able to provide a basis for understanding the East Germans' pre-revolutionary arrangement with their state, which had lent the GDR such apparent stability, as well as their current nostalgia for their state. What is more, in uncovering the causes of communism's stability and collapse in the state where its beginnings had been most precarious but its successes perhaps greatest, I should offer a more general understanding of communism's relative successes, its ultimate failure, and its contemporary legacy in Eastern and Central Europe.

3 Popular Explanations of the Popular Revolution

Few other unforeseen events have lent themselves to as much explanation as the fall of the Berlin Wall. It should come as no surprise, though, that the collapse of East German communism has prompted such a surfeit of retrospective analysis. As we saw in the last chapter, the GDR was at once the most vulnerable and the most successful of the Eastern bloc regimes, and its collapse can thus find explanation both in the particular challenges facing the East German rump-state and in the inherent contradictions of even the most successful state socialist regime. In hindsight the GDR would appear to have been doomed from birth: an incomplete nation coupled with an inflexible state can hardly hope to survive.

By its very perfection, however, hindsight may be the historian's worst enemy; it makes the unforeseeable appear foreordained, even overdetermined. But too many explanations of an event bring us no closer to discerning historical causality than too few. From the jungle of explanations we must weed out spurious and incidental causes of the event and expose its necessary and – more importantly – its sufficient causes. In this chapter I shall attempt to evaluate some of the more popular of the numerous journalistic and scholarly explanations of communism's collapse in the GDR. Relying in part on the results of my survey of ordinary East Germans, I shall argue that some of the common explanations point to necessary causes of communism's collapse but in the end fail to identify the sufficient causes of the popular mobilisation that brought down the regime.

REUNIFICATION AND THE REVOLUTION

A common mistake in the historiography of revolutions is the confusion of outcomes with causes. The question 'cui bono?' does not often provide a lead in the search for the

origins of revolution. Revolutions rarely end where they began
and those who launch them seldom profit from them. Disillusioned revolutionary radicals like to quip that the outcome and the cause of revolution are diametrically opposed:
'Revolutions always begin at the bottom left and end at the
top right.' But even such cynicism is too deterministic. As
Barrington Moore has remarked, despite all the efforts of
Marxist historiography to prove that an ascendant bourgeoisie
launched the great early modern revolutions, the term 'bourgeois revolution' describes only where a revolution ended,
not where and how it began (Moore, 1966: 427). Unless we
embrace some essentially ahistorical teleology, the outcome
of a revolution tells us nothing about its causes. The point
bears repeating in the context of the East German revolution, for especially outside Germany, where the divisions
among Germans are not so obvious, popular and sometimes
scientific opinion has mistaken German reunification for the
cause of the 1989 revolution. Viewed from afar, the easy
switch in the fall of 1989 from the democratic revolutionary slogan '*Wir* sind das Volk' to the nationalist refrain "Wir
sind *ein* Volk' suggests that nationalist motivations underlay from the beginning the mass protest movement that
toppled communism. A closer reading of events casts doubt
on such a facile linking of outcome and cause, but the notion
that pan-German national sentiment or a desire for unification caused the popular uprising of autumn 1989 remains a
hypothesis worth testing.

No one has seriously argued that the East German revolution was some kind of national liberation struggle, yet given
the GDR's perpetual crises of identity and legitimacy, it is
hard to imagine that national sentiment did not underlie
popular mobilisation against the regime. This national sentiment need not have sprung from the idealistic desire to
reunite politically the ethnic community alone; the democratic freedoms and material prosperity available in the West
sufficed to generate opposition to Germany's division. To
be sure, for some older East Germans, the ideal of a united
German nation-state, in which they had been born and whose
wrenching division they had suffered, motivated a sentimental
opposition to the GDR regime quite independent of any
desire for greater political freedom. Other East Germans,

particularly in the younger generations, had a more materialistic interest in overcoming the division of Germany. For them unification, whether at the individual level through emigration or at the societal level through the fall of the Wall, afforded a greater satisfaction of the consumer desires that the post-Stalinist 'social contract' of the 1970s and 1980s had awakened but not satisfied. For young and old, materialists and idealists alike, the division of Germany frustrated the most basic desires and motivated opposition to the regime.

Thus, it is possible to see the origins of the collapse of GDR state socialism in persistent internal opposition to the division of Germany, or more precisely to the frustrations it entailed. This opposition gnawed away at the foundations of the regime until its Wall began to crumble in earnest in 1984. That year the regime authorised the emigration of 41 000 malcontents, but this effort to quell the demand for exit visas backfired as it only emboldened tens of thousands of others to risk their careers and family welfare by applying to emigrate. The government's capricious stop–go policy in granting emigration and visitors' visas simply served to heighten frustration and opposition until on 2 May 1989, Hungary made its fateful decision to dismantle its border fortifications with Austria and suddenly opened a new channel for emigration. Even before the emigration flood of August–September 1989, a whole sub-culture of potential emigrants (*Ausreisewillige*) had arisen, particularly within the shelter of the church. As a nationalist-minded demonstrator from Leipzig whom I interviewed recounted:

> Leipzig's Nikolai Church developed as a centre of opposition only with the emigration wave of the late 1980s. *Ausreisewillige* from the whole country met in the sacristy to exchange information about emigration possibilities. I started going to the Monday evening peace prayers with my son, who wanted to leave the GDR, in early June 1989, just as the prayers were beginning to develop into the kernel of the fall's protest movement. My son got arrested after the June 13 prayer during a peaceful confrontation with the police. Of the 22 people arrested that evening, 16 had applied for emigration visas. That proves that it was the *Ausreisewillige* who brought the *Wende* into motion.

To be sure, the massive emigration wave of August–September and the small groups of protestors in Leipzig and Berlin crying 'Wir wollen 'raus' ('We want out') in September were the final precipitants of October's mass demonstrations. 'Wir wollen 'raus' gave way to the even more regime-threatening 'Wir bleiben hier' ('We're staying here', implying 'and things had better change') and 'Wir sind das Volk', but the issue of travel-freedom remained central to the protests. In fact, the fall of the Wall was the (intentional?) result of the government's clumsy efforts to save itself with the ultimate easing of travel restrictions. The emotional rediscovery of the German nation atop the Berlin Wall on the night of 9 November 1989, allowed the inchoate protest movement to articulate its underlying motive. At the following Monday's demonstrations, the chorus 'Wir sind *ein* Volk' united the East Germans in their fundamental desires for reunification, be they idealistic or materialistic.

Such an interpretation of the fall of 1989, however, contradicts the view of those who pretend to have been the authors of a popular democratic revolution and not of nationalist revival. For them the shout 'Wir sind *ein* Volk' represented a betrayal of the revolution, the result of the revolution's kidnapping by Western politicians looking for easy votes and businessmen eager to quench a new market's consumer thirst. For the democratic revolutionaries, the issues of emigration and travel restrictions were not the be-all-and-end-all of the *Wende*. The prominence of these issues in 1989 was symptomatic not of a yearning to restore national unity but of the people's opposition to a repressive party-state increasingly disdainful of its own citizens. The protestors did not aim to destroy the GDR but to democratise it.

For the democratic revolutionaries the *Ausreisewelle* (mass exodus) merely provided the context in which the regime betrayed its popular illegitimacy. In their view, 7 May rather than 2 May was the decisive starting-point for the *Wende*. The blatant fraud in the reporting of that Sunday's local election results gave the citizens of the GDR a much clearer signal than did Hungary's decision the preceding Tuesday to ease its border controls. Hungary's complete opening of its borders on 11 September did provoke a mass hysteria culminating in the storming of the West German embassies in Prague and Warsaw later that month, but it was the government's reaction to the *Ausreisewelle* that prompted the mass protest movement. The statement, attributed to Erich Honecker, that the party shed no tear over those who had fled left no doubt about the government's unwillingness to introduce reforms. Thus, the first mass organisations, most notably Neues Forum (founded on 9 September) and Demokratie Jetzt (founded on 12 September), and the first mass demonstrations (beginning 2 October in Leipzig) demanded political reforms within a socialist GDR. The freedom to travel figured as but one of the democratic citizenship rights demanded on the protestors' petitions and banners. Free elections headed the list of demands, as befitted a movement that had started in early May with formal protests against electoral fraud. The fact that the first free elections gave a majority to parties favouring immediate reunification did not prove that the democratic reformers and their followers had secretly desired unification all along but that reforming the GDR was an exceedingly difficult task, especially when West German parties and politicians had taken control of the political system.

The debate over the democratic versus nationalist character of the *Wende* continues today with the costs of unification lending it particular acrimony. The reformers of the fall of 1989 are bitterly disappointed over the lost opportunity to construct a democratic society while the conservative architects of unification hope that national sentiment will hold the divided country together. Both the nationalist and democratic revolutionary interpretations of the *Wende* appear credible, and it would be tempting to conclude that the truth lies somewhere in between and leave it at that. Nationalist and democratic impulses for revolution do not exclude one another, and some combination of them may have underlain the East German revolution. A closer look at events and at my survey data, however, strongly calls into question the role of nationalism in the *Wende*.

The sequence of events in 1989 does not automatically suggest that nationalism or the desire for reunification played a decisive part in the collapse of communism. First, although the *Ausreisewelle* was certainly an immediate precipitant of the popular revolution, little evidence shows that the desire to emigrate before or during 1989 was linked to a desire for national unity or even to a particularly strong disaffection towards the GDR. My own interviews with East Germans whose friends or relatives had fled lead me to believe that those who left did so for inarticulable, even irrational reasons. Most were relatively successful members of GDR society, who left behind cars, careers, and houses (cf. Voigt, Belitz-Demiriz and Meck, 1990). The psychoanalyst Hans-Joachim Maaz argues that precisely the most successful East Germans emigrated in order to fulfil even higher ambitions as part of a strategy to avoid confronting emotions that the GDR social and cultural system conspired to repress (Maaz, 1990: 123 ff.). He goes on to suggest that emigrants in fact desired the persistent division of Germany as a mechanism for further repressing past emotion (Maaz, 1991: 78). Second, at the mass demonstrations of October, particularly the decisive ones in Leipzig, nationalist sentiment and calls for unification were almost entirely absent. The masses shouted down those few who did voice pan-German nationalism. Third, the call for reunification became widespread only after the fall of the Wall when East Germans for the first time acquired or recovered their pan-German identity. The vast majority of survey respondents told me that, despite Western television and personal contacts, they had not felt part of a broader German community until visiting the Federal Republic after the fall of the Wall. Nationalist sentiment followed the collapse of the Wall – the communist regime's concession of defeat – and was therefore a consequence and not a cause of the revolution.

Still, it is possible that the dismantling of the GDR and the unification of Germany – and not the democratic renewal of socialism – were the protestors' goals from the beginning. As the nationalist demonstrator from Leipzig cited above insisted:

> The reformist intellectuals placed themselves at the head of the movement only after those who wanted to emigrate set it in motion. They have no right to claim they were betrayed. The people stopped listening to the Neues Forum in November (1989) because the reformers hadn't

recognised that the whole system had to go. The people knew that from the beginning. The masses were clever, though, and expanded their demands bit by bit each week. From the very start we all wanted reunification, but it would have been a tactical blunder to demand it right away. The left-wing intellectuals, like that well known pastor (Friedrich) Schorlemmer are spreading a historical lie: that the revolution was betrayed. They never were the revolution. They claim today that they were active dissidents for years. Big deal! They were allowed to be dissidents because they posed no threat. The people never respected them.

Our Leipzig demonstrator might be hard-pressed to prove that the masses secretly harboured a desire for reunification and cleverly used 'salami' tactics to attain it. Reunification may nonetheless have been a subconscious wish, the expression of which the harsh reality of the Wall allowed only in fantasies or jokes. Such a latent desire for reunification was evident, for example, in a joke one survey respondent told me about membership in the Society for German–Soviet Friendship (DSF): 'In case of reunification, the years of DSF membership would count in the calculation of pensions as time spent in a Soviet prisoner-of-war camp.' She added, 'People still laughed at that joke as late as October 1989 because the premise of reunification still sounded implausible.'

Individuals' arguments and anecdotes may be illustrative, but an appeal to my survey data might yield some more convincing evidence about the role of open, secret, or subconscious wishes for reunification in the mass mobilisation of autumn 1989. Two survey questions directly offered an opportunity for respondents to assess the importance of the desire for reunification during the *Wende*. One open-ended question (F48b)[1] asked respondents about their motives for participation or non-participation in anti-government demonstrations before the fall of the Wall. Of the 45 per cent who had demonstrated, only 5.5 per cent spontaneously mentioned reunification as a motivating goal as compared to 22 per cent who spoke of improving socialism and 58 per cent who expressed unspecified desires for political change. Another question (F54) offered a choice of two among five explanations of the massive demand for reunification that arose in November–December 1989. Only 17 per cent saw (as a first or second choice) the demand for reunification as springing from a longstanding, if repressed, German national sentiment whereas nearly 60 per cent attributed the pro-unification sentiment to a desire to obtain the level of material welfare that the East Germans had seen in the West after the fall of the Wall.

These survey results would thus suggest that a desire for unification did not directly or consciously motivate East Germans during the *Wende*. Indirectly, however, an unarticulated or subconscious desire to overcome the division of Germany may have underlain participation in the demonstrations that toppled the regime. We might expect that East Germans who had contact with friends or relatives in the West (F68a), who regularly watched Western television (F62c), who thought life chances were better in the West (F36a), or who had considered emigration (F37a) would have been more likely to participate in protest. None of these variables, however, correlates strongly (either individually or in a multivariate regression model) with the level of protest participation (F48a).[2] The strongest – but still very weak – correlation coefficient (+0.27) was that between Western media exposure and demonstration participation. It would be wrong to conclude, however, that Western broadcasts kept the dream of unification alive or otherwise encouraged opposition to the regime. Most survey respondents stressed that the artificiality of television prevented the development of a strong identification with West Germany. What is more, with Western television exposure nearly universal (except in the extreme north-east and south-east of the GDR), the media variable tends to be a better measure of pre-existing regime support than of an independent cause of opposition: only those who blindly supported the regime loyally avoided watching Western television. In cross-tabulations with both more and less stringently defined dummy variables for demonstration participation, the variables 'West relatives' (F68a,b) and 'considered emigration' (F37a) also proved positively and significantly related to protest though, as we shall explore further in Chapter 5, the relationship holds for only certain categories of survey respondents.

In short, variables linked to the problem of Germany's division have a positive statistical relationship with demonstration participation for at least certain survey respondent groups, but these findings hardly lend credence to the argument that the desire to reunify Germany primarily or consciously motivated the 1989 demonstrators. No doubt, the division of Germany fundamentally threatened the legitimacy of the GDR, but overcoming Germany's division was not the central concern of the East Germans who took to the streets to topple their government.

The outcome of the popular revolution in the GDR – German reunification – sets it apart from the other Eastern European 'refolutions' (Garton Ash, 1990). Elsewhere the national question has taken a contrary form, with disintegration instead of unification as revolution or reform's result. As in East Germany, though, nationalism – whether integrative or disintegrative in effect – was sooner an outcome than a cause of the refolution, except perhaps in Poland. The totalitarian party-state had more or less effectively 'normalised' or neutralised social divisions as the pervasive state apparatus repressed independent societal forces, including those based on ethnicity or nationality. A prerequisite for the rekindling of nationalist movements was therefore the suppression of the party-state and a rebirth of an autonomous society. As we saw in Chapter 1, theories of revolutions, including those in Eastern Europe, tend to emphasise either the erosion of the state or the mobilisation of society as the primary cause of revolution. We have just seen that the exceptional circumstances of the GDR as a partial-nation-state did not necessarily generate the revolution there. We shall now turn to an assessment of the applicability to the GDR of the more general theories of communism's collapse through erosion from above or mobilisation from below.

THE SELF-DESTRUCTION OF THE PARTY-STATE

Along with the exact circumstances of the fall of the Wall, the great mystery of the *Wende* is the failure of the state to engage its repressive mechanisms. With more information the mystery has only grown, for in the months following the Wall's crumbling, citizens' committees and other investigators discovered how extensive and how perfected the Ministry for State Security's (Stasi's) information gathering and repressive means were (cf. Bürgerkomitee Leipzig, 1991; Gauck, 1991; Hahn, 1990; Loest, 1991; Riecker, Schwarz, and Schneider, 1990; Wawrzyn, 1990; Wilkening, 1990). In fact, the discovery of the Stasi's pervasiveness led virtually all parties to agree on the necessity of dissolving the GDR. The questions surrounding the Stasi's inaction or even complicity during the *Wende* have given rise to various accounts of communism's collapse in East Germany, and throughout the bloc, as a kind of carefully planned revolution from above. These accounts are popular in the press (even the serious German news magazine *Der Spiegel* thrives on them), but they verge on conspiracy theory. Nonetheless, I shall briefly present some of them because they evoke and even support theories that explain communism's collapse with its erosion from the top.

At the very top of the world communist hierarchy stood none other than Mikhail Sergeivitch Gorbachev, and many a disappointed Stalinist and some scholars, too, would attribute the collapse of communism to his connivance (or brilliance) alone. According to this conspiratorial reading of Gorbachev's role in the world anti-communist revolution, the First Secretary of the CPSU was not a great reformer who inadvertently unleashed the furies with his new thinking but a clever tactician who orchestrated each regime's collapse. A well-timed phone-call to tell a subordinate leader, such as Polish Premier Rakowski during his Round Table negotiations with Solidarnosc, to make concessions (Gati, 1990: 168) or a secret order to a general or a KGB officer not to suppress a demonstration (Urban, 1990: 117) could suffice to bring down a government. In the case of the GDR, Gorbachev's crucial intervention came during his visit of 6–7 October 1989 to East Berlin on the occasion of the GDR's 40th anniversary celebration. In one fell swoop, Gorbachev allegedly decapitated the leadership with a Politburo speech critical of Honecker, deprived the regime of its ultimate means of repression with a non-intervention order to the Soviet military command in the GDR, and single-handedly mobilised the masses with his mere presence (Gorbimania) and with his oft-cited admonishment: 'Life punishes those who come too late.'

Another, somewhat more sophisticated and less conspiratorial theory recognises Gorbachev's personal contribution to the 'refolutions' but argues that his ability to influence events depended on the power-plays of various factions at the top of the party hierarchy. This 'Kremlinological' approach explains the collapse of communism as an unintended consequence of a fratricidal struggle between communist hardliners and equally communist reformers (cf. Gedmin, 1992). Not surprisingly, among the chief proponents of this type of analysis are the memoir-writing former Politburo members themselves, including Gorbachev. Thus, Erich Honecker explains his downfall as the result of Politburo scheming behind his back during his protracted illness over the summer of 1989 (Andert and Herzberg, 1990: 30–6). His successor, Egon Krenz, while in office tried to claim that the party under his leadership had in fact introduced the *Wende*, and later on insisted that he had personally prevented violence at the fateful 9 October demonstration in Leipzig by countermanding the order for armed intervention (Krenz, 1990: 205). More credibly, Politburo member and Berlin party-chief Günther Schabowski has explained the fall of the Wall as the result of a misunderstanding among Central Committee members debating the reform of travel restrictions (Schabowski, 1990: 134–40).

The most popular conspiratorial reading of events attributes the collapse of communism not to factional feuds or bumbling in the leadership but to the concerted actions of one branch of the state – the security apparatus. Here the variants of conspiracy theory are boundless, the possibilities for intrigue beyond imagination. With the likes of Stasi major and GDR arms-dealer Alexander Schalck-Golodkowski today freely roaming the Bavarian Alps and with Stasi revelations daily rocking every level of German society, East and West, it is impossible to exclude the hypothesis that the Pope, the CIA, the Trilateral Commission, the gnomes in Zurich, and all the other usual suspects were involved in organising the collapse of communism. More generally, though, these conspiracy theories contend that the Stasi was a state within the state, a diabolically pragmatic party above the party. Loyal only to itself, militarily organised, and perfectly informed, the Stasi escaped external control and ultimately destroyed the party for which it was to serve as sword and shield. The reasons for the security apparatus's alleged decision to scuttle the socialist state – prescience, perhaps, of an economic collapse or of profits and political opportunities in a Wild East – remain obscure, but evidence that secret-police agents infiltrated and even led every level of opposition in Eastern Europe seems to prove that the security forces controlled or at least condoned the popular uprisings. Typical was the East German case of Wolfgang Schnur, who led the Demokratischer Aufbruch movement into a pro-unification electoral alliance with Chancellor Kohl's CDU and then resigned under allegations that he was a Stasi mole.

Whatever form they take, the conspiracy theories of the 1989 revolutions share one trait: they are practically unverifiable. Based on fragmentary evidence and self-serving statements of former officials, they rely too heavily on speculation to be convincing. To be sure, events would have unfolded differently in 1989 if security forces had intervened (as they did in part in Rumania), if Politburos had not been fractured, and if Gorbachev had not been so charismatic and clever (or too clever by half). All these factors may have been necessary, but the theories of revolution from above signally fail to explain the distinctive characteristic of the 1989 revolutions: their popularity. Gorbachev may have planned palace coups, but he (and subsequent conspiracy theorists) did (and do) not predict the mass upheavals that would put playwrights into the castle. Rival Politburo factions may have done the dirty work of doing in each others' leaders, but like Egon Krenz and his reformers, they were merely rushing to catch up with a social movement over which they never had control. What is more, every second opposition group member and every tenth demonstrator may have been a Stasi informant, but even such an exaggerated proportion of Stasi participation cannot explain from where all the other regime opponents came. Although, as I shall argue in the next chapter, Gorbachev probably played an essential, if unwitting role in spurring popular mobilisation in the GDR, no individual, no faction, no organisation can claim credit for launching the mass uprising that toppled East German communism.

The conspiracy theories do, however, point to an important truth about the collapse of communism: the extent and the success of popular mobilisation at least partly depended on the breakdown of the normal functioning of state and party leadership. As we saw in Chapter 1, the post-Stalinist party-state witnessed a Weberian 'routinisation of charisma' involving the ritualisation of ideology and the bureaucratisation of organisation. During the Brezhnevite stagnation, communist ideology lost its mobilisational, millenarian appeal, becoming a formalistic shell where conformism replaced conviction. Similarly, the personnel of the party-state ceased to be a revolutionary vanguard and became a self-interested, self-reproducing political caste, the *nomenklatura*. Ideologically and organisationally, the totalitarian communist state disappeared well before 1989. What remained was a party-state staffed with ideological hypocrites motivated by self-interest, if at all. Equipped with a powerful military and police, such a moribund system could survive for several decades but had to collapse between the unconcerted efforts of those who hoped to reform or revive the system and those who wanted it to linger on in sweet decadence. Even the slightest opposition would suffice to bring down a regime that was but a shell of its former self.

In retrospect it is hard to know whether this description of communism's withering-away applies to the GDR or any other case. How dead does the ideology have to be? And how entrenched and inflexible need the bureaucracy be for the communist party-state to cease functioning? Just because the system died does not mean that it was terminally ill. In the GDR it was by no means clear that Marxism-Leninism was a dead letter in the 1980s, and the bureaucracy continued to work with Prussian efficiency down to the bitter end. In order to test a systemic breakdown theory, we must identify its testable component hypotheses. It would be difficult but not impossible to find reliable and revealing measures of bureaucratic self-reproduction (e.g. social origins of *nomenklatura* members) and self-interest (e.g. incidents of non-implementation or alteration of policy). In the absence of such demographic and behavioural data, attitudinal data might uncover bureaucratic cynicism reflective of a ritualisation of ideology. Without some sort of subjective measuring stick, though, it is virtually impossible to distinguish ritual motions from active belief. Psychological case-studies or survey research among party elites might provide such measuring sticks, but more readily available public opinion research would also permit the testing of the hypothesis that ideology for society at large, and by extension presumably for party elites, had become a matter of conformism rather than conviction, that a general erosion of faith in communism precipitated its collapse.

Unfortunately, reliable survey data on the evolution of East German public attitudes towards socialist ideology has until recently been unavailable (cf. Förster and Roski, 1990: 15–17; Gensicke, 1992; Schweigler, 1975: passim; Ludz, 1977: 224). The survey research that did occur in the GDR suffered not only from strict political control but also from researcher and participant self-censorship.[3] The wording of survey questions had to conform to party orthodoxy, with the result that surveys often measured knowledge of and attitudes towards official slogans rather than belief in underlying principles. Confronted with such questions, survey participants well-versed in public mimicry also tended to answer in a manner reflecting their anticipation of sanctions more than their personal point of view. When survey results nonetheless failed to flatter the party, they became classified materials, which researchers could discuss only informally and in guarded terms, especially if they wanted to pursue further research. For survey researchers, as for artists, a ban on publishing or presenting work became almost a badge of honour proving the originality and daring of their work. Furthermore, since general public opinion research was officially unnecessary in a state where the party perfectly represented the interests and aspirations of the people, surveys addressed only the problems and concerns of particular population segments, most notably the youth, who came under the careful scrutiny of the Zentralinstitut für Jugendforschung (ZIJ) in Leipzig.

Since the *Wende*, sociologists from the ZIJ have been able to publish previously classified survey data revealing the extent of ideological disillusion among youths in the late 1980s. Although the survey samples the ZIJ gathered over two decades included only apprentices and students aged 14 to 25, the clear trends in the ZIJ data presumably reflect the evolution of public opinion at large. The apprentices responded to a number of simple questions about personal identification with the GDR, satisfaction with life there, historical prospects for socialism's success, identification with Marxism-Leninism, and confidence in the SED and the youth movement FDJ (Förster and Roski, 1990: 38–44). Because the questions were posed at irregular intervals, it is not possible precisely to identify a historic attitudinal turning-point, but the ZIJ findings unambiguously reveal a dramatic decline in favourable attitudes towards the GDR and its socialist system in the late 1980s. Despite their temporal imprecision, what is striking about the ZIJ findings is the timing and speed of the attitudinal shift. The data show that attitudes towards the GDR and socialism were, by and large, stable and favourable from 1970 until 1985. Then, and apparently especially between 1987 and 1989, opinions rapidly soured. In 1970, for example, 23 per cent of the apprentices disagreed with the statement 'The SED has my trust' while in 1986 only 21 per cent disagreed. In May 1989, by contrast, fully 53 per cent disagreed (Förster and Roski, 1990: 44). Similarly, in an analysis of two surveys conducted by the East Berlin Akademie für Gesellschaftswissenschaften (AfG) in 1987 and late 1988, Thomas Gensicke concludes that despite their different target populations and questions, the AfG surveys measure a rapid and substantial drop in popular satisfaction with the GDR regime (Gensicke, 1992: 18).

The ZIJ and AfG evidence of such a sudden reversal of opinion suggests that socialist ideology in the GDR entered into a sudden crisis in the late 1980s and did not suffer from a gradual erosion over the preceding decades. An explanation that traces communism's collapse back to what Weberian sociology would call a routinisation of charisma, however, would normally predict that utopian ideology and confidence in the vanguard party would slowly grow ritualistic and devoid of sense, if not entirely hypocritical. The ZIJ and AfG data, inasmuch as they represent the state of general public attitudes towards real existing socialism in the GDR, imply not that an erosion of faith in communist utopia preceded the system's collapse but that a crisis of faith accompanied it.

The relatively simple formulation of existing East German survey questions, however, does not really permit an assessment of popular faith in socialism. Statements about trust in the party or identification with Marxism-Leninism tell us little about belief in or acceptance of socialist values such as equality and security. Quite possibly, the persistence of socialist utopianism rather than its disappearance as a source of legitimation brought down the party-state. In an ironic historic twist, the vanguard party may have succeeded in converting the masses to socialist ideals, and the masses in turn may out of utopianism have revolted against party leaders, whom they found cynical or impure. Certainly, the utopian character of opposition groups and of the first anti-government protests in the GDR would be consistent with such an interpretation. The first major public demonstrations in the GDR since 1953 occurred in January 1988 and January 1989 upon the occasion of the annual commemoration of the deaths of Karl Liebknecht and Rosa Luxemburg, with the protestors claiming to represent the true revolutionary heritage. The first declaration of the citizens' movement Demokratie Jetzt dated 12 September 1989, was typical of the ideological character of the opposition groups:

> We are in danger of losing the social justice and the solidaristic society for which the socialist working class movement has strived. Socialism must now take its true democratic form or else be lost forever. It must not be lost because endangered humanity in its search for sustainable forms of community needs alternatives to Western consumer society, whose welfare comes at the expense of the rest of the world. (Schüddekopf, 1990: 32)

Official declarations and public statements by opposition leaders, however, do not necessarily reflect the ideological orientations of the population at large or even of their followers. Evidence allowing us to conclude that either disenchantment with or true loyalty to socialist ideology brought the GDR regime asunder would thus seem to be lacking.

My own survey findings provide some evidence about the

decay or survival of socialist utopianism and its role in the collapse of state socialism, but it is inconclusive. As a one-time retrospective questioning, my survey can say little about the evolution of popular attitudes towards socialism. Instead it provides a reconstructed snapshot of attitudes during socialism's final hours. Overall the members of my survey sample demonstrated loyalty to the fundamental principles and to the founders of socialism but dissatisfaction with the form socialism had taken in the GDR. Thus, 81 per cent agreed with the statement that East German state socialism should not be confused with true socialism, which might still be attainable (F44g).[4] Similarly, Karl Marx, the German revolutionary martyrs Rosa Luxemburg and Karl Liebknecht, and the GDR's first president Wilhelm Pieck still enjoyed positive sympathy scores whereas latter-day real existing socialists such as Walter Ulbricht and Erich Honecker were scarcely less despised than Adolf Hitler (F43a–m). Among the anti-government demonstrators in the sample, ambivalence towards socialist values was somewhat stronger, suggesting that rank-and-file protestors did not necessarily share their leaders' utopianism. As we have already seen, 22 per cent of the demonstration participants wanted to improve socialism, but 58 per cent simply wanted things to change. The protestors' attitudes towards socialism followed no clear trends. None of the attitudinal variables from the questionnaire correlated strongly with the level of demonstration participation. Only disagreement with the statement that the anti-fascist background of the founders of the GDR and of the SED justified their leading role (F44a) had a correlation coefficient with demonstration participation worthy of mention: $+0.34$. The demonstrators also showed particular antipathy towards GDR politicians, surprisingly particularly towards the otherwise beloved worker-president Wilhelm Pieck ($r = -0.43$). Still, several demonstrators – in statements that reminded me of the French peasants' supplication of their 'good king' in their *cahiers de doléances* of 1789 – expressed their conviction that top leaders really did want 'only the best for the people' but had been deceived by ill-willed mid-level functionaries. The overall ambiguity of my findings, however, does not permit any conclusions about the role of socialist ideology in the GDR's collapse.

SOCIETAL MOBILISATION AGAINST STATE SOCIALISM

In discussing the role of ideology in communism's collapse, I have slipped away from a model of party-state erosion to one of societal mobilisation. In the totalitarian party-state, socialist utopianism legitimated and motivated single-party rule and also mobilised popular support for the regime. The corruption or ritualisation of ideology would therefore not only have undermined the functioning of the party-state but demobilised society. In the last section, I tried to determine whether the ideological demobilisation of society – through its members' loss of faith either in socialism or in the party-state's ability or will to realise socialism – precipitated the collapse of communism in the GDR. Implicit in the discussion was the notion that an ideological remobilisation of society, be it anti-socialist or neo-utopian, was necessary to topple a regime that had lost its idealistic underpinnings. Such a line of interpretation, in which a ideologically recharged society gives the *coup de grâce* to a corrupted political system, differs sharply from the theory of the mobilisation of civil-society. As we saw in Chapter 1, in the civil-society perspective, society does not mobilise to fill the vacuum left by the ideological retreat of the post-totalitarian state but in opposition to the party-state's continued effort to control society. This opposition can take both cultural-ideological and organisational form. In an almost hydraulic model, the rise of oppositional culture and groups, i.e. of a civil society, engenders the fall of a state with totalitarian aspirations.

The civil-society perspective has dominated explanations of communism's collapse in Hungary and especially Poland. Because of the weakness of organised opposition groups in the GDR and the forced expatriation of cultural dissidents, East Germany tended to be left out of discussions of the revival of civil society in Eastern Europe before 1989. Still, the GDR experienced the rise in the 1980s of oppositional culture and groups (cf. Kroh, 1988), and various scholars have drawn a causal link between this small opposition movement and the collapse of communism. Combining sociological analysis with literary criticism, Antonia Grunenberg has argued that in a significant rupture with official ideology and culture, an alternative youth scene and literary counter-culture arose in the GDR during the 1980s, though she concedes that these groups remained too small and of too little influence to constitute a veritable civil society (Grunenberg, 1990a, 1990b). Christiane Lemke, by contrast, contends that the broader rift that emerged in the 1980s between what she calls the official political culture and the dominant culture signalled the emergence of an East German civil society. According to Lemke, the contradiction between public norms and private values grew untenable in the late 1980s as traditional communist methods of political socialisation proved incompatible with the modernisation of society. Young people in particular escaped the ideological and organisational control of the party-state and brought it down with the *Ausreisewelle* and protests of 1989 (Lemke, 1991).

Alienation of large segments of the population from the ideology and institutions of the state, however, does not in itself guarantee the formation of a civil society capable of contesting the state's authority. A civil society must articulate alternative ideas and generate new forms of social organisation in order to pose a threat to the state. Although East German alternative thinkers regularly faced forced expatriation, both they and opposition groups found refuge in the Protestant Church (cf. Rein, 1990). Neither its Lutheran doctrine of church subordination to state authority nor its organisational strength – only one in three East Germans claimed any church affiliation – allowed the Church to become a veritable pole of opposition to the party-state. In fact, the officially atheistic regime at times relied on the Church as one of its support props as, most blatantly, during the Luther Year, 1983 (cf. Goeckel, 1990). Nonetheless, the Church was the one societal organisation that stood outside of state control, and logically regime opponents had to come together there. Peace and human rights activists, environmentalists, feminists and young people just looking for something different met each other, formally organised, and even opened libraries and information centres in Church buildings (cf. Kroh, 1988; Israel, 1991; Rein, 1990). In the fall of 1989, churches were the places whence protest meetings spilled on to the streets to become demonstrations; the opposition groups that had formed in the Church organised and set the non-violent tone of the mass actions; and pastors took the leadership of the new political movements and parties. In short, a civil-society model of the collapse of communism would seem to fit the East German case: an alienated society, particularly its youth, could articulate demands and organise opposition in the shelter of the Church and thus gathered the force to overthrow a state with totalitarian ambitions.

Although a church-led, or rather church-facilitated opposition may have been a necessary precondition for the peaceful revolution in the GDR, the actions of the nascent East German civil society hardly sufficed to bring down the communist regime. By the late 1980s large segments – if not a majority – of the GDR population were alienated from the regime, but organised, articulate opposition remained minuscule. The Leipzig sociologist Detleff Pollack estimates that membership in opposition groups, which were widely socially derided, numbered at most 10 000 to 15 000 in the entire GDR (Pollack, 1990: 18), while the Berlin political scientist Rolf Reißig places the number at a mere 2500 (Reißig, 1991: 24). Even this small opposition seemed to be losing rather than gaining strength in the GDR's final years (Henkys, 1990: 30). Still, a tiny and tired organised opposition may have been able to bring an alienated society – not yet well enough organised to be called a civil society – to the barricades. Opposition group members did found mass movements such as Neues Forum and lead the anti-government demonstrations in the fall of 1989. What is more, the predominance of young people in the *Ausreisewelle* and in the first demonstrations suggests that this group, which the state had failed politically to socialise, formed the natural constituency for the opposition culture that undermined the party-state.

Although both were highly visible during the *Wende*, my survey findings suggest that neither organised opposition nor youth played a decisive role in the regime's demise. Because the survey sample had an unavoidable self-selection bias towards politically active citizens (cf. Chapter 1), it was surprising that the sample included such a small number of *Bürgerbewegung* (citizens' movement) members. Of 202 survey participants, only 11 claimed to have belonged to or participated in one of the mass citizens' movements of 1989 (nine in Neues Forum, one each in Demokratie Jetzt and Demokratischer Aufbruch), and several of these activists entered the sample only because friends or neighbours had transmitted to them my request for survey participation.

Of course, the quantity of organised opposition may not carry as much weight as its quality. It is more important to know how many people a group such as Neues Forum influenced than how many it enrolled. To make its existence and demands known to the population and to the state, the Neues Forum circulated its founding declaration of 10 September 1989, in the form of a petition, which allegedly over a million East Germans signed during the following weeks. Among my survey respondents 64 per cent of those who participated in anti-government demonstrations signed the Neues Forum declaration as compared to only 34 per cent of the non-demonstrators.[5] It would be wrong to conclude, however, that the Neues Forum appeal mobilised the demonstrators. To the contrary, those who had already decided to protest subsequently signed the Neues Forum petition when it was circulated at demonstrations or special candlelight church services. In fact, as Karl-Dieter Opp and Peter Voss have confirmed with a survey of 1300 randomly selected Leipzigers, the decision of individual East Germans to participate in public demonstrations occurred quite independently of previous integration into oppositional groups. Mobilisation was spontaneous and not organised (Opp and Gern, 1992). While organised opposition groups may have given demonstrations a focus and some direction, they apparently cannot take credit for bringing about the fall's massive demonstrations. As one demonstrator from Greifswald put it with a baker's metaphor: 'The *Bürgerbewegungen* were like the raisin that happens to sit atop a risen bread dough and exclaims, "Look what I have done!"'

The unwrinkled youth, moreover, seems to have had as little to do with the rising-up of East German society as did organised opposition groups. Media images of young people confronting police lines and leaping over the Wall gave the impression that the autumn of 1989 was a revolution of disenchanted youths. To be sure, youthful idealism sometimes places young people at the head of demonstrations, but more often it is simply youthful vigour and fitness that puts young people in position for dramatic camera angles. My survey data, in fact, suggest that younger people were no more likely than their elders to be disenchanted with state socialism or to participate in anti-government demonstrations. Although Christiane Lemke, on the basis of the ZIJ apprentice survey data mentioned above, argues that the political socialisation of East German youth broke down in the 1980s, rendering it the revolutionary agent *par excellence* (Lemke, 1991: 152), my own data do not reveal an attitudinal generation gap. Youths may have lost faith in party and state in the late 1980s but no more so than did their elders. If anything, younger people with no other political life-experience may have had a stronger identification with the GDR and with socialism, though my survey found no statistically significant relationships between age and political attitudes. Similarly, young and old showed no significant differences in their behaviour during the fall of 1989. Several older survey respondents admitted that they had followed their children's lead in going to demonstrate, but overall age and level of demonstration participation showed virtually no correlation ($r = -0.07$).[6]

In short, my survey data do not support a civil-society model of communism's collapse in the face of growing organised opposition and (youth) counter-culture. While groups of young people meeting under the protective wing of the Church may in the 1980s have begun to generate an East German civil society capable of resisting the authoritarian party-state's stranglehold on social life, those opposition groups in particular and young people in general can certainly not alone claim credit for making the revolution that brought down the SED regime.

THE ECONOMIC UNTENABILITY OF COMMUNISM

The final fiasco of Marxism-Leninism has ironically proven the fundamental veracities of Marxism and Leninism. Marx correctly asserted that the strength of social and political systems rested on the performance of their economic substructure. He mistakenly believed, however, that revolutions

occurred when the development of the forces of production (substructure) surpassed and rendered obsolete the relations of production (superstructure). Lenin recognised that
revolutions seldom break out in the economically most advanced countries and therefore predicted and organised
revolution in the peripheral parts of the capitalist world.
Marx and Lenin can both rest assured that the collapse of
the Eastern European system that bore their names confirmed their ideas. The bureaucratic party-state could not
survive the breakdown of its economic system, and revolution erupted in the most backward part of the industrial-
ised world.

Economic disaster and its counterpart, ecological catastrophe, are no doubt the most visible causes for communism's collapse in East Germany as in the rest of the Eastern
bloc (cf. Maier, 1991). The absurdities of the planned
economy, the stupidity of a universal, unidimensional heavy
industrialisation strategy, the naïveté of marginal economic
reform efforts over the past decades, and all the other fol-
lies of state socialist economics do not need enumeration
here. It is clear that whatever turn the events of 1989 had
taken, the communist economic system could not have survived much longer and that radical social and political changes
would have been necessary. It is not clear, however, why
the economic crisis, which in some estimations had been
more severe in the early 1980s (cf. Drach, 1990), should
have provoked a popular uprising precisely in 1989 or
whether, in fact, economic concerns played an important
role in that year's events.

Economic explanations of communism's collapse gain much
of their credibility from two common prejudices. The first,
which we have already encountered, is the confusion of
consequences for causes. The radical drop in production
and the virtual halt of trade between former Comecon countries followed the disappearance of communist regimes and
the introduction of radical economic reform. Economic conditions were not as bad in the final years of state socialism
as during the transition to capitalism: the hardship of the
1990s could not possibly have brought on the uprising of
1989. The second common mistake is the very notion that
economic hardship causes revolutions. Desperate people,

common sense tells us, make desperate moves, but the rarity of revolution also tells us that neither absolute nor relative deprivation suffices to bring about revolution. To the contrary, years of hardship can forge the strongest loyalties to a regime.

In the case of East Germany, an economic explanation of revolution proves particularly inapplicable. Although economic planners and even the general public recognised in the 1980s that the technological gap between the GDR and the West was widening, real regression in production and living standards was not apparent as it was in Poland, Hungary, and especially Rumania. After the fall of 1989, former communist officials such as Alexander Schalk-Golodkowski conceded that the economic system was running on reserves and would not have survived much longer, but before 1990 such information circulated only at the top of a few ministries. Knowledge of the system's imminent economic collapse might explain why the regime so weakly resisted the popular revolt of autumn 1989, but it cannot explain why people who neither experienced nor foresaw certain hardship revolted.

Even more subjective relative deprivation (Gurr, 1970) or J-curve (Davies, 1962) economic models of revolution do not apply to the East German case. Such models contend that economic dissatisfaction, whether based on objective regression or on frustrated expectations, leads to political protest and/or social violence. Economic demands, however, were entirely absent from the East German protests of 1989. What is more, my survey data suggest that economic discontent was not an underlying or subconscious motive for protest. Quite surprisingly, the survey found that 90 per cent of respondents felt that their personal economic situation had remained the same (55 per cent) or improved (35 per cent) during the five years ending in 1989. No relationship existed between individuals' assessment of their economic well-being (F32a) and their participation in demonstrations (F48a). To the contrary, among Berlin respondents there was a tendency for precisely those who had improved their economic situation in the years before the *Wende* to participate in demonstrations.[7] Individuals' political judgements, however, do not rest entirely on their own experiences but on their assessment of the overall performance of the system. Thus, despite economic stability or improvement in their own lives, 87 per cent of the respondents thought that the overall economic situation of the GDR had deteriorated during the five years leading up to the *Wende* (F33a), and retrospectively 75 per cent believed that the economic crisis was a decisive cause of the *Wende* (F55a). These negative assessments of the regime's economic performance did not, however, influence respondents' decisions to demonstrate, for economic performance assessment variables do not correlate at all with demonstration participation for any category of respondents.

Another imputed motive for political protest in Eastern Europe was disgust with the environmental degradation that reckless industrialisation engendered. Upon observing the health risks and the flagrant natural and aesthetic damage caused by air and water pollution, acid rain, strip-mining, urban misplanning, and the like, Western observers have leapt to the conclusion that such horrors must have been at the source of widespread protest. Those who do not live on a daily basis amid obvious and ubiquitous environmental damage cannot imagine accepting such degradation as normal, but sadly my survey found such acceptance widespread. Even in Halle-Neustadt on the banks of the foaming, dead Saale River and next to the stinking, pestiferous Leuna and Buna chemical plants, survey respondents claimed to be unaware of any grave environmental problems. Among 13 possible causes for the popular uprising of 1989 (F55), survey respondents were least likely to rank ecological catastrophe (F55l) as a decisive cause of the *Wende* and for the greater part (56 per cent) dismissed environmental concerns as unimportant for the popular mobilisation. Although the citizen groups that played an important part in initiating the demonstrations of autumn 1989 often had environmentalist roots, my survey suggests that the bulk of East Germans who joined in the protest movement unfortunately had few worries about environmental pollution.

FROM STRUCTURAL TO INDIVIDUAL EXPLANATIONS

In assessing the popular explanations of the *Wende*, from rising national consciousness to impending natural disaster, I have judged them by voluntarist criteria. Because the collapse of communism in the GDR ultimately resulted from a popular uprising, I have asked whether the various accounts can identify the motives of the ordinary people whose mass mobilisation brought down their regime. It is, of course, not entirely fair to judge essentially structural explanations by voluntarist criteria. A structuralist does not particularly need or care to know what specifically motivated people to rebel against their government if that government's international, organisational, societal, economic and even ideological position is untenable. As we saw in Chapter 1, structural explanations are by and large functionalist models that derive their power from the *a priori* logic of a particular closed system. Even if such models always allowed accurate prediction of social outcomes (e.g. war-waging, fiscally strapped states with parasitic dominant classes armed with self-contradictory ideology always succumb to revolutions [cf. Skocpol, 1979]), they would nonetheless have to confront the theoretical problem of the translation of structural determinants into individual actions. At some point, human agency has to enter the picture in even the most determinist structural theory.

Contemporary social science has attempted to integrate individual-level and structural explanations in a theory known as rational choice, in which individuals act to maximise their interests within the constraint and incentive structures of particular social systems. The revolutions in Eastern Europe have not escaped rational choice explanations (cf. Bunce and Chong, 1990; Kuran, 1991; Opp, 1991; Porsch and Abraham, 1991), and the approach has succeeded in integrating international, political, economic and psychological variables into a coherent model. Mikhail Gorbachev's new international thinking, culminating with the announcement in late 1989 of the 'Sinatra Doctrine' (allowing the bloc countries to 'do it their way'), signalled a fundamental change in constraints throughout Eastern Europe. From Berlin to Bucharest, armed Soviet intervention was no longer a threat to potential reformers or revolutionaries. *Perestroika* not only reduced constraints but provided new incentives for reform. Change was possible – with the blessing of Moscow, to boot – and the rise of reformist factions in Hungary in 1988 and the Jaruzelski regime's dramatic democratic concessions in early 1989 proved as much to the rest of Eastern Europe. At the same time, the erosion or stagnation of living standards meant that the relative risks of demanding or attempting reform were diminishing. With the chances for change improving and the risks of repression in retreat, small opposition movements could snowball into mass mobilisation as the new and (with each increment of mobilisation) more favourable incentive structure pushed more and more citizens over their thresholds for political action. With a simple but clever mathematical model, Timur Kuran (1991) has shown that this mobilisation process had to take on an explosive, unpredictable revolutionary quality because previous repressive structures had led to a form of public preference falsification (or concealment of private, true preferences), which made it difficult for Eastern Europeans to recognise the extent of regime opposition and hence to act according to the veritable incentive/constraint structure.

Because rational choice models tend to identify incentive structures after the fact, they take on a tautological quality that calls into question their empirical validity (cf. Green and Shapiro, 1994). In a world where individuals always maximise their interests, the rational choice theorist need never prove what actually motivated individual actions but merely imagine what incentives or constraints might have channelled the self-interested actor's behaviour. With a survey of 1300 Leipzigers, however, Karl-Dieter Opp and Peter Voss have empirically tested a rational choice model of political protest in East Germany. True to their expectations, they found that protest participants had relatively high levels of political discontent and of perceived influence and belonged to networks of critical friends, who backed them in their actions. Quite unexpectedly from the rational choice perspective, though, Opp and Voss discovered that for first-time protestors the fear of repression relative to hopes of success rose with each demonstration up until the decisive demonstration of 9 October, when the amassed forces of order retreated before the throng. In other words, the protests in Leipzig grew as individuals joined in despite their expectations of repression or failure.[8] Like revolutionaries elsewhere, the East German demonstrators acted 'irrationally', or at least with motives that belie a simple calculation of interest. My own survey interviews confirm this finding that contradicts the suppositions of rational choice theory. Respondents who participated in the early, dangerous demonstrations spoke of fear, of anticipation of failure, and even of the futility of their action. Virtually none, moreover, mentioned the success of reform efforts in Hungary and Poland as an incentive or as evidence that repression was unlikely. Most expected a 'Chinese solution' since the SED had praised the restoration of order in Tienanmen Square in June 1989. Demonstrators in the sample seldom were able, even retrospectively, to articulate precise motives for participation. Instead, they spoke of an emotional need to participate, a need that overcame all fear and better judgement.

This emotional state that made protest possible or even necessary reappears in another model that links individual choice to social structures. Albert O. Hirschmann's concepts of exit, voice and loyalty have found great applicability to the case of the GDR's collapse (cf. Brubaker, 1990; Pollack, 1990). Hirschmann (1993) himself has written a masterful article in which he argues that the circumstances of the Hungarian border opening and the occupation of the Prague and Warsaw embassies transformed the anonymous, secret pursuit of the private good of exit (from the GDR) into a public event. Because the authority of the East German state symbolically and actually rested on the control of exit, the *Ausreisewelle,* or the public availability of the exit option, made it possible for regime critics to voice demands for the public good reform. At the same time, the regime's loss of authority either rendered regime loyalists immobile or pushed them also to demand reforms in order to restore their state's legitimacy. Thus, Hirschmann's model explains both mass mobilisation in a society where regime opposition had been small and the failure of the regime to crack down on protests. It also describes the moral and emotional confusion that the breakdown of authority entailed.

Although Hirschmann bases his argument solely on a close

reading of events and the logic of the exit, voice and loyalty options, the psychological conditions and motives that he deduces for different actors correspond closely to what I found in my survey interviews: uncertainty on the part of staunch loyalists and, on the part of the rest, indignation at having been abandoned by private good-seeking emigrants and at the government's inaction. In fact, only Hirschmann's model can make sense of one of my survey's most anomalous findings. The single best predictor of survey respondents' participation in anti-government demonstrations was their having had a friend or acquaintance leave during the *Ausreisewelle.*[9] By contrast, those who had had a family member flee were no more likely to demonstrate than those who had not. Since Hirschmann's model distinguishes between private acts (exit, normally) and public acts (voice), it suggests an explanation of the disparate reaction to friends' and family members' emigration. The flight of a family member, even in a massive public exit, remains a private event for those left behind, who have a personal sense of loss or of joy upon seeing their loved ones leaving for the West. Friends and acquaintances, by contrast, belong less intimately to the personal sphere, and their departure becomes more of a public event that provokes indignation and the public response of voice.

While Hirschmann's exit, voice and loyalty options provide insight into individuals' responses to the deteriorating quality of goods or organisations – in this case, the East German state, his model remains schematic in its description of individuals' motives. To be sure, the emigration wave of late summer 1989 undermined the authority of the SED regime, thus prompting the massive exercise of voice even among regime loyalists. Indignation at the departure of friends and colleagues and at the government's refusal to respond to the country's haemorrhaging allowed the demonstrators to chant with one voice: 'Wir bleiben hier! Wir sind das Volk!' The model thus well accounts for the outburst of voice, but it cannot really explain the content and meaning of voice. Hirschmann argues that the polysemic character of the protestors' slogans such as 'We are the people!' betrayed their inability to articulate a coherent set of demands which might have permitted the reform rather than the dissolution of the GDR. Although consistent with the final outcome of the *Wende*, such an argument needs to be tested with an inquiry into individual protestors' aspirations and motives.

In the end, like the other explanations of the *Wende* that we have examined in this chapter, Hirschmann's model imputes motives to individual actors on the basis of the logic of structural circumstances. Certainly, individuals do respond to the scientifically discernible circumstances that surround them, be they material or ideal. Economic, political, social, ideological and psychological structures shape and constrain behaviour, but only in conjunction with individuals' subjective appreciations and choices do they determine it. As we have seen in this chapter, various explanations of East German popular revolution, from the resurgence of national sentiment to the crisis of the communist economy, have proved inconsistent with or unconfirmed by the findings of a survey of ordinary East Germans who made or experienced the revolution. In the next two chapters, we shall take the opposite tack and try to build up a model of revolutionary mobilisation on the basis of my survey respondents' recounted experiences and motivations.

4 The Modest Germans: The Cultural Context of Mass Mobilisation

By 1989 bureaucratic state socialism in the GDR was a moribund system surviving apparently by inertia alone. The SED gerontocracy had lost touch with the rank-and-file of its own party, and the unbreakable bond between party and people had long since dissolved as citizens withdrew into the private sphere, if not into active opposition. East Germany's perfection of the planned economy had exhausted all growth potential – and at the price of consumer dissatisfaction and environmental degradation. To make matters worse, the GDR lost its propping as the Warsaw Pact's Western walled bastion against NATO imperialism. The decay and disappearance of communist orthodoxy in Poland, Hungary and especially the Soviet Union meant that the East German regime no longer had recourse to the ultimate guarantor of its survival: Soviet-backed force. The breakdown of the GDR's political, social, economic and international alliance systems were no doubt necessary preconditions for the state socialist regime's collapse, yet as late as the summer of 1989 few East Germans and outside observers foresaw the GDR's imminent demise.

As many of my survey respondents recalled, East Germans were aware of the regime's grave difficulties in 1989, but they also recognised that the regime had suffered almost constantly over the past 40 years from problems of political legitimacy and of economic performance yet had somehow always managed to survive. They saw no reason why the regime's most recent crisis should be its last. This subjective expectation of the regime's ultimate survival no doubt contributed to the system's staying-power. Fatalism and habit were indeed sources of the inertia by which the state socialist polity and economy continued to function even during the social upheaval of the autumn of 1989. If therefore we are more fully to understand how East German socialism survived as long as it did and why it finally collapsed in 1989, we must first investigate East Germans' subjective orientations to the political and social structures in and with which they had to live, i.e. we must study their political culture. In the previous chapter, we saw that systemic, or structural, explanations of East German communism's collapse fail adequately to explain the motivations and subjective states of the ordinary East Germans (represented in my survey) who brought down their regime. In this chapter, after a discussion of the theories and methodologies of political culture, we shall try to uncover the cultural context and causes of the popular revolution on the basis of a qualitative interpretation of my survey findings.

POLITICAL CULTURE AND INTERPRETIVE METHOD

The study of political culture in communist societies poses both methodological and conceptual problems. As originally formalised by Gabriel Almond and Sidney Verba in their classic comparative work *The Civic Culture* (1963), the study of subjective (cognitive, evaluative and affective) orientations to political objects largely depended on the possibility and reliability of survey research. In communist and other closed societies, however, politically unhampered opinion research verged on the impossible, though even the orthodox East German regime, as we saw in Chapter 3, did commission some more or less reliable survey research; now at last accessible, this survey data does allow a certain retrospective analysis of East German political culture. Despite their restrictions on opinion research, communist regimes actually had a particular interest in keeping track of the attitudes and values present in their societies since an important part of their political project was the propagation of new socialist ideals and behavioural norms. The existence of an ideologically defined goal culture in communist societies, however, rendered the study of political culture there methodologically and conceptually even more difficult because of the competition and confusion between expressed official political norms and actual but often concealed beliefs and behaviour.

Archie Brown (1984; Brown and Gray, 1977) addressed this problem by distinguishing between the official political culture and the dominant culture consisting of various subcultures including elements of alternative and even oppositional cultures. By contrast, Kenneth Jowitt (1992 [originally 1974]: 55), in defining political culture as the informal behaviour and attitudes by which individuals adapt to and permit the functioning of formal political structures, avoided the distinction between official and dominant cultures since ideological goals (towards which individuals must of course develop adaptive postures) belong to the realm of formal organisation, or structure. Jowitt, however, distinguished between political cultures at different levels of society, with élite political culture referring to the adaptive postures leaders developed from their own historical experiences and struggles; with regime political culture referring to informal postures adapted to the regime's particular institutional configuration; and with community political culture referring more generally to the adaptive responses of society at large to formal state structures.

My own understanding of the concept of political culture and my application of it here to the East German case tend to follow Jowitt's definition, though with some restrictions. First, I am interested almost exclusively in what Jowitt calls community political culture (or what Brown would label the dominant culture). Since I seek to explain popular mobilisation, rather than élite intransigence in 1989, the study of élite political culture is not necessary.[1] Also, regime political culture (a term unique to Jowitt) would be primarily of interest to students of comparative communism and institutions. Second, in his definition of political culture as 'informal, adaptive postures', Jowitt includes behaviour as well as attitudes. Although behaviour is culturally determined, its inclusion in a definition of culture can lead to an inference of cultural norms from behaviour, a practice which is problematic, since one and the same act can have different cultural meanings and causes. I therefore exclude behaviour from my definition of political culture and try to avoid inferring norms and values by its observation alone. Finally, although like Jowitt I see culture as existing in interaction and interdependence with formal structures, I object to his characterisation of culture as merely an intervening variable that fills the 'black box' between systemic stimuli and regime performance (Jowitt, 1992: 58). Assigning culture only such an intermediate, systemic-functional role, which among other things it no doubt fills, tends to overlook the possibility of independent cultural development and, worse, to encourage the functionalist inference of culture from the observation of structures.

Since we should not infer subjective orientations, or culture, from observed behaviour and structures, and since communist regimes restricted survey research and freedom of expression in any case, it would seem that the study of political culture in communist societies must have been a nearly impossible task, at least until after 1989. On the basis of available survey data, careful reading (between the lines) of journalistic and literary sources, interviews of expatriates, and informal personal observations and conversations inside the country of study, however, specialists succeeded in discerning the fundamental features of political culture in most communist societies (cf. Brown and Gray, 1977). In the case of the GDR, the amount of communication with the West, despite the regime's best physical and moral efforts at *Abgrenzung*, facilitated the task. West German observers, in particular, benefited from personal and familial contacts, from a common language and cultural heritage, from the relative facility with which East German authors could publish critical texts in the West, from the presence of a large number of expatriated GDR citizens, and, after the relative normalisation of relations in 1972, from the growing number of academic and political exchanges between the two states.

One of the most insightful observers of East German political culture, in fact, was the first permanent representative of the Federal Republic in the GDR, Günter Gaus, who coined the well-circulated term '*Nischengesellschaft*' to describe East Germans' tendency to retreat into a petty bourgeois private sphere and into consumerism (Gaus, 1983). West German journalists on frequent or long-term assignment in the GDR also rendered regular reports on daily life and popular culture (e.g. Marlies Menge's articles in *Die Zeit*) and sometimes compiled analytically useful collections of essays (cf. Dönhoff, Leonhardt, and Sommer, 1964; Bussiek, 1979; Filmer and Schwan, 1985; Menge, 1990). East German novelists, poets and playwrights of course offered a wealth of more or less fictionalised insight into their country's cultural values and norms, allowing the study of political culture through literary analysis (cf. Grunenberg, 1990a). The quantitative and qualitative content analysis of official documents, ranging from politburo pronouncements to teaching plans, also gave indirect access to East German political culture (cf. Opp de Hipt, 1989; Lemke, 1991). Occasionally, East German authors were able to publish in the West uncensored studies of daily and political life. Irene Böhme's essays in *Die da drüben* (1982) provided one of the first frank looks at East German political culture from the inside, while Gabriele Eckart (1984), an FDJ youth functionary, painted an unflattering (for the regime) picture of youths' political and social attitudes with the transcripts of interviews with young people in a rural area near Berlin. Finally, in a rare example of East German *glasnost*, the author Landolf Scherzer in 1988 was allowed to publish in the GDR an honest and remarkably revealing account of a county first party secretary's daily activities (Scherzer, 1989 [West German edition]).

These various studies of East German political culture served as points of reference and of departure for my own research, which, as we shall see, in fact confirmed many earlier findings. In undertaking my study, however, I wished to profit from the new possibilities for direct and relatively uninhibited opinion research in the expiring GDR and to apply an alternative approach to the study of political culture. As I mentioned in Chapter 1, the intensive survey allows the collection not only of potentially representative (or at least indicative) quantifiable behavioural and attitudinal data but also of qualitatively interpretable personal statements and testimonials. In other words, the intensive survey permits the application of both positivist and interpretive methods. While the positivist method seeks to predict behaviour on the basis of observation and (statistical) inference, the interpretive method tries to understand (*verstehen*), or find the meaning of, behaviour. Although partisans of these two methods within the social sciences wage an endless, often polemical struggle, the two approaches are actually complementary; for as Max Weber, the father of interpretive social science, observed, a statistically probable prediction without meaning is as useless as a meaningful interpretation without probability (cf. Weber, 1947: 99–100). In this chapter, I shall try to uncover the meaning of the East German popular revolution on the basis of a general interpretation of my survey interviews, leaving for the next chapter an attempt to test that interpretation's statistical probability.

In seeking the meanings, or subjective motivations, of social action, the interpretive method must first describe the culture, or the more or less coherent system of shared meanings and values, in which action occurs and takes on significance. Because the interpretive method as I understand and use it here considers culture in its broad, anthropological sense (cf. Geertz, 1973: Ch. 1), it differs from the standard approach to political culture, which concentrates on individuals' attitudes, knowledge and beliefs about the political system and their roles within it. Although political systems do have their own immanent logics and incentive structures, the motivations for political behaviour also lie outside the political system in economic, social and ideational values or goals. The interpretive method therefore situates political culture within the general culture that gives collective decision-making, or politics, its particular finalities. In other words, the understanding of political phenomena depends on the identification of the broader cultural values that motivate political action.

Since the values that can motivate action are as limitless as the human imagination, the challenge of interpretation consists in its ability to discern values, their origins, and their sources of change. The social sciences have tried to overcome this challenge by introducing various reductionist models of behaviour, of which rational choice theory (as discussed in the last chapter) is perhaps the best contemporary example. Already at the turn of the century, however, Max Weber combated the tendency of social science, particularly that of Marxist or other economic-materialist inspiration, to reduce the determinants of behaviour to instrumental rationality. Weber did not question the assumption of rationality. To the contrary, he argued that rationality, the human capacity to apply appropriate means to given ends, made human events, as opposed to natural phenomena, meaningful and therefore uniquely subject to scientific understanding. He recognised, however, that humans have the capacity freely to choose different ends, or ultimate values (*Wertideen*), and that rationalities vary with those ends. Thus, behaviour that would appear irrational in the light of one value-orientation and its concomitant rationality makes sense in another; for example, the worldly asceticism of early capitalists that violated the instrumental rationality of pre-capitalist production for consumption found its meaning and motive in the transcendent rationality of Calvinist doctrine (cf. Weber, 1958). In the Weberian view, then, interpreters of social actions must succeed in uncovering the particular ideas and values that make behaviour rational or meaningful. After properly identifying actors' value-orientations, social scientists can also judge in a value-free manner, i.e. without regard to their own value-orientations, whether behaviour is rational, or appropriate to chosen ends (cf. Weber, 1949).

Because interpretive social science recognises the competition of rationalities, it is necessarily an inductive science. Interpreters of social actions cannot *a priori* apply a particular rationality to a social situation; they must first engage in a dialogue with the actors in question (either directly or through the examination of documents and other artifacts) in order to discern the meanings and motives of actions. The simple observation of behaviour, no matter how complete or generative of predictive power, cannot suffice, for the same, even entirely predictable act has different significance in different cultural contexts. Students of culture, however, always suffer from the imperfect access they have to the individual subjective states in which values and meanings exist. The best they can offer, in fact, always remains only an interpretation, a partial understanding of reality always subject to refinement and open to complementary interpretations that take into account other parts of the infinite stream of events and ideas that make history (cf. Weber, 1949; Geertz, 1973).

The interpretive account of the stability and then the collapse of East German communism that I offer here is therefore necessarily incomplete. It has scientific value, however, as a complement to other, notably structural accounts of communism's collapse. As I argued in the previous chapter, those accounts are inadequate in themselves because they do not identify the actual motives of the East Germans who brought down their regime through mass protest. According to the interpretive method, we must look for those motives in the repertoire of values that directed East Germans' behaviour or, more generally, in their culture. The peaceful demonstrations of the autumn of 1989 had their particular meaning in the cultural context of East German real existing socialism, and to uncover that meaning we must first face the daunting task of describing East German culture. The magnitude of the mass upheaval of 1989, however, suggests that the most basic elements of East German culture came into play and that a subtle, detailed cultural analysis would surpass our needs; after all, 'it is not necessary to know everything in order to understand something' (Geertz, 1973: 20). Still, before we can examine even the most basic values characteristic of East German culture, we must have a clearer notion of what values are and whence they come.

The values that guide social action are not always evident even to actors themselves. As the finalities, norms, or desires towards which individuals strive, values can be multiple, contradictory, and more or less conscious and strong. They also certainly need not correspond to espoused virtues, as anyone who has watched a slick television evangelist preach Christian charity can attest. Interpreters of social action must of course take into account actors' self-proclaimed motivations – not everyone is unselfconscious or a liar – but also be prepared, on the basis of contextually informed observation, to ascribe values (for example, greed to the TV preacher). Weber (1947: 112–18) suggested four types of values and of consequent orientations to social action depending on the strength and consciousness with which the values are held. Strongly and consciously held values, such as a concern for religious salvation, leads to behaviour according to a rationality of absolute ends (*Wertrationalität*), whereas the conscious holding of more fungible values leads to the instrumental rationality (*Zweckrationalität*) of behaviour based on the calculation of relative preferences and of expected costs and benefits. By contrast, in the case of affectual rationality, strongly held values (e.g. sexual love) can motivate behaviour without the full consciousness of the (sexually repressed) actor. Finally, relatively unimportant values more or less consciously inherited through imitation or developed through habit guide traditional rational behaviour that verges on the automatic and therefore on the meaningless.

Weber's ideal-typical typology of rationalities suggests several sources of values that we might explore to uncover the basic contours of, say, East German culture: namely historical tradition, evolving ideas and philosophy, human psychology, and, not least, material conditions and structures. Both absolute and traditional values can find their origins in historically more or less freely developed religious and ideological doctrines. Thus, we might expect that at least some East Germans would act in accordance with the traditional Lutheran doctrine of subordination to state authority or with the traditionally strong as well as officially promulgated ideals of socialism. Affectual values that have their origins in individual psychology and intensely personal experiences may be difficult to characterise as part of a common culture (i.e. shared values), though the East German psychoanalyst Hans-Joachim Maaz (1990) insists that a common emotional repression (the so-called *Gefühlsstau*) characterised East German society and was unleashed only briefly in 1989. What is more, students of cultural modernity see the tension between the individual psychological values of self-control (rationalism) and self-expression (romanticism) with the growing dominance of the latter as a fundamental feature of modern cultures (cf. Schmidt, 1991). Since reunification, in fact, East German intellectuals have debated whether the limited opportunities for self-realisation in the GDR had rendered their culture backward and in need of modernisation (cf. Brie and Klein, 1991; Koch, 1992; Woderich, 1992).

While affectual rationality thus may have its place within modern culture, the defining characteristic of modernity has nonetheless been the dominance of instrumental rationality, or the individual calculation and maximisation of interest in accordance with predictable material conditions and structures. Weber, the modernist pessimist, considered such behaviour in accordance with material incentives and structural constraints (of capitalism) to be trapped within an 'iron cage' (Weber, 1958: 181). Despite the determinism of structures, the values, norms and adaptive strategies of what we might call modern instrumental culture are not simply reflections of material conditions or superstructures. Not only can instrumental rationalists pick different paths to the same goal (there is more than one way to skin a cat, after all); they will in reality pick at least somewhat different goals depending on how traditional, absolute-value, and affectual rationalities shape their relative preferences. Thus, just as different collectivities have developed different adaptive strategies to the common exigencies of advanced industrial capitalism, so too might we expect that the societies of Eastern and Central Europe varied in their cultural adaptation to Soviet-style state socialism. Still, the basic values of a culture such as East Germany's had to be consistent with and conducive to the functioning of the state socialist system.

Although we may know that East German culture was an amalgam of German traditions, socialist ideals, more or less modern psychological needs, and systemically functional (or instrumental) values, we could not even with perfect knowledge of these elements predict their particular admixture in East German culture. Only a dialogue with social actors permits the inductive description of actual cultures. Through my survey interviews I was able to gain at least partial access to ordinary East Germans' subjective orientations, and in my interpretation of these interviews, I am able to describe a set of values that drew on German traditions, socialist ideals, and psychological needs and that were systemically functional, that is, until their undermining in the late 1980s opened the door to revolutionary mobilisation.

EAST GERMAN CULTURE AND ITS CONTRADICTIONS

As I set out with my lengthy questionnaire to conduct 202 two- to four-hour interviews with randomly selected East Germans, I was not sure how I would organise the flood of facts and opinions that my questions elicited, and hoped that some serendipitous inspiration would allow me to paint an accurate picture of East German society and culture. Inspiration finally did strike when a retired school teacher from Thuringia shared an old saying with me: 'There are no dull landscapes, only dull eyes.' His saying not only reminded me that as an interpreter of culture I had to sharpen my vision if I wanted to distinguish the features of a foreign landscape but opened my eyes to the possibility that the seemingly dull East German landscape might hold a key to the country's culture.

Westerners who visited the GDR or still today visit the former GDR immediately think they know why the East Germans revolted. The decay of the cities, the pollution of the environment, the grey uniformity, the entire charmless landscape compels revolt. The short-term visitor sees, however, with dull eyes still. With time the ugliness fades and the eyes begin to delight at, for example, a tiny ornament from the Imperial era jutting out from a dirty Leipzig façade. And people who have grown up in the (ex-)GDR find their surroundings entirely normal. I shall never forget the first time I drove past the Buna Chemical Works. Suddenly I thought I was suffocating. There must have been an accident. Surely all Schkopau would choke to death in a poison cloud. I looked around: bicycle riders waved to one another; children played in a side-street; two women leaned over a garden fence, talking; a perfectly normal day in Schkopau!

The East Germans[2] were not blind to the decay, the daily drudgery, to the red posters calling for further success in the realisation of the goals of the most recent party congress, and to all the unpleasant things that leapt into a Western visitors' eyes. On the one hand, the East Germans bore the ugliness with fatalism; on the other, they made life attractive in those places where a Westerner without close contacts never came, that is, in their private lives, or what Günter Gaus (1983) described as their niches. Everybody's niche was a bit different, but most East Germans lived for their house (or apartment) and garden. There was a saying in the GDR: 'Nothing is available but everyone has everything.' The saying's meaning becomes clear with a visit to a perfectly outfitted East German home hidden behind a dilapidated façade. Through countless hours of free-time work, through the maintenance of a thousand-and-one connections (or 'Vitamin B' for *Beziehung*), and sometimes through the appropriation of state property (even the ubiquitous security forces turned a blind eye lest they infringe the social norm 'Privat geht vor Katastrophe', private concerns take precedence over public catastrophes), the East Germans turned their niches into the real 'achievements of socialism'. A majority of East Germans (64 per cent of my survey sample) recognised themselves as members of what Gaus had dubbed the *Nischengesellschaft*, and in their niches, according to my survey, they felt safe, happy and economically secure.

In Gaus's analysis, the *Nische* provided East Germans with a private shelter from the public exigencies of state socialism, a refuge in which traditional German petty-bourgeois values flourished. Although Gaus stressed its cultural continuity, the *Nischengesellschaft* was in fact much more than an anachronistic vestige of prewar culture;[3] it perfectly reflected the historically unique social structure of the GDR, the functional requirements of real existing socialism, and the particular psychological needs of East Germans.

Throughout Eastern and Central Europe socialist citizens commonly withdrew into private life (cf. Havel, 1978), but East Germans did so in a remarkably consistent manner reflective of the uniformity of their social origins. The expropriation of landowners and businesspeople – beginning with the Soviet land reforms of 1945 and culminating with the nationalisation of most remaining small businesses in the early 1970s (cf. Pickel, 1992) – and the relative permeability of the border to West Germany up until 1961 left the GDR with a homogeneous social structure: only the 'little people' (Gaus) remained. The emigration of social and cultural élites opened great opportunities for social mobility, particularly during the first two decades of the construction of socialism, but as the sons and daughters of workers and peasants rose to the top of the social hierarchy, so too did working-class and petty-bourgeois cultural values, including the pursuit of modest comfort and *Gemütlichkeit*, a levelling sense of equality, obedience, conformism and sociability. In a cultural sense, the party could correctly claim that the people and the leadership shared the same aspirations (cf.

Woderich, 1992: 25–6), though the modest origins of the leadership also tended to undermine its legitimacy as citizens questioned the political competence of a roofer (Honecker) and a bricklayer (Premier Willi Stoph).

While it is possible to identify the historical roots of the *Nischengesellschaft*'s values in the social origins and concomitant cultural traditions of the East German population, a society's values must be consistent with contemporary social, economic and political conditions. In fact, as the engines of social action, values must be not only consistent with but conducive to a society's functioning. From a historical repertoire of values, only those that meet this functional criterion will thrive, though other, non-functional values may survive, possibly to determine a society's particular response to changing structural conditions. A closer look at the values that my survey interviews uncovered will show that they permitted the functioning of East German society until the late 1980s, though often at the cost of psychological denial on the part of individual East Germans. I shall argue that this psychological tension erupted into the motivational energy for the popular uprising of 1989 after certain structural changes in the late 1980s rendered East Germans' basic social values and the niche-society as a whole dysfunctional.

As already mentioned, a large majority (64 per cent) of my survey sample recognised themselves as members of the *Nischengesellschaft*. That is, they acknowledged their voluntary withdrawal from the public into the private sphere. Ralf Dahrendorf has identified (and denounced the illiberal political consequences of) a longstanding German cultural preference for private over public values (Dahrendorf, 1967: 285ff.), but a withdrawal into the private sphere was both politically and psychologically necessary in the GDR of the 1970s and 1980s. Socialist ideology officially called for the active engagement of citizens in public life. In practice, however, this engagement became almost purely ritualistic, a lip-service necessary to assure social security and advancement. Students and workers spent hundreds of hours every year in political meetings and debates usually in conjunction with a formal curriculum of study, the so-called FDJ or party *Lehrjahr*, but not even the most ideologically orthodox of my survey respondents considered these indoctrination sessions to be more than a mindless pastime or, at best, an occasion to socialise. On holidays such as May Day and 7 October, citizens were expected to make a greater show of enthusiasm, with those wishing to display particular conformism hanging a red flag rather than a GDR flag from their window. To avoid even such superficial political engagement, some of my survey respondents made a special effort to get away to their garden plots on patriotic holidays. The case of one of the schoolteachers in the survey sample, however, is particularly illustrative of the formalism of expected political engagement. For years, her school director had hounded her to subscribe to the party newspaper *Neues Deutschland* because she alone was preventing the teachers' work collective from having a 100 per cent readership rate and thus from winning points in 'socialist competition'. When she complained that she already received the CDU paper and the local paper and had no time to read *Neues Deutschland,* her director responded: 'That's not the point. You're just supposed to subscribe.'[4]

This ritualisation of – and even retreat from – citizen participation was typical of political life throughout Eastern and Central Europe in the 1970s and 1980s. Following the fiasco of the Prague Spring of 1968, the ruling communist parties in Eastern Europe had tacitly proposed a social contract in which the party encouraged citizens to pursue private material well-being in exchange for political complacency (cf. Ekiert 1990). In the GDR the social contract was sealed at the Eighth Party Congress in 1971, when the new party-leader Erich Honecker promised the 'unity of social and economic policy'. New social programmes such as marriage bonuses, large-scale housing construction, and the continued encouragement of private garden plots – 'Laubenpieper machen brave Bürger [roughly: Garden enthusiasts make good citizens]', explained one survey respondent – were supposed to lure young people in particular into the quiet comfort of home and family life. At the same time, the ritualistic reinforcement of ideological orthodoxy in public life further pushed people to cultivate a private sphere where they could 'live in truth' (Havel). Psychologically, the division of the self into public and private personas verged on the schizophrenic but was necessary for people to live with themselves.

Thus, withdrawal into the *Nische* helped to maintain the regime's political arrangement with society and to compensate individuals psychologically for their extreme public conformism.

Although I specifically asked survey respondents about their withdrawal from public into private life, I posed no direct questions about the values around which they built up their private lives. As they talked of their lives in the *Nischengesellschaft*, however, respondents did reveal their principal value-orientations. While it is possible to identify their historical antecedents, these expressed values were essentially virtues born of societal and psychological necessity, and as such they pointed to the weaknesses and contradictions that underlay East German society. My survey respondents liked to insist on the modesty of their personal needs, and often in the same breath they praised their society's solidarity. People were happy with what they had and were glad to share it with neighbours. These expressed ideal values competed, however, with less overt and less virtuous cultural norms. Modesty concealed and helped assuage the frustration of consumerist desires, and behind solidarity hid dependence and a certain obsequiousness. People had to be happy with what they had because often they had had to wage a small war with full mobilisation of personal connections in order to obtain it. To be dependent on personal connections might fulfil the need for human contact, but maintaining vital connections and a painstakingly acquired modest well-being often required trickery and two-facedness. Thus, most respondents (57 per cent) felt that East Germans had morally debased themselves despite their proclaimed modesty and solidarity.

Closely linked to the values of modesty and solidarity were a certain pride in the GDR, a strong sense of family and friendship, and an appreciation of social security and stability. My interview partners insisted on the GDR's economic achievements in particular not only to counter the West German accusation that East Germans do not know how to work but also because they were truly proud of the modest well-being they had attained under difficult circumstances. This pride, however, obscured the jealousy with which they viewed their Western neighbour and the greedy joy with which some received packages from the West. Several respondents felt compelled to confess their shame at having written 'beggar's letters' to their Western relatives.

Much greater and more honest than GDR pride was the pleasure in togetherness with family and friends at home, but this pleasure in private life barely covered up the drabness of public life. Although traditional family structures were not particularly strong (the GDR had birth-out-of-wedlock and divorce rates among the highest in the world), close personal bonds took on particular importance in a society permeated with distrust. Outside the immediate family and a small circle of friends, people dared not speak freely, and outside the home a comfortable place to meet friends hardly existed. Getting a table in a nice restaurant was practically impossible, and the waiters, if they were not off on a meal-break themselves, would have been rude anyway.

Tucked away in their familial nests (which the typical over-heating of apartments rendered almost oppressively cosy), the East Germans relished a feeling of security. They knew that their jobs and basic needs were safe and could foresee their futures with an infallibility of which economic planners could only dream. 'Alles geht seinen sozialistischen Gang [very roughly: Everything goes with predictable socialist mediocrity],' they said with satisfaction. Such contentment with socialist stability, however, concealed and compensated for the absence of spontaneity and choice in the ordinary citizens' lives. Some survey respondents described the somnolence of East German life as a kind of Sleeping Beauty's slumber (*Dornröschenschlaf*) while others claimed with a certain perverse pride that the GDR was the most boring country on earth.

As we saw in Chapter 3, both during and after the revolution the East Germans continued to praise the values of socialism. Socialist ideals had inspired German working-class culture since the mid-nineteenth century, and in the wake of the Nazi experience they offered a positive model for the reconstruction of German society. When my survey respondents praised socialist ideals, however, they primarily meant the value of social equality, for that was the glue that held their modest society together. Equality of condition was a necessary value not only because it was supposed to conceal the monotony of life and political privilege but because it permitted modesty and solidarity. Without a certain equality of living conditions, which despite political privileges did exist in the GDR, people might not have been so modest in their needs, for inequality encourages competition in consumption as well as work. Solidarity usually develops only between people on an equal footing, or better yet on an equally bad footing. Many respondents described their lauded solidarity as a community of hardship (*Notgemeinschaft*). If hardship or its commonality disappears, so too does solidarity.

In sum, modesty, solidarity and, above all, equality were the values that held the *Nischengesellschaft* together until 1989. These values not only had their origins in the cultural tradition of the German lower classes; they permitted the survival of a society that penury, dependence and privilege constantly threatened. What is more, these values were consistent with the official ideology of the ruling party, whose leaders shared the same modest origins and values as the people. The GDR, it would seem, could have been the thousand-year Reich of happy homemakers. Yet in the fall of 1989 hundreds of thousands of East Germans streamed out of their niches and on to the streets. What had changed? What had made so many East Germans so unhappy that they were willing to risk even their lives to topple a regime with which they had apparently made a complaisant arrangement for so many years? Most demonstrators told me they had an ineffable psychological need to go, but one woman summarised that feeling most clearly: 'The hate became so great that I had to crawl out of my niche.'

Hans-Joachim Maaz, a psychotherapist from Halle, has identified in *Der Gefühlsstau* (1990) the origins of the hate that led to the *Wende* in the constant psychological repression from which East Germans suffered from the moment of their particularly traumatic births in inhumanly cold maternity wards to their deaths in regimented, under-serviced *Feierabendheime* (literally, 'after-work homes'). It is not necessary to psychoanalyse individuals in order to discover the origins of the revolution. The source of hate existed also at the level of society as a whole, namely within the tensions of East German culture. Already before the fall of 1989, students of East German political culture had identified destabilising cultural contradictions and tensions. As we saw in Chapter 3, Christiane Lemke (1989, 1991), following Brown's (1984) cultural dissonance theory, considered the contradiction between the public self of the official political culture and the private self of the dominant culture, and the competing socialisations into these cultures, to be generative of an oppositional (youth) culture capable of forming a regime-contesting civil society. In an analysis of the political culture of 'socialist paternalism', Gerd Meyer (1989) identified a tension between the integrative and disintegrative effects of the regime's exchange of social security for citizens' subordination. The paternalistic largesse and discipline of the socialist welfare state infantilised citizens, making them both entirely dependent on state bureaucracies and socially irresponsible. (Rudolf Woderich [1992] thus described East Germans as being torn between obedient conformism and self-interested stubbornness.) In the short run, a source of regime legitimacy, the guarantee of social security in the long run undermined incentives to work (and even to obey party-state authority) as citizens came to consider economic security an egalitarian right.

East German political culture in the 1970s and 1980s thus no doubt suffered from latent contradictions that threatened the system's ability to function. I have argued that behaviour in accordance with the ideal values of equality, modesty and solidarity provided psychological compensation for or concealed the limited possibilities for individual consumption and independence and thus secured the East German regime's stability. The undermining of these ideal values, however, could reveal more clearly the unpleasant underside of East German social and psychological reality: monotony, decay, privilege, disenfranchisement, material need, dependence, lies, shame. It was precisely the exposure of this ugly reality, I would argue, that generated the psychological tension, or hate, that culturally rendered East German society dysfunctional and motivated at least some East Germans to take to the streets in protest.

What, however, undermined the ideal values that hid society's shortcomings and contradictions? We have seen that values have their origins and thus their sources of change in social, economic and political structures, in the independent force of ideas and their evolution, and in human psychology. In the previous chapter, I argued that neither the structural crisis of the socialist economy, the erosion of the party-state, the rise of oppositional organisations and culture, the German nationalist ideal, nor the decay of socialist ideology motivated the demonstrators of late 1989. Although, like Vaclav Havel, we might see the collapse of communism as part of a world-historic crisis of modernity, it would be difficult to identify a link between the motives of demonstrators and the evolution of human consciousness and psychology. If we can attribute the mass upheaval of 1989 to neither the long-term structural deficiencies of East German state socialism nor the global transformation of mentalities, then perhaps we might find the motives for revolution in the particular short-term economic and political problems of socialism in the late 1980s. During its final years, the GDR experienced a decline in its economic growth rate, eased restrictions on travel to the West, and witnessed the rise to power of a great reformer in the Soviet Union. I would argue that the economic crisis, the easing of travel restrictions, and the reform policies of Gorbachev conspired – though all in an indirect and generally unexpected manner – to undermine the East German value hierarchy and thus to motivate mass mobilisation.

Although, as the last chapter's analysis of my survey data suggested, economic hardship drove not a single demonstrator on to the street, the *Wende* makes sense only against the backdrop of the economic crisis of state socialism. 'No one hungered or suffered otherwise', nearly every respondent emphasised, yet the East Germans nonetheless feared for their economic welfare. People who today expect to receive their Trabant automobile in eight years but who tomorrow learn that they will have to wait ten do not suffer an actual decline in their standard of living, but they do begin to fear they might not be able to build up their modest little paradise as planned. Indicative of the potentially serious psychological consequences of a still relatively small economic crisis was one survey respondent's observation: 'I knew the system was in trouble when I went to the butcher shop and could buy only sausage when I wanted sliced ham.'

When modesty starts to require doing without something more, it can become too much of a good thing; the tenuous psychological balance between modest satisfaction and consumer frustration began to tip in favour of the latter.

Much more serious than the economic threats to well-being, however, was the introduction of privileges designed to encourage productivity, for privilege directly attacked the values of equality and solidarity. As Freya Klier shows in her book *Lüg Vaterland* (1990), for example, the GDR's efforts to redress its technical-scientific lag behind the West through educational reform in the 1980s reinforced the self-reproducing character of the intelligentsia in blatant violation of the egalitarian goals of educational policy. Similarly, the expansion of wage differentials and bonuses to encourage the scientific-technical revolution and greater efficiency (in accordance with the much-touted *Leistungsprinzip*) threatened solidarity and equality, though monetary incentives had limited effect in a penurious economy based largely on informal exchange mechanisms.

Even more than the introduction of further privileges to combat the economic crisis, the easing of travel restrictions in the mid-1980s undermined the values of equality, solidarity and modesty. Before the revolution nearly one in three East Germans had visited the golden West. While these trips opened the eyes of many to the decay in the East and aroused an appetite for consumer goods among some, most of my respondents who had been West said that they had quickly readjusted to the grey reality of daily life in the East. The trips to the West seem to have meant more to those in my survey sample who had not gone. They were outraged that they had not received a travel authorisation either because they had no relatives in the West or because they were too honest to invent a great-aunt there or, even worse, because precisely out of loyalty to the state they had taken on one of countless positions of responsibility requiring an oath of secrecy. Their solidarity-destroying jealousy towards those who went West grew even more severe because the travellers returned with Western goods and currency. With that, solidarity, equality and modesty were out the window. A grandmother returning from Hamburg, one respondent recounted, could send her grandchild back to school in the fall with a book-bag from the West, and if this book-bag looked just like one from the GDR, or even if it was made in the GDR (exclusively for export, of course), it was a marvel for the other children to behold – and to covet. And people with D-Marks in their pockets could afford anything, or so it seemed. They could short-circuit the whole connection network by offering 'blue tiles' (100 DM notes) for barter on the grey market. A little Western currency could go a long way to stir up jealousy, too, for it was always enough to buy some special, unavailable treat in the hard-currency 'Intershop'.

To combat the rise of a parallel hard-currency economy and to contain jealousy, the state had already in the late 1970s introduced 'Exquisit' and 'Delikat' shops, where it was possible to purchase Western and high-quality Eastern merchandise at outrageously high but East-Mark prices (cf. Bussiek, 1979: 93ff.). Most of my survey respondents remembered the 'Exquisit' and 'Delikat' shops as an innovation of the 1980s, though, and indeed their socio-economic significance grew exponentially during the GDR's final years with 'Exquisit', for example, in the late 1980s expanding from 5 per cent to 25 per cent of turnover in retail clothing sales (Ernst, 1989: 168). When a coveted can of pineapple cost 18 Marks in the 'Delikat' and a standard shirt or blouse at 'Exquisit' easily cost 200 (or nearly a fifth of the average monthly pay-cheque), wage differentials took on a significance they had never had when there was nothing much to buy. Marks, West or East, now made it possible for people to buy their way out of modesty.

A Western visitor to the Wandlitz Woods Settlement (the home of the Politburo) would probably find it hard to believe that inequality and privilege tore East German society asunder, for even the houses of the most privileged East Germans of all lay within the bounds of modesty. Any mid-level bureaucrat in West Germany or any hard-working craftsman in East Germany could have built a house as nice as the uniform grey houses of the Politburo. For the East German people, however, ideal and not material values were at stake. My interview partners told me that they did not care how well or poorly the Politburo members lived. What bothered them was that the party leaders preached water but drank wine.[5] The party and the people had always agreed on the ideal of equality. Yet in the late 1980s equality evidently no longer existed. Was there any way to resolve this contradiction? The people desired equality and the party stood for equality. That had been the party's saving grace, moreover. Numerous comrades and non-party members I spoke with had put up with a lot from the party because they believed that the party shared their hope of building through socialism a just society with material well-being for all. How then could they attack the party?

Mikhail Gorbachev's reform efforts allowed the East Germans to turn the weapons of socialism against the party. Without Gorbachev, the mass mobilisation of the *Wende* would perhaps not have been possible, though it would be a mistake to attribute his influence to the appeal of his reform policies. Most East Germans had only the foggiest notion of the contents of Gorbachev's ideas and programme, and those few who were really interested had little access to them. Gorbachev's works were purposely published in only small numbers in German, and when the party banned the Soviet magazine *Sputnik* in November 1988 because it contained revelations about the Stalinist era that might have discredited the SED leadership, the censorship of information on *glasnost* and *perestroika* became blatant. Gorbachev's role in the East German revolution remained therefore mostly symbolic. The *Sputnik* ban clearly betrayed the conflict between the GDR leadership and Gorbachev. The content of the conflict, however, was secondary to the mere fact that a conflict existed at all. Until then the slogan had always been 'Learning from the Soviet Union means learning victory!' Now the East German leadership was in blatant self-contradiction. In a twist on the fairy-tale, the emperor had shown that his cronies wore no clothes. Thus disappeared the final tattered shred of ambiguity which until then had covered the leadership's naked lust for power.

With his visit to East Berlin in early October 1989, Gorbachev provided the East Germans the means to express their frustration with the decay of their society's values: he not only lifted the threat of Red Army intervention but again exposed the illegitimacy of the SED leadership. When the first demonstrators in the GDR chanted: 'Gorbi! Gorbi! Gorbi!'

they were not only calling for the extension of his reformist agenda (whatever it was) to the GDR but were trying to show their own potentates that they (the demonstrators) stood on the side of superior strength. When the party leadership – the anti-fascist resistance fighters who allegedly did all for the good of the people – had revealed themselves through their arrogant rejection of *perestroika* as old men incapable of any reform, the people could do nothing but cry: 'We are the people!' We alone now have the right to speak in our interest.

The revolution had to end with the nationalist cry 'We are one people!' ultimately also because of the collapse of the GDR's value-system. Since the primary values of modesty, solidarity and equality had eroded, East Germans needed to find new values with which to confront and conceal the grim reality of material frustration, decay, dependency, deception, monotony and jealousy. The collapse of the old value system did not leave East Germans in a cultural vacuum, though. Various secondary and latent values gained in relative importance and came into play during the weeks before the fall of the Wall, as we shall explore further in the next chapter. With the fall of the Wall, however, East Germans came into intensive contact with West German society, which offered them alternative and often already familiar values. In addition to shared traditional German values including nationalism, the Federal Republic offered the new democratic ideal values of individualism and pluralism, which could combat dependency, two-facedness and grey uniformity.

More importantly, though, wealthy West Germany offered material values which one object perfectly embodied: the D-Mark. The hard currency had already, before 1989, divided East Germany into haves and have-nots, and the opening of the border only intensified the social divisions of a dual currency economy. The immediate introduction of the D-Mark could patch up this division and ease jealousy and consumer frustration. Thus, when the first free elections of 18 March 1990 presented East Germans a choice between a conservative 'Allianz für Deutschland', promising immediate currency union, and parties favouring slower steps towards unification, they gave an unexpected landslide majority to the markedly anti-socialist CDU-led alliance. Most observers

had predicted a Social Democratic victory since the SPD
had not been compromised in the SED regime and embraced
the egalitarian values that East Germans still favoured. These
observers had not necessarily overestimated the East Germans' loyalty to socialist or social democratic ideals, though.
Unaware of the social and economic consequences of their
act, East Germans may have voted for a rapid currency
union because they thought it would restore the value of
social equality.

The collapse of the East German value-system built around
the ideals of modesty, solidarity and equality thus can explain not only the psychological frustration that underlay
protest but also the nationalist outcome of the demonstrations, as East Germans sought new values and found them
in the West; it may also even explain the surprising results
of the first free elections as East Germans voted to restore
equality. Such a cultural interpretation of the *Wende* suggests some possible motives for East Germans' political behaviour during the six months from September 1989 to March
1990 that sealed the GDR's fate, but is such an explanation
really necessary or accurate?

I have argued in this chapter that the breakdown of the
values that maintained the *Nischengesellschaft* resulted from
the extension of privilege to combat economic decline, from
the rise of a dual-currency economy and accompanying inequality, and from the resistance of the party leadership to
the reform efforts of Gorbachev. In other words, the weakness of the GDR within the international economy and the
rigidity of its political system lay at the root of the crisis of
values that prompted popular revolution. My cultural explanation of the *Wende* thus ultimately rests on a structural
foundation. Nonetheless, it goes beyond structural accounts
because a cultural interpretation not only shows how structural forces translate into political action but suggests, as
we shall see in Chapter 6, what structural and cultural consequences that action can have.

Although a cultural interpretation may thus be a necessary complement to structural accounts of communism's collapse, the question remains whether my interpretation of
East German culture and its shaping of behaviour in the
autumn of 1989 is accurate. I have contended that the erosion

of psychologically and systemically functional values in the late 1980s created the frustration that mobilised the East German population against the communist regime. Like any cultural argument, mine suffers from its generality and temporal imprecision. While it may be true that the East German population as a whole tended to embrace the values modesty, solidarity and equality and that these values became increasingly untenable in the late 1980s, this knowledge cannot tell us precisely when and why some East Germans (a minority in any case) decided, as consciously motivated social actors, to express their purported frustration through public protest; why others (a majority) stood by as silent opponents or grudging supporters of the regime; nor why still others (a considerable minority) remained outspoken regime loyalists. In the next chapter, I shall test the accuracy of my cultural interpretation by more closely examining the behavioural motives of individual East Germans represented in my survey.

5 Different Strokes for Different *Volks*

No matter how bitter or violent, political protest in itself does not a revolution make. In East Germany in the fall of 1989, the revolution did not begin when *Ausreisewillige* shouting 'Wir wollen 'raus!' scuffled with police outside Leipzig's Nikolai Church nor even when others stormed the Dresden railroad station to try to board the trains carrying refugees to West Germany from the embassies in Prague and Warsaw. Although they may have precipitated the demise of the GDR, these protestors did not challenge the existence of the state socialist regime; they merely wanted out. The revolution began in earnest only when crowds began to chant, 'Wir sind das Volk!' With this slogan that mocked the party-state's claim to do all for the good of the people ('Alles zum Wohle des Volkes'), the protestors reclaimed their sovereignty and put an end to the state's authority. As the people denied the indissolubility of the bond between them and their alleged vanguard party, the Volkskammer, the Volkspolizei, and the Volksarmee lost their power to the *Volk*, and for a few brief weeks in October–November 1989, the East German people were drunk with the feeling of their own power and freedom.

The revolutionary slogan 'Wir sind das Volk!' proved so intoxicatingly successful not only because it emptied the party-state of all its claims to authority but because it perpetuated the illusion that 'the people' actually existed. Through its ambiguity the slogan allowed the East Germans to believe they were united in their motives and aspirations and thus gave them the strength to overthrow their regime. With the fall of the Wall and the rush to reunification, however, it became clear that the East Germans were divided among themselves and incapable of finding common solutions for the reconstruction of their society. The revolutionaries cried betrayal and lamented the loss of popular unity. In fact, there had never been unity, for just like the abstract concepts society and culture, 'the people' has never actually existed. People exist, but 'the people' is merely a figure of speech to describe a particular aggregation of individuals. As Charles Tilly (1984: 20ff.) has pointed out, the elevation of such figures of speech into real social forces belongs to the 'pernicious postulates' of eighteenth-century social philosophy and its child, nineteenth-century social science. In the twentieth century, the reification of abstract concepts has given rise to obtuse social theories and, much worse, to totalitarian violence of the left and right in the real-life pursuit of a purity that exists only in the mind.

In the previous chapter, I too indulged in pernicious postulation as I developed a theoretical model of the East German revolution in which the collapse of the *culture* that held together *society* prompted the *people*'s mobilisation. My point of departure had been a series of interviews with individual East Germans about their motives and experiences before and during the *Wende*. Through the inductive process of interpretation I abstracted away from concrete individuals and their attitudes and behaviour to speak of a society and its value system. Society, however, is nothing more than the indeterminate sum of social relationships between concrete individuals. Similarly, culture is not a self-contained system of meanings and values but an unfixed set of individuals' unequally shared meanings and values. Neither society nor culture has precise boundaries: individuals from opposite sides of the planet can engage in relationships and share certain meanings and values. Of course, the number and intensity of contacts and shared meanings tend to be greater within particular geographical areas, so that it is possible, for example, to speak of an East German culture or society that also belongs to a European culture/society and encompasses a Thuringian culture/society.

Hence, when I argued that systemically functional values such as modesty, solidarity and equality held together East German society up until the late 1980s, I did not of course mean that all and only East Germans shared all and only these values. Instead, within the nearly infinite constellation of social contacts and cultural contexts in which East German individuals found themselves, they tended to recognise and interact with each other on the basis of modesty, solidarity and equality. At the same time, countless other values motivated East Germans in their interactions. In fact, with the erosion of the common, functional values, alternative values gained in importance and East Germany lost some of its cultural coherence. During the *Wende* and increasingly as the dissolution of state authority removed conformist constraints, a broad range of values came into play to motivate demonstrators, whom only a loss of the primary values partly united. In this chapter, through the quantitative analysis of my survey data, I shall lay bare some of the differing motives of the various East Germans who brought down their regime and thus show why the revolution had to end not in the reconstitution of an East German 'society' but in the remaining option of reunification. In doing so, I shall try to test the veracity of my cultural interpretation of the *Wende* and, in the end, shall propose an alternative explanation that my statistical analysis suggests.

QUANTITY vs. QUALITY: PROBLEMS OF VERIFICATION

Before turning to this analysis, however, I must address several methodological problems confronting the empirical verification of my argument about the role of value-erosion in the motivation of East German revolutionaries. Most serious is the problem that my argument would in itself seem to preclude the possibility of finding the evidence to confirm it. If the undermining of the values modesty, solidarity and equality rendered real existing socialist society dysfunctional, generated psychological and political frustration, and finally unleashed a slew of other competing values before and during the *Wende*, how are we to know that those basic values (and the response to their erosion) ever really motivated East Germans? My survey research unfortunately does not provide a very satisfactory response to this question. Although I inductively developed the cultural account of mass mobilisation on the basis of qualitative interpretation of my survey interviews, the quantifiable survey questions do not well lend themselves to testing my interpretation. What is more, even if the questions permitted the adequate operationalisation and measurement of my account's components, it would be disingenuous, if not tautological to test hypotheses with the same data that generated them. As we saw in Chapter 3, little other reliable East German survey data on pre-revolutionary attitudes is available, though the existing Zentralinstitut für Jugendforschung and Akademie für Gesellschaftswissenschaften data showing a sudden drop in confidence in the GDR and socialism in the late 1980s would tend to confirm my argument about a conjuncturally induced value collapse (cf. Förster and Roski, 1990; Gensicke, 1992). These surveys' questions, like my own, however, do not permit the verification of a more subtle cultural analysis.

In the search for confirmation of my interpretation, I extended my dialogue with the survey respondents by sending a summary of the findings to all of them and a fuller analysis to about 50 of the most interested. I was curious to see whether the respondents recognised themselves and their social experiences in my interpretation of their culture. The French sociologist Alain Touraine calls such an attempt to engage research subjects in a more abstract, theoretical dialogue about themselves a 'sociological intervention' (cf. Touraine *et al.* 1981, 1983). Such a technique, as Touraine himself has found, unfortunately bears little scientific fruit. Although the written responses to my analytic 'intervention' have tended to voice agreement with my cultural account of the *Wende*, most respondents were not really concerned about its theoretical validity. Some probably read my analysis as they would an astrologer's horoscope, picking out the parts with which they agreed and ignoring those they felt did not apply to them. Others did not even consider the account's accuracy but simply latched on to the concrete problems mentioned in the analysis that concerned them. Their exclusive interest in details was in effect a clear confirmation of Max Weber's observation about social scientific theories: 'Meaningfulness naturally does not coincide with laws as such, and the more general the law, the less the coincidence. For the specific meaning which a phenomenon has for us is naturally not to be found in those relationships which it shares with many other phenomena' (Weber 1949: 76–7).

This Weberian anti-nomotheticism is a particularly pertinent reminder to anyone trying to explain an event as complex as a popular revolution. The result of an incalculable number of more or less conscious individual decisions to promote or resist the overturning of a socio-political order, a revolution necessarily defies all attempts to impose causal generalisation. As the seemingly endless historiography of the French Revolution attests, the meaningful explanation of complex events depends on the discovery more of decisive particularities than of all-encompassing generalities. Indeed, in studying the East German revolution by conducting an intensive survey with many open-ended questions in an interview format, I intended to avoid reducing my respondents to mere cases confirming some general and therefore not particularly revealing trend and to uncover some of the richness of individual experience and choice that brought about popular mobilisation. A few very brief examples drawn from my interviews illustrate how complex and personal the final decision to join into anti-regime protest could be:

(1) A practising Christian, Doris K. had always had difficulties with the state. In order to attend high school beyond the 10th grade, she had had to sign a letter renouncing her religious beliefs. Since then Doris had always felt she was under observation. The resulting stress finally became unbearable in early 1989 when the police, employing a common practice to discourage visits to the West, waited until two hours before her only allowed departure-time to give her an exit visa. From that point on she vowed not to bite her tongue any more and told her child's teacher that her daughter would no longer participate in Pioneer activities after school. This minor but open resistance did not become active opposition, though, until Doris saw a Western television report on the arrest of protestors in late September 1989. She decided to participate in the decisive 2 and 9 October protests in Leipzig because (despite 'rational' incentives to free-ride) she could not bear to see other people arrested and beaten on her behalf.

(2) Jürgen B. described himself as a 'convinced communist', at least up until 1988, though he did not quit the party until late 1989. As an economic planner, he realised

the system was far from perfect, but to forget his frustrations at work he spent his free time building up his stamp collection. His correspondence with stamp-collectors around the world allegedly attracted the attention of the Stasi and cost him a demotion at work in 1988. He himself was not prepared to participate in the growing public protest movement until he heard that the district party secretary who had played a part in his demotion was going to address the demonstrators. Jürgen immediately drove to town to join the demonstration and went straight to the open microphones to denounce the party secretary.

(3) André F. had grown up like everyone else he knew: he split his personality between his public and private selves. Thus he had had no particular difficulty in volunteering to perform extended military service since he knew this display of public virtue might help him fulfil his private ambition to get a spot in medical school. In the army, however, the tension between his public and private selves became untenable. 'Even when I was in the shower,' he complained, 'I would get party congress resolutions shoved under my nose to read! I wanted to rebel.' The demonstrations of October 1989 at last gave André the outlet he sought.

(4) Gerd V., a software engineer, had lost all interest in his work. How could he take it seriously when official reports of success contradicted his daily work experience? Fortunately, he had a small garden plot in a complex where the club director did not take the officially required political activities seriously, so Gerd could lead a peaceful life at home and in his garden. Then, after a business trip to Bulgaria, he noticed a clicking in his phone-line and never again felt free of interference in his private life. When the first demonstrations occurred in the early autumn of 1989, Gerd's department director called a meeting and announced, 'Everyone is free to express their opinion but we shall decide to be against the demonstrations.' Gerd 'flipped out' [*ausgeflippt*] and had to go see the works' psychiatrist, who responded to Gerd's complaints by telling how he could no longer tolerate the political interference into his own work. Both Gerd and his psychiatrist went to their town's first demonstrations.

(5) A former competitive athlete, Lutz R. was an athletics instructor for handicapped children until he took an early retirement as a disability pensioner. He was proud of the GDR's achievements, particularly its generous social benefits, and appreciated the social justice of the country's uniform living conditions. A native of Thuringia, Lutz had never felt at home in Leipzig and retrospectively he despised his fellow Leipzigers for having led the revolution against socialism. He himself, however, had joined the Monday-night demonstrations, swept away with the enthusiasm of the moment: 'It was little people like me who did it; we showed that a revolution really is possible.'

Although the particular and true motivations for political mobilisation lie deep within individuals' personal experiences (well beyond what I have sketched above), generalisation across cases can have some value if not for predicting particular behaviour then at least for the contextual understanding of social phenomena. Even the five disparate cases I have summarised here suggest a certain similarity. Whether Doris K.'s desire to be true to her convictions, Jürgen B.'s desire to avenge his professional frustrations, André F.'s desire to protect his personal space, Gerd V.'s desire to speak his mind, or even Lutz R.'s desire to empower the socially protected little person, the motivation for protest participation seems to have lain in the contradiction between personal aspirations and public conformism.[1] This contradiction, however, for many years confronted nearly all of my survey respondents, those who did not join the demonstrations as well as those who did. Similarly, the generalisation across over 200 cases that I offered in the previous chapter, namely that the erosion of common functional values motivated the protestors of 1989, cannot tell us why particular members of the survey sample went to demonstrate against the regime, since the purported cultural crisis affected the whole society. Nonetheless my generalised interpretation can situate individual protest motivations in the general cultural context that gave them social meaning and consequences: the panoply of individual motives for revolt could come to the fore only in the context of the cultural crisis that the erosion of common functional values entailed. Unless they found themselves in a common cultural crisis, it is difficult to imagine how individuals as diverse as 'convinced communists' and Christian dissidents could all individually motivate themselves for revolt at the same historical juncture.

Since, following Weber, we cannot discover the precise meaning and therefore the adequate explanation of motivated individual behaviour in causal uniformities, a statistical analysis of my survey data would appear to be all the more fruitless. Still, a quantitative analysis of my survey data, revealing the social, behavioural and attitudinal attributes of the respondents who participated in the protests that brought down the East German regime should allow us to determine whether the survey's statistical findings are at least consistent with my interpretation of the survey interviews. That is, a statistical analysis should show that the variables associated with protest participation at least do not contradict my interpretation nor suggest another more plausible explanation for popular mobilisation. The analysis that follows necessarily runs roughshod over the richness of individual detail that I collected in my survey interviews, though I have tried to offer as qualitatively informed interpretations of the statistical findings as possible. (Readers who have little patience for statistical jargon or who are unable to suspend their disbelief in the explanatory value of statistical inference may wish to skip ahead to the chapter's concluding section.)

QUANTITATIVE ANALYSIS OF A QUALITATIVE PROBLEM

For the analysis of my survey data, I have used only the simple statistical techniques of correlation, cross-tabulation, and elementary multiple regression. Such techniques are more readily accessible and intuitively more trustworthy than sophisticated procedures for massaging or torturing data such as probit or log-linear regression. What is more, simple and sophisticated techniques usually equally identify any statistical relationships strong enough substantively to merit reporting. The relationships I sought to uncover in my analysis were of course those that might suggest explanations for participation in the mass demonstrations that ultimately brought down the SED regime. Among the variables the 235 survey questions generated (cf. Appendix: Survey Questionnaire), the best measure of the dependent variable demonstration participation was a question (F48a) asking respondents to place themselves on a seven-point scale ranging from opposition to the demonstrations to active leadership in their organisation.[2] The questionnaire also yielded about 150 operationalisable independent variables, including measures of socio-economic status, group memberships, political behaviour, attitudes towards socialism and the GDR, and sympathy for historical figures and contemporary politicians.

In a first brush with the data set, I looked for correlations between the continuous or at least ordinal independent variables and the dependent variable demonstration participation (F48a). I also cross-tabulated bivariate independent variables with a dummy variable for demonstration participation. Table 5.1 lists the variables having a correlation coefficient with demonstration participation equal or superior to ±0.30, i.e. those variables that in a simple regression could explain at least almost 10 per cent of variance. Table 5.2 identifies the bivariate independent variables having a statistically significant association with demonstration participation. It is interesting to note that Tables 5.1 and 5.2 do not include socio-economic variables that we normally associate with political participation such as income, education, and professional status, though the 'classic' variables, party membership, church affiliation, and geographic region do appear. The tables' inclusion and exclusion of variables do not, however, allow us to draw conclusions about the East German population's motives for participating in demonstrations or not since the findings of an intensive survey are indicative but not as potentially representative as an extensive survey with a larger random sample size.

The sample size of an intensive survey, however, is large enough to identify statistically significant differences among categories of respondents and thus to suggest the existence of similar differences, among many others, within the population at large. The data set includes variables that allow a categorisation of survey respondents by party membership, church affiliation, age, region and gender. Although the crude

Table 5.1

Selected* correlates of demonstration participation for various respondent categories
(Pearson's R and adjusted-R^2)

| Variable | | | | | | | Respondent categories | | | | | |
| | | | not | | | | not | | | | | |
Name	Description	All n=202	SED n=60	SED n=142	Young n=92	Old n=110	Church n=70	Church n=132	South n=110	North n=46	Berlin n=46	Men n=109	Women n=93
F4a	Town's quality of life in decline, 1985–89	0.17			0.31 (0.08)	0.07			0.32 (0.10)	−0.12	0.08		
F16a	Felt safe/free in 'Nische'	−0.24	−0.38 (0.13)	−0.16					−0.29	−0.10	−0.33 (0.09)		
F32a	Personal economic situation declining, 1985–89	−0.03							0.04	0.10	−0.30 (0.07)		
F25a	Size/status of private automobile	0.17	0.34 (0.10)	0.12					0.30 (0.08)	−0.03	0.13		
F36a	Thought life chances better in FRG	0.17							0.17	0.39 (0.14)	−0.03		
F42a	Favourable to GDR's provision of women's rights	−0.18							−0.35 (0.10)	0.23	−0.22		
F42b	Favourable to GDR's promotion of world-class sports	−0.23			−0.32 (0.09)	−0.20	−0.07	−0.33 (0.09)	−0.23	−0.28	−0.35 (0.09)		
F42c	Favourable to GDR's collective agriculture	−0.18	−0.33 (0.06)	−0.06	0.01	−0.36 (0.11)			−0.21	−0.24	−0.32 (0.05)		
F42d	Favourable to Marxist critique of bourgeois society	−0.24	−0.32 (0.07)	−0.14	−0.07	−0.35 (0.09)			−0.42 (0.14)	0.17	−0.27		
F42h	Favourable to GDR's grass-roots democracy	−0.20							−0.31 (0.09)	0.06	−0.21	−0.12	−0.37 (0.12)
F42i	Favourable to GDR's promotion of popular sport	−0.18	−0.32 (0.07)	−0.11									
F42k	Favourable to GDR's right to work	−0.17			−0.06	−0.32 (0.09)						−0.14	−0.30 (0.08)
F42l	Favourable to GDR's universal child day care	−0.27	−0.40 (0.15)	−0.21	−0.34 (0.10)	−0.25	−0.12	−0.33 (0.11)	−0.32 (0.09)	−0.11	−0.41 (0.18)		

Variable												
gdrgood Favourable to GDR's features (composite F42a–1)	−0.42 (0.17)	−0.51 (0.25)	−0.32 (0.10)	−0.36 (0.12)	−0.46 (0.20)	−0.29 (0.07)	−0.42 (0.17)	−0.53 (0.27)	−0.06	−0.48 (0.21)	−0.42 (0.17)	−0.41 (0.16)
F43f Personal sympathy for Ernst Thälmann	−0.37 (0.14)	−0.31 (0.09)	−0.35 (0.11)	−0.40 (0.15)	−0.37 (0.13)	−0.49 (0.13)	−0.19 (0.23)	−0.53 (0.27)	−0.21	−0.38 (0.13)	−0.39 (0.15)	−0.36 (0.12)
F43g Personal sympathy for Wilhelm Pieck	−0.43 (0.18)	−0.38 (0.14)	−0.40 (0.15)	−0.43 (0.17)	−0.44 (0.18)	−0.43 (0.17)	−0.36 (0.12)	−0.54 (0.28)	−0.17	−0.30 (0.07)	−0.44 (0.18)	−0.43 (0.17)
F43j Personal sympathy for Walter Ulbricht	−0.35 (0.12)	−0.37 (0.13)	−0.28	−0.39 (0.14)	−0.34 (0.11)	−0.22	−0.31 (0.09)	−0.51 (0.25)	−0.16	−0.40 (0.14)	−0.45 (0.19)	−0.21
F43m Personal sympathy for Erich Honecker	−0.34 (0.12)	−0.34 (0.10)	−0.29	−0.36 (0.12)	−0.35 (0.10)	−0.35 (0.08)	−0.29	−0.44 (0.19)	0.05	−0.53 (0.26)	−0.39 (0.14)	−0.29
procomm Symp. for communist leaders (composite F43)	−0.41 (0.16)	−0.40 (0.14)	−0.35 (0.12)	−0.42 (0.16)	−0.42 (0.17)	−0.39 (0.14)	−0.31 (0.09)	−0.58 (0.33)	−0.07	−0.36 (0.11)	−0.41 (0.16)	−0.41 (0.16)
prowest Symp. for Western figures (composite F43a, h, k, l)	0.16	0.36 (0.11)										
F45a 'Easier travel would not have prevented Wende'	0.18										0.09	0.30 (0.08)
F55c 'Electoral fraud not important cause of Wende'	−0.14											−0.30 (0.08)
F61a Father's profession (higher social origins)	0.28			0.24	0.30 (0.08)			0.33 (0.10)	0.10	0.26		
F68a Contacts with friends/relatives in West	0.29	0.30 (0.08)	0.24	0.31 (0.09)	0.29			0.35 (0.12)	0.25	0.14		

*Table reports correlation coefficients for those variables that correlate with demonstration participation for at least one category of respondents at a level of at least ±0.30. For the sake of comparison it also reports the correlation coefficients for complementary categories. Adjusted−R^2 statistics appear in parentheses immediately below the correlation coefficients superior to ±0.30

Table 5.2

Bivariate associates of demonstration participation for various respondent categories*

Variable				not SED				not Church					
Name	Description	All	SED	SED	Young	Old	Church	Church	South	North	Berlin	Men	Women
F5a	Felt hometown to be disadvantaged	+				+?	(+?)					+!	
F9a	FDGB (official trade union) member	−!		−	−!			−			−!	−!	−!
F11a	Confirmed in Church				+								
F11c	Member of Church	+!		+	+?	+!			++!		+	+	+
sed	Member of SED	−?			−				−!				
F14	Saw self as part of Nischengesellschaft	+		+	+?		+?		+				+
F23a	Had a private garden					(+?)							
F35a	Happy with life in early 1989	−!	+	−?		−!	−	−	−!	−	−?		−!
F37a	Had considered emigrating before 1989	+!	−!	+		+!	+!	+!	++!				++!
F38a	Saw different East/West national characters	−	−			−!	−	−	−	−		−	
F38e	Personal identification as 'DDR–Bürger'				−?			−					
F46b	Acquaintance/friend left during Ausreisewelle	++!	++!	+!	++!	+!	+!	+!	++!	+	+	+!	++!
F47a	Would have left in Ausreisewelle too	++!	++	+!	+	++	++	++	++!	+		+!	++!
popnazi	Father was member of NSDAP	+?	+?			+?	(+?)	(+?)				++!	++!
novote	Refused to vote for official candidates	++!	++?	++!	++!	++!	++!	++!	++!	++!	++!	++!	++!
south	Lived south of Berlin	+!	+!	+!	+	+!	+!					+?	+!

*Table summarises results of cross-tabulations of bivariate independent variables with a dummy variable for demonstration participation for various categories of survey respondents.

Key

+ = positive association, where gamma is greater than 0.30 but less than 0.60

++ = strong positive association, where gamma is greater than or equal to 0.60

− or −− = negative or strong negative association

! = strong statistical significance, where p is less than 0.01

? = weak statistical significance, where p is greater than 0.05 but less than 0.10

( ) = association disappears with control for additional group membership

categorisation of respondents according to such variables
goes against the grain of my methodological concern to
respect individuality, I nonetheless consider these categories to correspond to qualitative differences I discerned in
the interview process. The second to twelfth columns of Tables
5.1 and 5.2 provide an overview of the correlates and bivariate
associates of demonstration participation for various categories
of participants. Fortunately, multiple regression analysis can
help us weed through the diversity and multiplicity of motives for demonstration participation that Tables 5.1 and 5.2
suggest. With the help of the twelve columns of Tables 5.1
and 5.2, it was possible to construct and test various regression models for each of the respondent subcategories as
well as for the sample as a whole. Tables 5.3a–f summarise
the best-fitting multiple regression equations for each group.
In the following sections I shall discuss and interpret the
different regression models for the group as a whole and
for each subgroup.

A MODEL FOR ALL RESPONDENTS

As Table 5.3a indicates, the regression equation that can
best describe demonstration participation for all 202 survey
respondents ($r^2 = 0.42$) includes no unexpected or counter-intuitive variables. In fact, the equation suggests a rather
banal explanation for the *Wende*: those East Germans tended
to demonstrate who had already dared prior to the autumn
of 1989 to vote against the official slate of candidates or to
practise electoral abstention (V1 or 'novote'); who had faced
the shock of a friend's or acquaintance's emigration during
the *Ausreisewelle* (V2); who would have been tempted to leave
the country then themselves (V3); who were dissatisfied with
their lives early in 1989 (V4); who through a composite index
('gdrgood') expressed disapproval of the ostensibly positive
features of East German society (V5); who never even liked
the popular founding president of the GDR, Wilhelm Pieck
(V6); and who lived in a town they felt to be relatively disadvantaged (V7). In short, those who were opposed to the
regime and were discontented not surprisingly demonstrated
against the government. However banal these variables may

Table 5.3a

Summary of the best-fitting regression equation for 'demonstration participation' (F48a) for *all* survey respondents

Independent variables	*Coefficient for All* (n = 202)
V1: 'novote': refused to vote for official candidates (cf. F63a)	+ **
V2: friend/acquaintance fled GDR during *Ausreisewelle* (F46b)	+ **
V3: would have left in *Ausreisewelle* too (F47a)	+ *
V4: happy with life in early 1989 (F35a)	−
V5: favourable to features of GDR or 'gdrgood' (composite F42a–1)	− **
V6: personal sympathy for Wilhelm Pieck (F43g) (first GDR president)	− **
V7: felt hometown to be relatively disadvantaged (F5a)	(+ *)
(south: lived south of Berlin)	+ **
Adjusted R^2 of regression equation	0.42
(Adj. R^2 of equation when 'south' added)	(0.44)

Key
+ = positively correlated coefficient
− = negatively correlated coefficient
** = significant at $p<0.01$ level
* = significant at $p<0.05$ level
no * = significant at $p<0.10$ level
( ) = variable loses reported significance and/or excluded from multiple regression equation when variable 'south' included

appear, each merits closer examination, for the fact that not even one of them reappears in all the best-fitting regression equations for the subcategories of respondents suggests that the equation for all respondents conceals more complex or subtle motives for demonstration participation.

The one variable that does appear in all but two of the subgroups' regression equations, 'novote', seems to provide a rather question-begging explanation for oppositional behaviour in the fall of 1989. It would appear obvious that the respondents who in May 1989 (the last SED-controlled elections in the GDR) or earlier had already taken the public and sometimes risky step of refusing to participate in the popular approbation of official candidates should also be more likely to take the public and sometimes risky step of protesting against the regime. Surely, refusal to support the regime's candidates and demonstration against the regime must be expressions of the same phenomenon: regime opposition, though in a simple regression 'novote' explains only 17 per cent of variance in demonstration participation (cf. adjusted-r^2 statistics in Table 5.1). Multiple regression analysis does indicate, albeit weakly ($r^2 = 0.21$), the significant correlates of 'novote' and hence additional possible determinants of regime opposition and protest. The best-fitting regression equation shows not only antipathy to Wilhelm Pieck (V6) – itself already a correlate of demonstration participation – but church membership, non-membership in the official trade union FDGB, residence in a larger city, and troublesome personal encounters with the Stasi to be associated with 'novote'. Of these variables, residence in a larger city is the most readily explicable correlate of 'novote': the anonymity of urban life makes the detection of abstention or of voting against official candidates more difficult. In Berlin, for example, it was possible to vote in advance of election day in a large central polling place, where in the throng oppositional voters could slip unrecognised into the polling booth to cross out candidates' names. Such petty protest still probably got noticed in the GDR and prompted some unpleasant encounters with the security organs. As a result, the correlation between the variable for personal difficulties with the Stasi and 'novote' probably reflects that run-ins with the Stasi were less a cause than a consequence of the decision not to endorse the National Front at the ballot box.

The other two variables related to 'novote' which in themselves do not significantly correlate to demonstration participation, church membership and FDGB non-membership, lend themselves to two different interpretations. From a sociological perspective, integration in an officially sponsored union would provide a mechanism for enforcement of electoral participation whereas integration in the one voluntary association free from state control would offer support to those who resisted state authority. From a psychological view, staying out of official organisations, joining unofficial ones, and refusing to vote for official candidates would all be characteristics of a risk-accepting personality. Such a psychological interpretation would in fact be consistent with the qualitative findings of my survey interviews. Respondents who obediently voted for candidates not of their choosing, who quit the church to avoid trouble at school or work, or who remained in a union that often did not even provide a vacation spot in one of its industrial-scale holiday resorts often claimed, in a manner reflecting more self-censorship than external compulsion, that they had no choice. Respondents who took the risk of staying out of the union or refusing to vote reported consequences no more grave than a superior's remark. Only active church members complained of material disadvantages stemming from their allegedly deviant behaviour, though membership in an alternative community compensated them for the material risks. Similarly, the likely non-voters who had ugly encounters with the Stasi said that even such experiences did not affect their behaviour whereas the mere thought of a run-in with authorities was enough to put risk-averse personalities on the path to the polling place.

Along with 'novote' (V1), one other variable (V2) appears in the regression models for almost every group of survey respondents. Fully 67 per cent of the respondents who participated in demonstrations had a friend or close acquaintance leave the GDR during the *Ausreisewelle* of August to October 1989. Paradoxically no substantively or statistically significant relationship exists between demonstration participation and the emigration of a family member at that time. As we saw at the end of Chapter 3, Albert O. Hirschmann's (1993) account of the transformation of private exit on a mass scale into the public voice of mass demonstrations can also explain the different effects on protest participation of losing friends versus relatives. Similarly, Hirschmann's account can make sense of the presence in the regression model for all respondents of the substantively related but statistically independent variable 'would have left too' (V3): demonstration participants were not only likely to know someone who had exercised the exit option (V2); they were likely to have considered exercising that option themselves (V3). As Hirschmann has argued, exit and voice do not always vary inversely as he originally posited (1970: 44ff.). Instead, the availability of the exit option can stimulate voice. Thus, the permeability of East Germany's borders following Hungary's decision to open its frontier with Austria coupled with the unique possibility for East Germans to obtain citizenship and social benefits immediately upon arrival in West Germany made protest a relatively risk-free operation for those who were willing to consider exit in case of voice's failure or repression.

While the exit–voice model thus shows how public protest could erupt in 1989 and accounts for the presence of variables V2 and V3 in the regression equation for all respondents, Hirschmann's model does not uncover the sources of the discontent that motivated East Germans' exit and voice. The remaining variables in the regression model, however, do point to the sources of discontent. Demonstration participants in the survey sample tended to recall having been dissatisfied with their lives in early 1989 even before they sensed the imminent demise of the GDR (V4). Although such general unhappiness would appear to be a natural precursor to protest, V4 is not a particularly powerful indicator of protest involvement. In a simple regression model for all respondents, the 'happiness' variable (V4) can explain only 6 per cent of variance in demonstration participation, and the variable for general dissatisfaction appears with powerful statistical significance ($p < 0.01$) in only two of the regression equations for sample subgroups (cf. Tables 5.3b–f).

A more unexpected predictor of demonstration participation is antipathy towards Wilhelm Pieck, the first president of the GDR (V6). In fact, in the regression models for all respondents and for several subgroups, antipathy towards Pieck proved a stronger predictor than a composite index measuring sympathy towards various figures in the German communist movement ('procomm'). The Pieck-antipathy variable, however, probably better measures overall hostility towards communist leaders than does the composite index, for two reasons. First, 'procomm' included sympathy scores for the martyrs of the 1918–19 revolution, Rosa Luxemburg and Karl Liebknecht, who were also popular in oppositional milieus. Second, because Wilhelm Pieck ('our little worker President') was the most popular politician in the history of the GDR (cf. question F43 in Appendix: Survey Questionnaire), those who showed antipathy towards even him were probably hopeless cases for the communist camp.

Another composite index that does appear in the best-fitting regression equation for all respondents (V5 or 'gdrgood') seems to capture well respondents' overall assessment of the GDR and its self-proclaimed virtues and positive features such as equal rights for women, the promotion of sport, the right to work, and the universal provision of day-care (cf. question F42). Respondents who saw little about the GDR to be worth preserving naturally found it easier to participate in demonstrations that brought down the regime. Again, it is interesting to note that 'gdrgood' does not appear in the regression equations for all subgroups. As we shall see, often dissatisfaction with particular features of the GDR seemed to suffice to prompt protest participation among some categories of respondents.

Finally, the presence in the overall regression model of variable V7 shows that demonstration participants were likely to feel that their hometowns were disadvantaged compared to towns of the same size and significance elsewhere in the GDR. This reasonable cause for protest loses its substantive and statistical significance, however, when we introduce a geographic context variable to the regression equation. As the second to last line of Table 5.3a indicates, the variable 'south' (respondent lived south of Berlin) increases the regression equation's predictive power by two percentage points and renders V7 insignificant. The introduction of 'south' has a similar effect on most of the subgroups' regression equations: it improves the equations' fit (i.e. increases their r^2-statistics) and reduces the number of independent variables necessary for prediction. Although it is clearly a good indicator of demonstration participation, I did not originally include the variable 'south' in the applicable regression models because it does not really tell us much about individuals' motives for demonstration. It merely indicates that respondents living in the south were more likely (with powerful statistical significance, moreover) to demonstrate (55 per cent of the subgroup) than respondents from Berlin (41 per cent) or from the north (32 per cent). Of course, the variable 'south' may conceal attitudes and conditions more common in the south than elsewhere, but my survey data do not reveal any regional attitudinal or material specificities and show only the 'exit' variables V2 and V3 to be associated with 'south'. Thus, the data suggest only that the greater propensity for southern survey respondents to demonstrate may have stemmed from their greater awareness of the exit option, though southerners may also simply have had more opportunities to participate in protest since, thanks to the tradition of Monday peace prayers in Leipzig's Nikolai church and to the routing of emigrant trains over Dresden, demonstrations began earlier and were more widespread in the densely populated south.

In short, the regression model that best predicts demonstration participation for the entire survey sample includes three kinds of variables. First, the variable 'novote' (V1) shows that protest participants were likely already to have had an inclination towards oppositional behaviour. Second, the 'exit' variables V2 and V3 suggest that the sample's demonstrators risked protest participation because they were aware of and willing to use the exit option. Third, the variables V4 through V7 identified – though only very generally – the sources of dissatisfaction that motivated protest. A look in the next sections at the regression equations that best describe demonstration participation for various categories of survey respondents should, however, allow us to uncover more precise motives for protest.

DIFFERENTIATING BETWEEN DEMONSTRATORS

Before trying to discover different groups' motives for protest participation, we must first consider a fundamental qualitative problem with our dependent variable, the degree of support for and participation in public protest. Although the measure based on survey question F48a does distinguish between levels of opposition and support for the demonstrations that preceded and ultimately engendered the fall of the Wall, the variable does not discriminate between respondents who participated in the earliest, most dangerous and decisive demonstrations in Leipzig, Berlin, Dresden and some other smaller centres of protest (such as Plauen) before 9 October and those who hopped on the protest bandwagon in the final days or even those who participated in the big Berlin Alexanderplatz demonstration of 4 November because they saw it as an occasion to stand up in defence of a democratised but still socialist GDR. Through a question directed to the survey interviewer (myself or my spouse) and asking for a subjective assessment of the respondent's protest participation, however, it was possible to identify the 'revolutionaries of the first hour', i.e. those respondents who through a strong and early engagement in the protest movement contributed (in a historically decisive way perhaps) to its initial impetus and success. This group included only 16 members of the survey sample.

The revolutionaries of the first hour in the sample numbered too few, of course, to allow a statistically significant quantitative analysis of their behavioural, attitudinal and biographical characteristics. Nonetheless, this group of 16 shared some features that distinguish it from the rest of the survey sample and that suggest a profile of the typical revolutionary. Not surprisingly, all 16 had already before the fall of 1989 engaged in at least one oppositional act; all had refused to vote for official candidates in an election ('novote'). Nine of the 16 (or 56 per cent as compared to 18 per cent of the total sample) had had personal run-ins with the Stasi, as would perhaps befit oppositional types, while 11 (or 69 per cent versus 30 per cent of the total sample) were members of the Protestant church, towards which dissident individuals gravitated and under whose protection they were able to organise oppositional groups. Otherwise the revolutionaries of the first hour did not strikingly differ from the rest of the survey sample, with one notable exception. Whereas only 11 per cent of all respondents considered their personal standard of living to have declined in the five years preceding the *Wende*, seven of the 16 most active revolutionaries (or 44 per cent) said theirs had deteriorated, though a majority described their living standard as stable.

In short, the 16 revolutionaries of the first hour in the sample resembled those oppositional church members who indeed organised the first formal protests against the regime and founded groups such as Neues Forum (to which seven of 16 belonged). Their small number in my survey sample, however, prevent our gleaning any more insights into the motives of this decisive group. Of course, other (auto)biographical and more formal studies of the East German revolutionaries of the first hour do exist (cf. Liebsch, 1991; Grabner, Heinze and Pollack, 1990; Rein, 1990; Marcuse, 1990; Philipsen, 1993). My purpose in my survey and here, however, was and is to explain not so much the first revolutionaries' initiation of protest in the fall of 1989 as the subsequent mass mobilisation of opinion against the regime. For that purpose the dependent variable measuring levels of support (or opposition) to the demonstrations is adequate, and we shall now see how the correlates of that variable differed for various groups of East Germans represented in my survey.

PARTY MEMBERS AGAINST THE PARTY-STATE

The most unexpected but perhaps most interesting group of demonstration participants in the survey were those who belonged to the SED. Surprisingly only a substantively weak, statistically not quite significant, negative association exists between membership in the ruling party and participation in demonstrations that chased the party from power: fully 35 per cent of the comrades (n = 60), as compared to 48 per cent of the partyless (n = 142), participated in demonstrations against the party-state. Whereas the general regression model for all respondents also best describes protest participation for the partyless in the sample, a rather different equation, for which it is tempting to offer an unflattering interpretation, fits best for the SED members. As we can read from Table 5.3b, like the general model, the equation for party members includes the variables 'would have left' (V3), 'happiness' (V4), and 'Pieck sympathy' (V6), but it

Table 5.3b

Summary of best-fitting regression models for 'demonstration
participation' (F48a) for SED party members and non-partisans

Independent variables	Coefficients for	
	SED *party members* (n = 60)	*not SED* *party members* (n = 142)
V1: 'novote': refused to vote for official candidates (F63a)		+ **
V2: friend/acquaintance fled GDR during *Ausreisewelle* (F46b)		+ **
V3: would have left in *Ausreisewelle* too (F47a)	+ *	(+)
V4: happy in early 1989 (F35a)	−	−
V5: favourable to GDR features: 'gdrgood' (composite F42a–1)		− **
V6: personal sympathy for Wilhelm Pieck (F43g)	− **	− **
V7: felt hometown to be disadvantaged (F5a)		+ (**)
V8: personal sympathy for Western personalities (F43a, h, k, l)	+ *	
V9: father was member of NSDAP: 'popnazi' (F61c)	+ **	
V10: favourable to GDR's child day-care sytem (F42l)	− *	
V11: had private telephone (F67)	+ *	
(south: lived south of Berlin)		+ **
Adjusted R^2 of regression equation	0.51	0.42
(Adj. R^2 of equation when 'south' added)		(0.46)
Adj. R^2 when best-fitted equation for all respondents applied to respondent category	0.36	0.42

Key
+ = positively correlated coefficient
− = negatively correlated coefficient
** = significant at p<0.01 level
* = significant at p<0.05 level
no * = significant at p<0.10 level
( ) = variable loses reported significance or excluded from multiple
regression equation when variable 'south' included

does not contain 'novote' (V1), 'friend fled' (V2), or 'gdrgood' (V5). Also neither 'hometown disadvantaged' (V7) nor 'south' improves the fit of the party members' equation. Although these variables do not appear as statistically significant components of the regression model for SED members, they are nonetheless associated with demonstration participation (cf. Tables 5.1 and 5.2). What distinguish the SED demonstrators from the others are their marked tendencies to disapprove of the GDR's universal day-care system (V10, a component of the index 'gdrgood'); to be offspring of fathers who had belonged to the NSDAP (V9 or 'popnazi'); to have a telephone in their home (V11); and to be sympathetic to famous Germans not generally revered in the GDR (V8 or 'prowest', a composite of sympathy scores for Otto von Bismarck, Konrad Adenauer, Willy Brandt and soccer star Franz Beckenbauer).

This rather peculiar hodge-podge of variables, which when put together in a regression equation explain 51 per cent of the variance in SED members' demonstration participation, can make sense, though, in light of an interpretation that would describe SED members who participated in anti-government demonstrations as opportunists. The attitudinal variables associated with protest suggest that the SED demonstrators from the sample were never convinced communists: not only were they hostile to Wilhelm Pieck (V6) and sympathetic to 'militarists' and 'revanchists' such as Bismarck and Adenauer ('prowest'); they also agreed with conservatives who attacked the GDR's infant day-care system, which gave mothers an equal opportunity to work, as unhealthy for children and destructive of the family (V10). If not out of conviction, then, the SED demonstrators appear to have come to the party in pursuit of privilege. The positive correlation of variable V11 with protest participation indicates that the SED demonstrators tended to belong to the lucky minority, usually people with positions of responsibility, who had a private telephone. As Variable F25a in Table 5.1 shows, the SED demonstrators also tended to enjoy the privilege of driving a large automobile such as a Wartburg or Lada, though in multiple regression the telephone variable proves more significant. Almost three times more often the children of Nazis than the partyless protestors, the SED demonstrators seem to have come from a family tradition of siding with the party in power. In the fall of 1989 these SED members may simply have sniffed the changing political winds and joined (or merely claimed to join) the demonstrations in order to secure their place in the new political system. The widespread denunciation today of so-called *Wendehälse*, i.e. of former SED petty functionaries who again occupy positions of power and prestige, suggests that the small group of SED demonstrators in my survey sample were not an anomalous bunch and that the interpretation of their behaviour as opportunistic is not too far afield. Another piece of evidence from my survey, however, should hold us back from such a prejudicial interpretation: the comrades who demonstrated against the party did not tend to be those who admitted having joined the party to advance their careers (cf. survey question F12b,c).

YOUNG AND OLD DEMONSTRATORS

Apparently less cynical than the SED members might have been in their motives for demonstrating were the younger members of the survey sample (i.e. those 40 and under in 1989). Although young people predominated in the *Ausreisewelle* and were highly visible in the first demonstrations of autumn 1989, my survey (as we saw in Chapter 3) found no correlation between age and demonstration participation. Younger and older demonstrators, however, seem to have had different motives for protest. Table 5.3c shows that demonstrators born before and after the founding of the GDR tended alike to have refused voting for official candidates (V1) and to have personally known someone who left during the *Ausreisewelle* (V2). Whereas the older demonstrators in the survey sample were prepared to leave the GDR themselves, no relationship exists between the variable 'would have left too' (V3) and demonstration participation for the younger ones. Even though a move to the West would have been easier for them, the younger demonstrators seem to have wanted to make the best of the GDR.

Youthful idealism (or perhaps naïveté) might explain this willingness to stay behind and work for the improvement of

Table 5.3c

Summary of best-fitting regression models for 'demonstration participation' (F48a) for young (born after 1949) and old survey respondents

		Coefficients for	
Independent variables		*Young* (n = 92)	*Old* (n = 110)
V1:	'novote': refused to vote for official candidates (F63a)	+ **	+ *
V2:	friend/acquaintance fled GDR during *Ausreisewelle* (F46b)	+ **	+ *
V3:	would have left in *Ausreisewelle* too (F47a)		+ *
V10:	favourable to GDR's child day-care system (F42l)	− **	
V12:	favourable to GDR's promotion of world-class sport (F42b)	− **	
V13:	town's quality of life in decline 1985–89 (F4a)	(+ *)	
V14:	rejected leading role of GDR founders (F44a)	+ **	
V15:	confirmed in church (F11a)	+[*]	
V16:	saw different East/West national characters (F38a)		− *
V17:	favourable to GDR's collective agriculture (F42c)		− *
V18:	father's profession (F61a) (higher social origins)		+[*]
(south: lived south of Berlin)		+ **	+ *
Adjusted R^2 of regression equation		0.54	0.47
(Adj. R^2 of equation when 'south' added)		(0.56)	(0.50)
Adj. R^2 when best-fitted equation for all respondents applied to respondent category		0.41	0.43

Key
+ = positively correlated coefficient
− = negatively correlated coefficient
** = significant at p<0.01 level
* = significant at p<0.05 level
no * = significant at p<0.10 level
( ) = variable loses reported significance or excluded from multiple regression equation when variable 'south' included
[ ] = variable gains significance or is included in multiple regression equation when variable 'south' added

the GDR, but so too might some other variables in the regression equation. The younger demonstrators who had been confirmed in a church (V15) during the ideologically tense late 1950s, 1960s or 1970s had not only shown a certain idealism with that act but learned to pay the price of their idealism as well. Children from families with 'bourgeois idealist [i.e. Christian] *Weltanschauungen*' often quite literally had a black mark next to their names on their teachers' class lists and were treated accordingly. Those who could bear the social burden that confirmation entailed usually came from solid, traditional families. Strong family bonds might explain further why young demonstrators did not want to leave the GDR and probably also why they tended to be hostile to the GDR's day-care system (V10), which helped dissolve the traditional family. Interestingly the younger demonstrators tended to be particularly hostile to the GDR's promotion of world-class sport (V12). Apparently the regime could not buy their loyalty with circuses, particularly when they perceived that bread was no longer forthcoming: younger demonstrators tended to have perceived a decline in the quality of life in their towns during the last few years before the *Wende* (V13), though this relationship loses its statistical significance when the regression equation includes 'south'. In any case, the younger demonstrators tended to consider the SED regime to have been illegitimate from the very beginning since they found even the anti-fascist achievements of the GDR's founders to be no justification of their leadership role (V14).

While the survey sample's younger demonstrators thus seem to have been idealists from strong traditional families, the older demonstrators tended, as the additional correlates of their protest participation (V16, V17 and V18) would suggest, to be German nationalists from bourgeois backgrounds. From Table 5.2 we can read that older demonstrators were likely to think that their life chances would have been better in West Germany (F36a), to have considered emigrating (F37a), and to believe that different East and West German national characters had not developed (F38a or V16). Of these substantively and statistically related variables, the last (V16) proves decisive in multiple regression analysis. That is, a belief in the indivisibility of the German national identity would appear to have motivated older demonstrators both in their thoughts of emigration to a West which offered greater opportunities and in their demonstration participation. The older demonstrators' faith in the superiority of the capitalist FRG, moreover, is not inconsistent with their social origins (V18). The older opponents of the 'Arbeiter-und-Bauern-Staat' did not themselves tend to be the children of workers and peasants but rather those of bureaucrats, professionals and small businesspeople. For them, the socialist state's attack on private property, particularly the forced collectivisation of agriculture, might have motivated opposition, as the older demonstrators' marked hostility to the GDR's cooperative farming system (V17) would suggest.

WHY THE RELIGIOUS AND THE HEATHEN RAGED

For older survey-respondents, who grew up in a time when almost everyone was confirmed in the church, variable V15 is not a correlate of demonstration participation as it is for the younger ones. Survey question F11c (church membership in 1989) offers a better measure of religious affiliation for the entire sample. In fact, church membership is by itself – but not in multiple regression – one of the better predictors of demonstration participation: 59 per cent of the survey respondents who said they belonged to a church went to demonstrate, as opposed to only 36 per cent of those without religious affiliation (in a cross-tabulation, gamma = 0.44, p = 0.002). As Table 5.3d indicates, these two groups of demonstrators also seem to have had different motives for demonstration, though aside from the common correlates 'novote' (V1) and 'friend fled' (V2), the variables in the two groups' regression equations for demonstration participation are not terribly revealing. Both demonstrator groups tended to have higher class origins (V18), and for the non-church member demonstrators these origins may have been linked, as they were for the older protest participants, to German national sentiment. The non-religious demonstrators tended not to believe in the development of distinctive Eastern and Western national characters (V16) and not to identify themselves as *'DDR-Bürger'*, the common

Table 5.3d

Summary of best-fitting regression models for 'demonstration
participation' (F48a) for church members and non-church members

Independent variables	Coefficients for	
	Church members (n = 70)	not Church members (n = 132)
V1: 'novote': refused to vote for official candidates (F63a)	+ **	+ **
V2: friend/acquaintance fled GDR during *Ausreisewelle* (F46b)	+ **	+ *
V3: would have left in *Ausreisewelle* too (F47a)		+ *
V4: happy in early 1989 (F35a)	− **	
V12: favourable to GDR promotion of world-class sport (F42b)		− **
V16: saw different East/West national characters (F38a)		− *
V18: father's profession (F61a) (higher social origins)	+ *	+
V19: personal sympathy for Ernst Thälmann (F43f)	− **	
V20: personal identification as '*DDR–Bürger*' (F38e)		− *
Adjusted R^2 of regression equation	0.58	0.37
Adj. R^2 when best-fitted equation for all respondents applied to respondent category	0.47	0.33

Key
+ = positively correlated coefficient
− = negatively correlated coefficient
** = significant at p<0.01 level
* = significant at p<0.05 level
no * = significant at p<0.10 level

self-description of East German citizens (V20). The churchless
demonstrators' particular hostility to the GDR's international
sport success (V12) may also have been an expression of
their pan-German nationalism since the regime promoted
Spitzensport in order to develop popular pride in the GDR.

Whereas for the religiously unaffiliated the variables correlated with demonstration participation lend themselves to
a fairly coherent possible interpretation, those for the church

members (aside from the common ones already discussed) do not. The best-fitting regression equation for the church-goers shows the demonstrators among them to have been unhappy with their lives in early 1989 (V4) and unusually antipathetic towards Ernst Thälmann (V19). Keeping in mind the possibility of statistical coincidence, it is possible to imagine that the German Communist Party leader of the 1930s and concentration-camp victim posthumously provoked the loathing of church members since the mandatory East German children's 'pioneer' organisation bore his name. During school-based Thälmann-Pioniere activities young Christians often suffered ostracism and ridicule.

REGIONAL VARIANCE IN PROTEST MOTIVES

We have already seen that the addition of the variable 'south' to various subgroups' regression equations could increase their predictive power. In fact, regression models for the three major regions where respondents resided – the south, the north and Berlin – reveal considerable regional variation in the imputable motives for demonstration participation. That variation should come as no surprise, of course, since these regions have obvious longstanding historical and cultural differences. From Table 5.3e we can see that the regression model for respondents living south of Berlin does not differ significantly from the model for all respondents. In fact, the general model explains 55 per cent of the variance of protest participation in the south. The replacement of the variable measuring sympathy for Wilhelm Pieck (V6) with a composite index of sympathy scores for various communist leaders (V21) and the addition of the variable measuring belief in a single German national character (V16) improve the equation's predictive power for the south by an additional four percentage points (and render the 'exit' variable 'would have left too' (V3) statistically insignificant).

By contrast, the general model has absolutely no predictive power for the demonstration participation of respondents living north of Berlin (adjusted-r^2 = 0.00)! Although the best-fitted regression equation for the northerners includes the variable 'novote' (V1), almost always associated

Table 5.3e

Summary of best-fitting regression models for 'demonstration participation' (F48a) for different regions

Independent variables	Coefficients for		
	South (n = 110)	North (n = 46)	.Berlin (n = 46)
V1: 'novote': refused to vote for official candidates (F63a)	+ **	+ *	+ **
V2: friend/acquaintance fled GDR during *Ausreisewelle* (F46b)	+ **		+ **
V4: happy in early 1989 (F35a)	− *		
V5: favourable to GDR features: 'gdrgood' (composite F42a–l)	− *		
V10: favourable to GDR's child day-care system (F42l)			− **
V14: rejected leading-role claim of GDR founders (F44a)			+ *
V16: saw different East/West national characters (F38a)	−		
V21: sympathy for communist figures (composite F43)	− **		
V22: favourable to GDR's cultural funding (F42f)		+ *	
V23: personal sympathy for Willy Brandt (F43k)		+ *	
V24: thought life chances better in FRG (F36a)		+ *	
V25: personal sympathy for Erich Honecker (F43m)			−
V26: felt free/safe in *Nische* (F16a)			− *
V27: personal economic situation declining 1985–89 (F32a)			−
Adjusted R^2 of regression equation	0.59	0.33	0.63
Adj. R^2 when best-fitted equation for all respondents applied to respondent category	0.55	0.00	0.43

Key
+ = positively correlated coefficient
− = negatively correlated coefficient
** = significant at p<0.01 level
* = significant at p<0.05 level
no * = significant at p<0.10 level

with regime opposition, its other three independent variables are not easy to interpret. The northern demonstrators tended to have a positive appreciation of the GDR's policy of subsidisation of culture in the provinces (V22), to show sympathy for Willy Brandt (V23), and to believe their life chances would have been better in the West (V24). These variables' association with protest could suggest (together with my subjective impression of the northern demonstrators in the sample) that the Pomeranian protestors may have been more intellectual or idealistic than their southern compatriots. Neither the shock of the *Ausreisewelle* (V2, V3) nor unhappiness with the GDR ('gdrgood' or V5) nor with life in general (V4) motivated the northern demonstrators. Instead, they appreciated subsidised culture, the genius of the author of *Ostpolitik*, and the chances for personal development the West offered. By all accounts, the relatively late and infrequent demonstrations in the north of the GDR in autumn 1989 were indeed more idealistic affairs than in the south. The observably superior quality of life in the agricultural, touristic north probably meant that material interest underlay political protest much less than in the over-industrialised south.

Similarly, in Berlin political principle seems to have motivated protest more than any material concerns. Although a decline in personal economic well-being (V27) does not correlate with demonstration participation for respondents living anywhere in the GDR, the Berliners from the sample who went to protest actually tended – albeit with weak statistical significance ($p = 0.09$) – to report an improvement of their standard of living in the years immediately preceding the *Wende*! East Germans from the provinces would understand why East Berliners had no material motives for protest. As one respondent from *Bezirk* Halle remarked: 'In [East] Berlin, they lived just as in the West.'

If the Berliners allegedly had it so good, what pushed them to protest? The variables in the regression model for Berlin, aside from the common ones 'novote' and 'friend fled', suggest that principled and personal opposition to the SED regime motivated the Berlin respondents' demonstrating. Like the younger demonstrators in the sample, the Berlin demonstrators rejected the GDR's founding myth, namely that anti-fascism justified the leadership of the creators of the SED and GDR (V14). In a manner apparently confirming the saying 'familiarity breeds contempt', the protestors from the 'Hauptstadt der DDR' not only disdained the party-state's founders but also markedly and statistically independently loathed its last leader, Erich Honecker (V25). The political hatred that protest in Berlin expressed may have had its origins in a greater politicisation of private life in the capital city. The Berlin demonstrators reported feeling unfree from state interference in their private lives, or *Nischen* (V26), and this resentment of state intervention into family life may also have lain at the root of the Berlin demonstrators' hostility to the GDR's universal day-care system (V10).

GENDER AND PROTEST

Although several categories of demonstrators tended to be hostile to the GDR's day-care system, the survey respondents as a whole expressed satisfaction with that and other policies facilitating women's entry into the workforce. Despite the advantages and formal guarantees offered to women, equal rights remained an unachieved goal in the GDR, as elsewhere. In the survey sample, men and women were equally likely to participate in demonstrations, but the different status of the sexes in the GDR meant that they went to demonstrate for somewhat different reasons. As table 5.3f shows, the regression equations for male and female demonstrators are both quite similar to the general regression model for the entire sample, though the men seem to have been particularly hostile to Walter Ulbricht (V28) rather than to Wilhelm Pieck (V6) and awareness of the personal availability of the exit option (V3) may have provided the female demonstrators extra motivation.

A few other gender differences in the apparent motives for protest also merit mentioning. The addition of the variable 'south' affects the women's regression equation more than the men's. Thus, as the table summarises, residence in the south, where the opportunities for demonstrating were greater, is a better predictor of women's participating in protest than their evaluations of the political importance of

Table 5.3f

Summary of best-fitting regression models for 'demonstration participation' (F48a) for male and female survey respondents

Independent variables	Coefficients for	
	Men (n = 109)	Women (n = 93)
V1: 'novote': refused to vote for official candidates (F63a)	+ **	+ *
V2: friend/acquaintance fled GDR during *Ausreisewelle* (F46b)	+ *	+ *
V3: would have left in *Ausreisewelle* too (F47a)		+ *
V4: happy in early 1989 (F35a)	− **	[−]
V6: personal sympathy for Wilhelm Pieck (F43g)		− **
V7: felt hometown to be disadvantaged (F5a)	(+ *)	(+)
V28: personal sympathy for Walter Ulbricht (F43j)	− **	
V29: FDGB (official trade union) member (F9a)	− **	
V30: favourable to GDR's grassroots democracy (F42h)		− *
V31: 'easier travel would not have prevented *Wende*' (F45a)		(+ *)
V32: 'electoral fraud not important cause of *Wende*' (F55e)		(−)
(south: lived south of Berlin)	+ *	+ **
Adjusted R^2 of regression equation	0.43	0.44
(Adj. R^2 of equation when 'south' added)	(0.44)	(0.46)
Adj. R^2 when best-fitted equation for all respondents applied to respondent category	0.41	0.40

Key
+ = positively correlated coefficient
− = negatively correlated coefficient
** = significant at p<0.01 level
* = significant at p<0.05 level
no * = significant at p<0.10 level
( ) = variable loses reported significance or excluded from multiple regression equation when variable 'south' included
[ ] = variable gains significance or is included in multiple regression when variable 'south' added

the electoral fraud of May 1989 (V32) and of travel restrictions (V31). The introduction of 'south' does not, however, affect the other independent variable unique to the women's regression model: their hostility to *Basisdemokratie* (grassroots democracy) as it was practised in the GDR (V30). Generally absent from positions of power and prestige in the polity and economy – Margot Honecker was a notable exception – women in the GDR, particularly those without full-time employment, found themselves relegated to maintaining the *basisdemokratische* institutions such as the Wohnbezirksausschüsse (neighbourhood councils) and the Volkssolidarität ('people's solidarity', or local social services). Some women found their grassroots involvement effective and fulfilling, but because democratic centralism extended all the way down to the neighbourhood level, other women through their local experience grew disillusioned with the entire political system and, as the statistical significance of variable V30 suggests, also grew prone to protest. By contrast, the male respondents who were involved in the official trade union (V29) seemed to find it difficult to participate in anti-government protests, though as we saw in the discussion of the variable 'novote', union membership may be a better measure of risk-aversion than political integration.

INTERPRETING THE INTERPRETATIONS

As the interpretation of the correlates of their demonstration participation would indicate, men and women in the survey – like northerners, southerners, and Berliners; church members and atheists; young people and old; party members and partyless – seem to have had different motives for joining in the political protest that brought down the East German regime. I have necessarily based my interpretations of the statistical correlates of the various subgroups' protest participation on the qualitative impressions that my survey interviews yielded. The question remains whether these interpretations are consistent with the qualitative analysis of the collapse of GDR state socialism that I presented in the last chapter. From the discussion of Tables 5.3a–f it is clear that for all categories of respondents (except the SED members and the northerners) the *Ausreisewelle* triggered demonstration participation among those who had shown a predilection for oppositional behaviour by refusing to vote for official candidates. The apparent sources of discontent underlying protest, however, varied from group to group. Although the independent variables present in the different respondent subgroups' multiple regression equations suggest some possible causes for protest participation, I did not intend to develop a generally valid predictive model for anti-government demonstrations with my statistical analysis. The survey data do allow the inference that dissatisfaction with certain features of GDR life drove some respondents to demonstrate, while – in gross simplification – opportunism, idealism or nationalism motivated others. The statistical findings are simply not rich enough, though, to allow a more subtle interpretation of the protestors' motives. As we saw with even a superficial examination of five individual cases, those motives lay within unquantifiable personal experience. Nonetheless, the different correlates of demonstration in the respondent subgroups' regression equations indicate that the East German protestors probably had a wide range of specific motives, possibly but not necessarily those I suggested in my interpretations. This finding, though admittedly hardly counter-intuitive, nonetheless tends to confirm my argument that the competition of often incompatible motives prevented the East German revolutionaries' creation of a coherent political programme, but it does not substantiate my claim that the collapse of a unifying value system unleashed this competition of motives. To the contrary, the statistical significance in various regression models of variables such as antipathy to the GDR's first leaders (V6, V21, V28), disapproval of the GDR's founding myth (V14), and belief in a single German national character (V16) suggests that the motives for popular mobilisation existed well before any erosion of common values in the late 1980s.

As I argued at the beginning of this chapter, the sharing of the values modesty, equality and solidarity did not preclude – and may even have permitted – a diversity of other values within the East German population. Since the chapter's statistical findings clearly point to a diversity of protest motives but not to a mobilising collapse of common values, they call into question my argument that the breakdown of the East German value system provoked and initially united the demonstrators of autumn 1989. Indeed, the findings suggest an alternative explanation more consistent with classic theories of totalitarianism. As Friedrich and Brzezinski (1956: 281) wrote, 'the totalitarian dictatorship seeks to divide and rule in the most radical and extreme way'. Thus, the state both encourages the fragmentation of society and contains the resulting tensions through repression. Totalitarianism is therefore an inherently unstable system since any erosion or lapse of state authority can allow the explosion of repressed social tensions. As we saw in Chapter 3, Albert O. Hirschmann (1993) has argued that the East German state based its repressive authority on the draconian control of 'exit'. When Hungary's opening of its borders undermined the SED state's means of repression, the party-state lost all credibility and unleashed the furies of 'voice' even among regime loyalists, as the correlations of the variables 'friend fled' (V2) and 'would have left too' (V3) with demonstration participation suggest. Behind the unison of the chant mocking state authority, 'Wir sind das Volk', however, hid the cacophony of interests and motives that my survey uncovered. In such a reading of events the decisive cause of popular revolution was much less the erosion of some common, systemically functional culture than the simple breakdown of state authority. Societal divisions and discontent thus were not the results of a cultural crisis but were more or less constants, just waiting for the opportunity to express themselves.

Although consistent with my quantitative findings and with the fundamentally repressive basis of totalitarian regimes, such an explanation of the East German revolution overemphasises the system-stabilising role of repression and neglects the informal arrangement that citizens made with the party-state and that generated a distinctive political culture. To be sure, the Wall, the ultimate symbol and concrete instance of repressive state authority, was constitutive of an East German community of fate, but within its confines the East Germans cultivated values that helped to stabilise the system and to facilitate life within it. The remarkable social stability of the GDR between 1961 and 1989, to which both events and more or less reliable existing East German survey data testify (cf. Chapter 3), suggests that positive values – beyond fatalism, fear and hypocrisy – formed the basis of a specific East German culture.

Since 1989, as they have had to confront the political and cultural insensitivity of West Germans, the former '*DDR-Bürger*' have grown more aware of the common experiences and values that continue to guide their behaviour. In their struggle to meet the challenges of democratisation and industrial restructuring, East Germans – like other peoples throughout Eastern and Central Europe – are reaching back to and becoming conscious of their communist cultural heritage. In fact, probably only this ongoing process of adaptation will fully reveal the values and meanings which for forty years shaped and distinguished East German culture. Although it is possible, as we have just seen, to explain the East German demonstrators' motives without referring to the broader East German cultural context, I shall argue in the final chapter that an understanding of pre-revolutionary culture, while not sufficient for explaining individual demonstrators' motives, is necessary for explaining both the relative stability of East German state socialism and the contemporary political consequences of the popular revolution of 1989 for the reunified Germany.

6 The Cultural Legacy of Communism

In 1989 the world marvelled at the revolutionary *élan* of ordinary East Germans as they took to the streets and peacefully reclaimed their sovereignty with chants of 'We are the people! No violence!' Marvel quickly turned to horror, though, as the world saw – live and in colour – ordinary East Germans, first in Hoyerswerda in 1991 and then in Rostock-Lichtenhagen in 1992, lean from their windows to egg on neo-Nazi assailants of refugee centres with cries of 'Foreigners out! Burn them alive!' The first democratic revolution in German history would appear to have been an aberration, and worse yet, the once heroic revolutionaries of the Democratic Republic would seem, despite half-a-century of allegedly anti-fascist education, not to have transcended the cowardly, genocidal racism of their Third Reich parents and grandparents. The latest outbreaks of popular but ugly protest, however, have not been restricted to eastern Germany. In fact, xenophobic violence began in the West before reunification, and since the incendiary murders in Mölln and Solingen it has taken on proportions even more alarming in the West than in the East. Throughout Germany, political violence in the streets and ubiquitous disillusionment with established politicians and institutions are beginning to echo the final years of the Weimar Republic. With reunification the forty-five years of Germany's division seem to have vanished without a trace.

The post-reunification political crisis, however, is not a resumption of German history after a half-century hiatus. History does not stand still (let alone end) and despite superficial similarities, today's racist violence and disenchantment with mainstream political parties and parliamentary democracy is as little a continuation of Nazism as the GDR was the perpetuation of Third Reich totalitarianism under a new name. To be sure, cultural forms repeat themselves – young skinheads shout, 'Heil Hitler!' and the Nationale

139

Volksarmee goose-stepped just like the Wehrmacht – but those forms' meanings are not the same in different historical and structural contexts. During the forty-five-year division of Germany, new social, economic, and political structures evolved in the East and the West. As I argued in Chapter 4, a particular culture, or set of common subjective orientations, developed in the GDR not simply as a superstructure but as a creative historic, social and psychological response to the structures of real existing socialism. Similarly, a more or less functional set of values emerged to motivate behaviour in the new West German liberal market society. With reunification, the East Germans and, to a much lesser extent, the West Germans have found themselves in an unprecedented structural context, for which the distinct identities and values they developed over four-and-a-half decades have not prepared them. In this final chapter, I shall argue that the political crisis gripping all of Germany today results from the clash of East and West German identities and cultural values. With this argument, I wish to establish the validity of the cultural interpretation I elaborated in Chapter 4 by demonstrating its analytic utility (the sole criterion for judging an interpretation) for elucidating the motives and meanings behind not only the popular revolution of 1989 but also the contemporary crisis of German democracy.

Quite obviously, the cultural heritage of the forty-five-year division is not the only cause of the reunited Germany's political problems. Indeed, the rise of xenophobia, of far-right parties, and of general disenchantment with democracy has afflicted nearly all Western societies in recent years. It is thus possible (and necessary) to see Germany's present political problems as a specific case of the general crisis of post-industrial democracy. In the Federal Republic, as elsewhere in Western Europe and North America, the loss of faith in mainstream political parties and in their seemingly incapable leaders as well as the rise of populist, racist and extremist parties and movements are linked no doubt to the erosion of the postwar forms of social organisation and representation. Confronted in the 1980s with de-industrialisation, structural unemployment, and global interdependence, the governing catch-all parties, which in the first three decades after 1945 successfully competed to manage economic growth and redistribution through the Keynesian welfare state (cf. Offe, 1983), lost the confidence and support of their electorates, making way for electoral abstentionism and for new parties and social movements. West Germany witnessed the rise, in the early 1980s, of the Greens on the left and, in the late 1980s, of the Republicans on the far right while, in the same decade, France saw the rise of the National Front and Italy the birth of its populist Leagues. (The United States did not trail far behind with the Perot phenonemon beginning in 1992.) At the same time, the weakening of integrative institutions (from labour unions to the family) and of the social safety-net increasingly generated anomic violence, often directed against foreigners accused of taking jobs and welfare benefits. Thus, even before the East German revolution of 1989 and the reunification of 1990, the Federal Republic, like its Western neighbours, experienced xenophobic murders and the election of far-right parties to local and regional governments. In fact, opinion researchers report that since reunification Germans have merely 'caught up' to their Western neighbours in their level of expression of illiberal attitudes (Falter and Schumann, 1993).

Nevertheless, the speed and the strength of the rise of the far right and of racist violence in Germany since reunification give grounds for concern, especially in light of Germany's traumatic past, and suggest unique, endogenous causes for Germany's current crisis. Because the first, most spectacular incidents of racist violence erupted in the East, (West) Germans and others initially saw the root of the evil in the survival in the East of authoritarian values perpetuated under a communist regime that had paid only lip-service to anti-fascist ideology and turned a blind eye on skinheads and other partisans of 'order' (cf. Hirsch and Heim, 1991; Süß 1993). Although on a per capita basis, xenophobic violence has indeed been – at least until late 1992 – more widespread in the former German Democratic Republic than in the West (Sur, 1993), virulent xenophobia is an all-German problem that alleged lingering East German authoritarianism alone cannot explain. What is more, the far-right parties with their more or less overt racist appeals have gained more (intended) electoral support in the West than in the

East (Roth, 1993: 291; Tournadre, 1993: 78).

Because it is thus difficult to blame the meteoric rise of the racist right on the East, the public debate in Germany has found another scapegoat in the very victims of xenophobia. According to German public opinion and politicians, the unprecedented influx of foreign asylum-seekers since the collapse of communism has provoked racist reactions through its strain on public order, housing and budgets. In line with this logic, a two-thirds majority of the Bundestag voted on 27 May 1993, to restrict severely the constitutional right to asylum. This illiberal constitutional amendment quickly proved the futility of fighting hostility towards foreigners by limiting the presence of foreigners, for within days of its passage racist youths launched a wave of terror beginning with the quintuple murder in Solingen. The victims of this terror, moreover, have been mostly Turks and other longstanding immigrants in the West and in a few cases homosexual, homeless or handicapped Germans (Stock, 1992; Sur, 1993), facts which suggest that racist violence is not a direct response to the recent 'flood' of asylum seekers. In the East, far-right-wing youths have attacked Mozambican and Vietnamese 'guest-workers' remaining from GDR-times as well as asylum-seekers, yet the frequency of these attacks has been entirely disproportionate to the small number of foreigners present in the East, be they new or old arrivals. In other words, it would be difficult to attribute xenophobic violence to the dramatic rise in the number of asylum-seekers in the past three years except in so far as the widespread perception that the quantity of foreign refugees is unabsorbable has generated a climate of tolerance for racist acts.

While neither the Federal Republic's acceptance of nearly a million refugees over the past three years nor its inheritance of authoritarian political cultural values from the GDR can directly explain the frightening resurrection of racist violence and extreme-right political parties in Germany, these factors nonetheless point in the direction of the underlying causes of the crisis of German democracy. The influx from Eastern Europe of asylum-seekers and of ethnic Germans with claims to citizenship did not cause but has highlighted the confusion surrounding German national identity ever since the defeat and division of 1945. At the same time, the incorporation of the GDR into the Federal Republic has not revived or preserved authoritarian values but has introduced into united Germany's political culture a new repertoire of values that developed in the East during the forty-five-year division. It is precisely the ambiguities of German national identity and especially the conflict between East and West German (political) cultural values that have provided fertile ground for anti-democratic sentiment and the growth of right-wing extremism.

THE LINGERING NATIONAL IDENTITY CRISIS

Nietzsche once observed that it is typically German to ask what it is to be German. The question of who or what should constitute the German political community has haunted Germans at least since the birth of the modern nation-state two centuries ago. Indeed, the debate over the appropriate ethnic and territorial composition of a German state stood behind several of the international conflicts of the nineteenth century and reached a paroxysm with Hitler's simultaneous pursuit of *völkisch* purification and *Lebensraum*. The defeat of 1945 and the subsequent division of Germany did not lay the national question to rest but simply adjourned the debate until the increasingly unexpected moment of reunification. In the meantime, the two German states (Austria having quickly re-established its distinct identity after its absorption into the Reich) developed, in mirror-image of one another, opposite conceptions of the nation in order to delegitimise and to place the blame for the war on the other (cf. Le Gloannec, 1989: Ch. 1).

The collapse of the GDR and the subsequent popular demand for rapid reunification suggest that the East German state did not succeed in forging a distinct national identity among its citizens, or at least not one strong enough to preserve an independent state. In contrast to the Federal Republic, the SED regime had tried, as we saw in Chapter 2, to develop a political as opposed to ethnic conception of the German nation. Prior to the construction of the Wall in 1961, when the East German communists still believed their system might win the hearts of all Germans, the GDR leadership clung to the ethno-linguistic conception of the nation. Over the course of the 1960s and especially after Willy Brandt launched his *Ostpolitik*, though, SED ideologues began to elaborate a political, class-based notion of the nation. The GDR, in their view, represented the culmination of all the positive democratic, proletarian traditions of German history while the revanchist Federal Republic embodied the bourgeois, authoritarian and militarist tendencies. Finally, in 1974, the GDR entirely abandoned references to German ethnicity when it constitutionally defined itself as simply 'a socialist state of workers and peasants'. Yet the GDR's efforts in the 1980s to reclaim as its own various periods and personalities from German and particularly Prussian history suggested the untenability of a purely contemporary, political definition of the nation (cf. Chapter 2).

Despite the GDR's apparent failure to forge a distinct identity, the priority the SED regime gave the *demos* over the *ethnos* in its conception of the nation represented a significant departure from the German national tradition as preserved in the Federal Republic. There the ethnic definition of the nation and of citizenship was not only a holdover from the past but a weapon in the Cold War and in electoral politics. In declaring itself the heir of the German Reich, the Federal Republic accepted the legal responsibility (including the payment of compensation) for the Nazi genocide but also gained the claim to represent the entire nation. This so-called *Alleinvertretungsanspruch* – legally based on the Potsdam agreement and on the preamble and Articles 23 and 146 of the Basic Law of 1949 (itself ostensibly provisional until the full-fledged political reconstitution of the nation-state) – allowed the Federal Republic to recognise citizens outside the territory under its control and to maintain claims to the territories of the Reich of 1937, except for the Soviet-annexed portion of East Prussia. In thus refusing to recognise the GDR's sovereignty and separate citizenship, the Federal Republic undermined its communist counterpart's legitimacy and lured away its unhappy citizens *en masse* until 1961. At the same time, the refusal to accept Germany's postwar boundaries as definitive made it possible for the Federal Republic's Christian Democratic governments to maintain the aspirations and electoral support of millions of organised expellees from the eastern territories. Although Brandt's *Ostpolitik* in the early 1970s normalised the Federal Republic's relations with its eastern neighbours, including the GDR, enough legal ambiguities remained to allow Helmut Kohl as late as 1990, before the conclusion of the Two-plus-Four Treaty, to scandalise world opinion, but to shore up his support on the right, by hesitating to acknowledge the finality of the Oder–Neisse border with Poland.

The Federal Republic's legal posturing with its *Alleinvertretungsanspruch* did not, of course, offer the only basis for national identity in postwar West Germany. In fact, in the wake of the war, the vast majority of West Germans would have gladly forgotten the Federal Republic's historical legacy and claims. For them 1945 marked the 'hour-zero' after which they had become performance masters of the social market economy, exemplary students of parliamentary democracy and committed members of the Western alliance system. The economic miracle and the political stability of the Federal Republic absolved West Germans of their war-guilt, at least until the generational break of 1968. Then a younger generation espousing post-materialist, participatory values questioned their parents' suppression of their Nazi pasts and, like students of German political culture of the 1950s and 1960s (Almond and Verba, 1963; Dahrendorf, 1967), doubted the sincerity of their elders' commitment to democracy. The repercussions of this generational challenge to West Germans' self-image included: left-wing terrorism; the rise of an alternative political culture and an extra-parliamentary opposition which eventually gave birth to the Green party; and ultimately in the late 1980s the *Historikerstreit*, in which intellectuals disputed whether Germans could ever put the horrors of Nazism behind them.

In opposing those (notably Ernst Nolte) who sought to re-establish historical continuity between pre- and postwar Germany and those (notably Jürgen Habermas) who argued that the singular barbarity of Nazism necessitated a conscious moral rupture with the past, the *Historikerstreit* reflected but did not resolve the ambiguities and contradictions of West German national identity on the eve of reunification (cf. Maier, 1988). On the one hand, the argument for continuity rested on the hereditary, ethnic conception of German national identity. It was thus consistent not only with living German cultural traditions but with the Federal Republic's official claim to be legal heir of the Reich, with its blood-based definition of citizenship, and with its policy (at least under centre-right governments) of non-recognition of Germany's eastern borders. On the other hand, the argument for rupture with the past mirrored the new forms of (West) German national identity that had emerged since the war. These included what Habermas derides as *D-Mark-Nationalismus,* i.e. the powerful identification with West Germany's economic achievements that developed in the 1950s and 1960s at the expense of historical memory and responsibility, and what he (among others) praises as *Verfassung-spatriotismus,* i.e. the allegiance to the liberal democratic principles enunciated in the Basic Law that emerged with the rise of a participatory political culture in the 1970s and 1980s. In short, the *Historikerstreit* laid bare the disparate historical, ethnic, economic, and political elements of postwar West German identity.

Reunification could or should have allowed a clarification and consolidation of German national identity, for with the dissolution of the second German state and the complete international restoration of German sovereignty, any uncertainty about the appropriate territory, citizenship and common values for the German political community should have disappeared. Precisely because reunification came as the result of the collapse of the GDR, however, it did not necessitate a re-examination of West German identity. For West Germans the failure of communism confirmed that they lived in the 'Modell Deutschland' (Weidenfeld, 1992: 382), and even critical intellectuals believed that the East simply (or rather not so simply) had to catch up to the more modern West (cf. Habermas, 1990; Brie and Klein, 1991).

Thus, the old ambiguities of the Federal Republic's identity have survived to nurture a climate favourable to the outburst of extreme right-wing xenophobic nationalism. Although the 'Two-plus-Four' Treaty of 1990 clearly established the finality of reunited Germany's borders, right-wing politicians continue to comfort the territorial aspirations of the *Vertriebene,* as did, for example, the Minister-President of Bavaria in May 1993, when he encouraged the Sudeten Germans in their quest for compensation from the Czech Republic. Even more troubling, though, is the maintenance of citizenship based on *jus sanguinis*. In the Cold War era this ethno-hereditary right to citizenship strengthened the Federal Republic's *Alleinvertretungsanspruch* and allowed it to defend the interests of ethnic Germans in the Soviet bloc. Today the *jus sanguinis* merely serves to prevent the integration of life-long 'foreign' residents into German society and to perpetuate a racialist if not racist definition of the German political community (cf. Welsh, 1993).

What is more, because West Germans saw reunification primarily as a technical problem of bringing the East up to their level (cf. Stassen, 1993), the high cost of unification has threatened their identity as economic miracle-workers. Students of West German political culture have long feared that a sharp decline in material performance might undermine the popular legitimacy of democracy (Sontheimer, 1990:26–7). Today Germany finds itself in just such a crisis, and *D-Mark-Nationalismus* seems to be haunting democracy as Germans rally around their magic currency against the encroachment of the European monetary union and strive to seal their borders against economic refugees from the south and east. Such a context of irredentism, racialism and economic defensiveness has placed few constraints on the violent impulses of a tiny minority of racist young men.

The massive candle-light processions and counter-demonstrations with which responsible citizens have responded to xenophobic violence prove, of course, that the democratic, participatory elements of postwar West German political culture and identity have survived reunification. The apparent *Verfassungspatriotismus* of the (silent) majority of Germans seems, however, to have taken on naïve, even counter-productive proportions. The efforts to solve Germany's political problems by constitutional tinkering (as with the amendment of the right to asylum) and by appeals to the Constitutional Court (as with the recent challenges by parties within the governing coalition to the new abortion law and to Bundeswehr participation in international peace-keeping operations) suggest a dangerous inability to settle conflicts through democratic debate and compromise. Liberal constitutionalism thus does not seem strong enough to compensate for the persistent ambiguities in German national identity that have spurred xenophobia.

As I shall argue more fully below, the very process of reunification not only failed to strengthen the participatory values present in German political culture but exacerbated the lingering crisis of national identity. What is more, because reunification did not resolve fundamental cultural antagonisms between East and West Germans, their mutual antipathy has grown over the past three years, and the deflection on to foreigners of hostility between 'Ossis' and 'Wessis' has become another source of xenophobic violence and right-wing nationalism.

THE CLASH OF CULTURES

In describing Germany's national identity crisis since reunification, I have so far mentioned only the inheritance from the old Federal Republic of the irredentism and racialism present in foreign policy and in citizenship laws and of the economic nationalism and constitutional liberalism present within the population. The German Democratic Republic, of course, also contributed its heritage to the new Germany's identity. Although, as I have already noted, the SED regime through its policy of Prussian revivalism admitted the failure of its efforts to establish a distinct class-based GDR national identity, another form of GDR identity did emerge within the population over the course of its forty-year experience with state socialism. That identity, as I argued in Chapter 4, existed within what students of communist political cultures call the dominant culture as opposed to the official socialist goal culture. While the dominant culture in East Germany developed in at least partial opposition to the official culture and under the direct influence – through mass media and personal contacts – of West German culture, it was by no means identical to Western culture. To the contrary, as a response to the challenges of daily life under socialism, East German culture incorporated values diametrically opposed to those appropriate to democratic capitalism in the West, and the partial survival of those values lie at the root of the current clash between East and West German cultures.

In Chapter 4 I argued that the democratic revolution of 1989 resulted from the undermining of the dominant East German cultural norms. I contended that the re-enforcement of privileges and of the parallel hard-currency economy in the late 1980s eroded the psychologically, socially and politically functional values (summarised by the triad modesty, solidarity and equality) that until then had stabilised the *Nischengesellschaft* and its arrangement with the SED regime. Although in Chapter 5 I could not show that the erosion of common functional values motivated specific individuals to participate in anti-regime protest in 1989, I argued that the political cultural crisis of late state socialism provided the context in which a general mobilisation of opinion against the regime and the specific individual motives for active protest could express themselves.

Given this alleged collapse of the East German cultural system in the late 1980s, it might seem that the cultural values of the GDR would be irrelevant for understanding the problems of the reunited Germany. Indeed, in 1990 most Germans, East and West, assumed that whatever cultural specificities the GDR had retained from German tradition or developed under socialism would quickly dissolve in the greater mass of modernised West German culture. The popular revolution of 1989 supposedly represented a conscious break with the past, and unification would mop up any communist cobwebs in the corners of people's minds. Thus, the well-known political scientist Kurt Sontheimer (1990) wrote that East German political culture would not be 'a factor that could independently influence the political culture of the Federal Republic'. Instead, the revolution had 'left behind a political and intellectual vacuum that [would] now be progressively filled from the West'. Although he acknowledged that the East German culture included positive, even desirable features, Sontheimer contended that these were imposed values that could not survive:

> We might wish that certain values from the *Nischengesellschaft's* political culture – namely the sense of neighbourly cooperation, a greater respect for social equality, a developed

sensibility for solidarity and fraternity – be strongly introduced into the Federal Republic's political culture because
they could strengthen democracy, but they developed in
the GDR thanks more to the economic exigencies of the
totalitarian system than to a free act of self-determina-
tion. The imperatives of a liberal market society will drive
them into the background. (Sontheimer, 1990: 87)

During the year of reunification, East German culture did
indeed appear fragile and doomed to disappear as the Easterners readily embraced Western values. The values of modesty, solidarity and equality, as I have argued, may have been
psychologically, socially and politically functional under real
existing socialism, but they were certainly not suited to a
society such as West Germany's, which offered unbridled
possibilities for consumption and for individual advancement.
It seemed, however, that East Germans could adapt easily
to West German society because real existing socialist society
and liberal market society had shared a fundamental value
orientation: both were consumer societies. In the aftermath
of the Warsaw Pact invasion of Czechoslovakia in 1968, the
Communist Parties of Eastern Europe governed on the basis
no longer of the millenarian appeals of utopian ideology
but of a pledge of improved living standards in exchange
for political acquiescence. This new social contract, as we
saw in Chapter 2, became explicit in the GDR in 1971 at
the Eighth Party Congress of the SED, when Erich Honecker
promised 'the unity of social and economic policy' (i.e.
economic policies designed to meet the consumer desires
of the population). Relative to the West, the possibilities
for consumption remained restricted, and only the development of the values modesty, solidarity and equality made
the satisfaction of consumer desires possible. The fall of the
Wall, however, suddenly expanded the opportunities for
consumption and seemingly rendered modesty, solidarity and
equality obsolete.

Thus, in an initial period of euphoria that lasted precisely
from 9 November 1989, until Chancellor Kohl's triumphant
victory in the first all-German elections on 2 December 1990,
it seemed that cultural unity had already come. East Germans went into a consumer frenzy that began as soon as

they crossed the Wall and pocketed their 100 D-Marks *Begrüßungsgeld* and continued in earnest with monetary union on 1 July 1990. One phenomenon in particular suggested that East Germans had cashed in their values of modesty, solidarity and equality for their West German counterparts of consumerism, individualism and status-seeking: their rush in the summer and autumn of 1990 to purchase automobiles. Thanks to the gift of monetary union at the exchange rate of one-to-one for wages and, in effect, for most savings, millions of East Germans were able to accede to the Western car-culture. With their new (if often used) cars, East Germans not only satisfied their repressed consumer fantasies but asserted their individual freedom to travel wherever (and as fast as) they wanted and joined the German status game of outdriving and outshining everyone else on the road.

Social mimicry may be an effective learning strategy, but even in their new cars East Germans have not been able to keep up in a value system that is not their own. Far from guaranteeing the East Germans' assimilation into the Western culture, the imperatives and opportunities of a liberal market society have provoked a cultural backlash in the East. To be sure, East Germans today still appreciate the new order's possibilities for consumption and for individual development and distinction. Since reunification, however, they have discovered that they are at home in neither the new society nor its culture. Inexperienced with the exigencies of a competitive, individualist consumer society, East Germans have found themselves at the mercy of unscrupulous salespeople, exploitative employers and business partners, and impatient friends and relatives from the West. Very quickly the East Germans coined a new word to describe the Westerners who did not hesitate to tell their fellow citizens in the East that they knew everything better: the *Besserwessis.*

The East Germans' treatment as second-class citizens in the new Germany has been particularly difficult for them to swallow. Few East Germans realistically expected the immediate or rapid attainment of economic parity with the West, but they did expect that reunification would bring social and political equality. The slogan with which the revolution of 1989 ended, 'Wir sind ein Volk', had not so much expressed nationalism as a desire for social and political equality. As they discovered in the winter of 1989–90 the extents of social control by the Stasi and of political corruption, East Germans came to think that reunification would bring them not only the much-prized D-Mark but the equal citizenship rights that had been denied them in what they now considered an irreformable GDR. Reunification has not brought those rights, though. West Germans have treated their new fellow-citizens not as social equals but as inferiors, 'half-Russians' who do not know how or care to work (cf. *Der Spiegel,* no. 3, 1993: 58). Even worse, the West has succeeded in politically silencing East Germans with accusations of Stasi involvement or simply of collaboration with the SED regime. Leading East German politicians in every party have lost their jobs or authority under the fire of accusations in the Western media (almost the only media left). Manfred Stolpe has survived as the last elected indigenous eastern Land premier only because the East Germans, fearing their total disenfranchisement, have rallied in support of him.

In effect, in response to their political, economic and social inferiority in the united Germany, the East Germans have regained their solidarity and their identification with, if not pride in, the GDR. Although Easterners and Westerners alike joke half-seriously about rebuilding the Wall (only this time higher and from both sides), a return to the past is, of course, impossible. Still, a growing majority of East Germans today identify themselves as former '*DDR-Bürger*', whereas in June 1990, in anticipation of monetary union, most had enthusiastically declared themselves 'Deutsche' (Le Gloannec, 1993: 71; also cf. extensive survey findings in *Der Spiegel,* no. 3, 1993). The East Germans have also come to express profoundly ambivalent, not to say self-contradictory attitudes. Public opinion surveys report East Germans to be simultaneously dissatisfied with the reunification process and unwilling to call into question the wisdom of the rapid political unification of 1990 (cf. Noelle-Neumann, 1991: 179 ff.; Bauer-Kaase, 1993; Gibowski and Jung, 1993; Veen, 1993; Yoder, 1993). Similarly, they feel that Helmut Kohl and other Western politicians have broken their promises and betrayed East German interests, yet they have not shown much support for the efforts of Gregor Gysi (former leader of the reformed communist party) and Peter-Michael Diestel (former right-wing DSU and CDU leader) to create a non-partisan 'Committee for Justice' in defence of eastern Germans' interests. Indeed, it is remarkable that the nearly universal perception of gross injustices in the reunification process has not given rise to specifically East German political organisations or parties, except, of course, for the once-dwindling but now recovering SED successor party, the Party of Democratic Socialism (PDS), and the inheritor of the citizens' movements of 1989, the tiny *Bündnis 90*, now fully merged with the West German Greens. The explanation for this lack of political mobilisation lies in part in the established West German parties' rapid and complete occupation of organisational space already in early 1990. More important, however, have probably been the immobilising ambivalent attitudes already mentioned as well as divisions within the East German population that have grown since reunification. As we saw in Chapter 5, significant motivational differences existed among East Germans on the basis (among others) of region, generation and gender. These differences have gained significance as different categories of the population have turned out to be net social and/or economic winners or losers from reunification. Most pensioners, mobile and younger skilled workers, and residents of some border regions have profited from reunification while older laid-off workers, women in general (cf. Ferree and Young, 1993), and workers in the heavy industrial regions have suffered losses. The dividing lines between the winners and losers of reunification, however, have not been clear. Most families include both clear-cut winners and losers, and almost every East German has been both a winner and a loser in terms of political rights, economic well-being and social status (cf. Koch, 1993). In such circumstances, even if everyone shares an identity as a disadvantaged 'Ossi' and has something specific to complain about, political mobilisation seems unlikely. As one of my interview partners in Leipzig recently exclaimed, 'Of course we want to stand up for ourselves, but for or against whom or what precisely?'

While the East Germans have thus not politically mobilised around their reclaimed identity and solidarity, they do seem to have fallen back on or rediscovered the functional value of modesty and two other values that were common in East German society: familism and security. Modesty has again become a virtue in part because unemployment and low incomes have made it functional but also because it allows a critique of West German consumerism and overbearing self-confidence. The East Germans' widespread retreat into their families, or private space, has come both as a reflex of people accustomed to subordination and as a result of their disappointment with the outcome of their daring venture into public space in autumn 1989 (cf. Yoder, 1993: 13; Henrich, 1989: 91). Finally, the disruption that unification has brought into their lives has given rise among East Germans to a nostalgia for the security and stability they enjoyed behind the Wall.

While reinforcing the East Germans' current political paralysis, this revival of the values of security and stability has probably also encouraged outbreaks of xenophobic violence. Before 1989, the GDR was one of the most socially and ethnically homogeneous (or, as some East Germans quipped with a certain perverse pride, 'the most boring') country in the world. The possibility for emigration that bourgeois and aristocratic East Germans had had before 1961 rendered the levelling effects of socialism more complete in the GDR than elsewhere (cf. Gaus, 1983: 31 ff.). As the former heartland of Prussia, the GDR was home to an almost exclusively German and overwhelmingly Protestant population. Despite its celebration of socialist internationalism, the GDR regime severely restricted contact to the few thousand foreign guest-workers and several hundred thousand Soviets living there. Thus, before the fall of the Wall, East Germans had had virtually no close contact with ethnically different or socially distressed people. Ignorance is the parent of racism and intolerance, and the greater willingness of East than of West Germans to express and perhaps to harbour racist attitudes has no doubt created – in conjunction with the general insecurity that rising, previously unknown unemployment and crime rates have engendered – a climate favourable to right-wing violence against asylum-seekers in the new Länder.

Racist violence, as the world now recognises, is not an East German but an all-German problem. Aggressive xenophobia is, at least in part, the extreme response of a small number of East and West Germans in the society-wide search to overcome the conflict between East and West German values and interests. Antipathy between East and West Germans has progressively grown since unification not only because Ossis and Wessis disagree on how much the West should contribute to the reconstruction of the East but because the economic, social and political difficulties of reunification have made the East Germans unable and increasingly unwilling to adopt West German cultural values.

A variety of strategies for living with this antipathy have emerged. As the East German sociologist Thomas Koch (1992) has observed, most East Germans have responded to the cultural contradictions between East and West with a more or less constructive re-identification with the GDR while a smaller number have denied their Eastern identity and values by moving West or mimicking Westerners. Reunification has not posed as great a cultural challenge to West Germans, of course. The collapse of communism has comforted most of them in their embrace of liberal economic, political and social values. But as they have come to recognise that reunification may cost them not only higher taxes but higher interest and unemployment rates, a growing number have lost faith in the Federal Republic's traditional democratic Volksparteien and are willing to cast protest votes in favour of far-right parties (cf. Roth, 1993).

Only a tiny number of West and East Germans have responded to the difficulties of reunification with acts of racist violence. While it is possible to see the violent reassertion of ethnic nationalism as the effort of the losers of reunification in East and West to combat their own social exclusion (cf. Le Gloannec, 1993: 71–2), the social character of the perpetrators of violence suggests a less instrumental cause. Usually carried out by mindless teenage boys, who, far from being socially isolated delinquents as Chancellor Kohl claims, are the children of traditionally conservative lower-middle class milieus (cf. Drieschner, 1993), racist violence seems to be more the extreme expression of society-wide scapegoatism than of individual frustration. In neither East nor West Germany have foreigners or asylum-seekers been the primary cause of economic hardship, but public

opinion – according to which, in the West, the presence of
foreigners is society's biggest problem and, in the East, the
third biggest after unemployment and crime (cf. Roth, 1993;
Gibowski and Jung, 1993; Kuechler, 1993) – has cast the blame
for general problems directly attributable to reunification
on them. In the West, it is migration from the new Länder
(at the rate of 1000 per day) and not the flood of asylum-
seekers and refugees that has heightened the housing shortage
and competition at the lower end of the job market. In the
East, it is obviously not foreign workers but industrial restructuring and mismanagement on the part of the Treuhand
privatisation agency that have caused massive unemployment.
Blaming foreigners for Germany's problems, however, allows
Germans not to have to blame each other (more than they
already do); hating others helps deny and deflect the
antagonisms that East and West Germans have for each other.

The wave of xenophobia that has swept Germany, East
and West, suggests that the cultural crisis that began in the
GDR in the late 1980s and brought on the collapse of communism there has culminated in a profound crisis of German political culture. Although mutual antagonisms have
not pushed the vast majority of Germans to the extreme of
racist violence, the extremists have succeeded in setting Germany's political agenda. The major parties' first response
to the violence that erupted in Rostock in August 1992 was
not a vow to crack down on extremists or to redress social
tensions in East and West but, as we have seen, a promise
to restrict foreigners' access to Germany by amending the
constitutional article allowing asylum. Such an inappropri-
ate and, as events have proven, ineffective response to a
direct attack on the liberal democratic order in the Federal
Republic leads me to fear that a retreat to ethnic nationalism may become – just as in the other troubled societies of
Central and Eastern Europe – the final solution to Germany's cultural division and antagonisms.

EXCURSUS: HOW SUCCESS SPOILED UNIFICATION

Germany's reunification in 1990 need not fatally have led
to the current national identity crisis, the clash of cultures,

and the accompanying outburst of extremist racist violence. Although Germany had inherited from its forty-five-year division an ambiguous sense of national identity and two distinct political cultures, reunification could have provided an opportunity to redefine German national identity, to forge common participatory political cultural values, and to strengthen liberal democracy in the Federal Republic. Indeed, as the result of the first successful democratic revolution in German history, reunification might have represented the 'revolutionary break with the past' essential for the establishment of democracy (cf. Moore, 1966: 431). The common German linguistic downgrading of the *friedliche* (peaceful) *Revolution* of 1989 to a simple *Wende*, or turn-about, however, seemed to express the Germans' inability to recognise or to seize the historic opportunity.[1] The last *Wende* in German politics had come with the parliamentary manoeuvrings of 1982, by which a Christian-liberal coalition replaced the social-liberal government without reference to the electorate. The resurrection and widespread adoption of the term *Wende* in 1989 marked the end of the popular revolution and the resumption of politics as usual in the form of élite bargaining. Thus, reunification became a technical problem for the existing West German political system, and not an occasion for its recasting.

While the collapse of the East German regime certainly did not in itself necessitate the reform of the West German regime, the Federal Republic's Basic Law actually foresaw such a situation and in Article 146 prescribed the drafting of a permanent Constitution to be approved by the democratic will of the reunited German people. At the same time, however, Article 23 provided for the accession of new territories organised as federal Länder into the existing constitutional order. In 1957, the Saarland had in fact acceded to the Federal Republic under Article 23, after having voted in 1955 against continued administration by France. The existence of Article 23 and the precedent of the reincorporation of the Saarland offered an escape-hatch from the obligations of Article 146. Thus, claiming a democratic mandate from the results of the first free Volkskammer elections of March 1990, in which the parties favourable to rapid reunification took a majority of seats, the Christian Democratic leaders of the GDR and the FRG negotiated an agreement whereby the reorganised five Länder of the East along with the reunited city-state Berlin would join the Federal Republic using Article 23 on 3 October 1990 (cf. Smith, 1991; Thaysen, 1993).

The main argument in favour of this form of reunification was expediency, though expediency is unfortunately rarely an attribute of democracy. To be sure, two important considerations did militate against postponing unification until after a lengthy democratic constitutional debate. Growing instability in the Soviet Union required a rapid agreement on the full restoration of German sovereignty and the withdrawal of Soviet troops from East German territory. Similarly, the deepening economic crisis, coupled with the continuing massive emigration to the West after the fall of the Wall necessitated rapid political action to restore confidence in the future economic well-being of eastern Germany. Immediate reunification at least initially seemed to hold up the promise of prosperity. The political decision in favour of an expedient reunification under Article 23 responded to these international and economic considerations but had nefarious consequences for post-reunification democracy. Because reunification under Article 23 entailed the immediate introduction of West German legal and political structures into the East, the entire process became a technical exercise in which the bureaucratic values of speed and efficiency, or what Manfred Stassen (1993) has colourfully called 'tachocracy' and 'machocracy', prevailed. Public participation and debate did not enter into the procedure. The German electorate had to embrace reunification as a *fait accompli*: the five new Länder joined the Federal Republic eleven days before the East Germans even elected their state governments, and the West Germans had no chance to express their preferences until two months after reunification in the first all-German elections.

Admittedly, the German people retroactively sanctioned their governments' decision in favour of quick reunification, and even today, amid sour relations between 'Ossis' and 'Wessis', few Germans seriously call reunification into question. Despite the high cost, the re-establishment of German unity remains a worthwhile and legitimate political goal. The goal of reunification, however, does not lie at the root of the crisis of German democracy. The problem lies in the means, or the process. Germany is paying the price of its failure to respect the obligations of Article 146. The decision in favour of the expedient solution offered by Article 23 certainly succeeded in speeding Germany to legal and political unity, but the concomitant silencing of time-consuming public debate left the reunited nation-state with a deficit of identity and democratic legitimacy. In fact, the success of German reunification bears remarkable similarity to another quick but ill-fated unification, that of the Italian Risorgimento. In a classic article, Raymond Grew (1962) described the rapid extension of the Piedmontese *statuto* to the rest of the peninsula in a process that sought to avoid foreign intervention and the social, economic, and administrative disruption that popular political mobilisation would entail. Success spoiled the Risorgimento, though, because without democratic mobilisation at its birth, the new liberal regime lacked identity and legitimacy right down until the fascist seizure of power.

Unlike the Italian élites who opted for expediency in 1861, the German politicians who chose to speed reunification along with Article 23 in 1990 have to live with the consequences of their decision and with the knowledge that they had another option. In fact, they had a constitutional obligation in case of reunification to mobilise and to rally the population around the democratic renewal of national identity and legitimacy. Although a constitutional convention in accordance with Article 146 would have cost time and energy and not rendered reunification a painless process, a discussion of constitutional principles (beyond that of the little-publicised activities of the joint constitutional commission of the the Bundestag and Bundesrat [cf. Krisch, 1993; Thaysen, 1993]) might have prevented the current climate favourable to right-wing extremism and violence by allowing Germans to define more clearly their identity and their common (political) values or at least to establish procedures for recognising and mediating conflicts, which will in any case grow in number as Germany unavoidably moves towards multiculturalism (cf. Welsh, 1993). Since reunification, the parliamentary debates on moving the seat of government from Bonn to Berlin and on Germany's military role in the post-Cold War international order have functioned as surrogates for such a public discussion (cf. Strassel, 1993), but only a fundamental constitutional debate could have brought reunited Germans closer to understanding one another and their country's place in the world. The question remains whether such a debate is still possible in the current climate of shock, mutual recrimination, and fading confidence in democratic institutions.

CONCLUSION: CULTURAL CONTINUITIES IN EASTERN GERMANY

My proposition that a constitutional debate might have allowed Germany to avoid its current political problems would seem to contradict my argument that those problems' roots lie in a fundamental conflict between East and West Germans' cultural values. A constitutional debate cannot, of course, magically dispel such a deep-seated conflict, but it can establish procedures for regulating social and cultural conflict. Or, as the Canadian example since 1982 suggests, a constitutional debate can itself become a forum into which society diverts some of its conflicts and tensions. Still, the question remains whether a political-cultural conflict really does lie at the root of Germany's post-reunification political crisis.

After all, even without any cultural differences, the reunification of East and West Germany would have been an enormously risky venture. In an international context of instability, recession and mass migration, the sudden political, economic and social integration of 16 million new citizens had to upset the smooth functioning of the Federal Republic. The simple conflict of East and West German material interests can suffice to explain societal antagonisms. Disillusionment with democracy and violent extremism, moreover, necessarily followed from the major political parties' failure to demonstrate leadership in the face of a pending economic and social crisis: Chancellor Kohl's governing CDU/CSU/FDP coalition in 1990 grossly misrepresented the obvious costs of reunification while the opposition SPD, in running a scare campaign evoking those costs, devalued the historic and moral significance of reunification. Like the collapse of communism, the misfortunes of reunification would in retrospect thus appear to have been overdetermined. Once again, a political-cultural explanation would seem entirely superfluous. Why then do we need a cultural account of Germany's current political crisis?

My cultural interpretation of Germany's post-reunification problems enjoys the advantage of being part of a consistent account of East Germans' behaviour and attitudes under communism, during its demise, and since unification. Although it is possible to explain East German communism's stability, the GDR's collapse, and the united Germany's political crisis without reference to cultural values (and some of my research findings have supported such explanations), my cultural interpretation can make sense of all three phenomena. In brief, my survey interviews suggested that East Germans had developed a set of values as an adaptive strategy to life within real existing socialism, that the erosion of those values in the 1980s underlay the popular mobilisation against the regime in 1989, and that the contradiction between those partially still-functional and surviving East German values and those of West German society have poisoned the social and political climate in the reunited nation.

At the same time, however, my interviews and statistical findings are open to competing interpretations. As we saw at the end of Chapter 5, my differentiated quantitative analysis of the survey results suggested a common precipitant for protest in the shock of the *Ausreisewelle* of the late summer of 1989 but diverse motives for protest, some of which easily antedated the alleged breakdown of cultural coherence in the late 1980s. These findings were consistent with an interpretation whereby the party-state's loss of authority, as represented by its sudden inability to control the 'exit' option, allowed the outburst of 'voice' of a long-repressed but divided opposition. If we were to accept such an account of communism's collapse, stressing long-standing opposition to state socialism, societal divisions and the breakdown of the state's repressive capacity, however, we would be hard-pressed to explain the resurgence of East Germans' self-identification as 'former GDR-citizens' except as a purely reactive response to the hardships of unification. Yet the fact that in opinion surveys East Germans increasingly accent their distinct identity even as they express greater optimism about their personal well-being within reunited Germany (cf. Bauer-Kaase 1993: 4–8) suggests that this revived GDR-identity is neither purely reactive nor interest-based but rather has a cultural content. East Germans identify with one another not only as possible allies in the distributional conflicts of unification but as holders of common experiences and values.

While the resurgence of GDR identity may prove that common, surviving values unite East Germans, it does not necessarily tell us that those values are the ones I have identified and upon which I based my analysis. As we saw in Chapters 3 and 4, other students of East German political culture have described it, using Archie Brown's distinction between official and dominant political cultures. Although the kinds of values characteristic of East German society they discerned are similar to those I identified through my survey, the cultural causes for communism's collapse that their analyses suggest differ sharply from my own. In their view, the growing rift between the official and dominant cultures, along with a breakdown of official political socialisation mechanisms, allegedly precipitated the collapse of popular support or tolerance for the regime. Christiane Lemke (1991) has most completely developed this line of argument for the East German case. As we saw in Chapter 3, Lemke contends that the incompatibility between the official cultural goals of modernisation and of renewed ideological orthodoxy rendered official political socialisation ineffective in the 1980s and hence allowed the dominant and alternative political cultures to generate a civil society capable of contesting state authority.

I argued in Chapter 3 that Lemke overestimates the strength of the GDR's nascent civil society, but the fundamental premise of her argument, namely that the contradiction between official and dominant cultures spurred regime opposition, requires closer examination. Dualism, or even duplicity (cf. Labelle, 1992), would seem to be a basic feature of communist (political) culture, particularly in the period after 1968 that Havel (1978: 68ff) calls 'post-totalitarian'. In exchange for lip-service loyalty to the regime, citizens could withdraw into an apolitical private life of consumption. For Havel, the existence of a space, no matter how apolitical, in which it is possible to 'live in truth', ultimately threatens the survival of the institutionalised lie upon which the regime rests. This space open to truth generates 'the power of the powerless' to contest the historic lie. Because any culture outside the official culture almost by definition becomes oppositional, the post-totalitarian dictatorship must repress or deny the existence of any cultural currents beyond official culture.

Although the notion of cultural dualism well reflects the contradictions of daily life under communism, I am suspicious of the dialectical political dynamic it suggests. To be sure, many of the East Germans in my survey sample described as schizophrenic their maintenance of prevaricating public and truthful private selves. What is more, my own description of East German culture in Chapter 4 had a strong dualistic element: the virtues of modesty, solidarity and equality served to conceal or compensate for the vices of consumer frustration, dependence, monotony and privilege that permeated GDR society. Cultural and psychological contradictions and tensions, however, do not in themselves provoke political opposition. Normal people throughout the world are capable of living placidly in self-contradiction. The distinctions that Havel makes between 'life in truth' and 'life in lies' (or that Brown and Lemke make between official and dominant/oppositional culture) are useful intellectual constructs, but they do not describe the cultural experience of ordinary people preoccupied more with their daily existence and the pursuit of life's small pleasures than with the critical appraisal of their lives' contradictions. Hence, the kind of moral dissidence that Havel admirably practised and advocated never extended beyond a small circle of intellectuals. Although intellectual dissidents did place themselves at the head of the popular revolutions of 1989 in Czechoslovakia and the GDR, in neither country did they launch the mass movement, and, as we saw in Chapter 3, they never even enjoyed much popularity in the GDR.

Even if the cultural dualism argument successfully identified the origins of regime opposition, it could not very well explain the survival and revival of communist cultural forms.

Since the opposition between the dominant and official cultures resulted in the overthrow of the party-state that championed the official culture, it would be surprising today to find the former official culture thriving outside small circles of communist die-hards. The example of the revival of the Jugendweihe in East Germany, however, suggests that the disjuncture between the official communist goal culture and the dominant popular culture was never that great and that ordinary citizens happily lived in a hybrid culture that has partly survived communism's collapse. In the late 1950s the SED regime reintroduced the old socialist working-class ceremony of the Jugendweihe in order to replace the traditional Lutheran confirmation. In their public Jugendweihe, young people (generally 14-year-olds) pledged their loyalty to the ideals of socialism and acceded to the circle of adults (henceforth their teachers addressed them with the *Sie*-form). The ceremony developed into a peculiar cultural concoction of socialist idealism, political conformism, familism and consumerism since parents used the quasi-mandatory ceremony as an occasion to throw a big family party and to obtain visitors' visas for gift-bearing relatives from the West. Although few East Germans (10 per cent of my survey sample) saw the Jugendweihe as an important step in their moral or political development, a majority of East Germans in many areas have since reunification not only continued to fête their 14-year-olds but have insisted on organising inspirational (humanist, if not socialist) public Jugendweihe ceremonies (cf. Roegele, 1992). Even after the demise of socialism, the event apparently would not have as much meaning if it did not maintain its old official cultural form.

While the survival of the Jugendweihe, like the revival of GDR-identity, is not consistent with the dualist conception of communist culture, let alone with the assumption of long-standing popular anti-communism, it does make sense in light of the cultural interpretation I offered in Chapter 4. East Germans' embrace of the values modesty, solidarity and equality allowed them to accept both communist party rule and the difficulties of daily life under that regime. Although the violation of these cultural values motivated popular mobilisation against the regime, the revolution of 1989 did not sweep aside the values that emerged under real existing socialism, so that today they continue to shape East Germans' beliefs and behaviour. Thus, the identification of these values provides a consistent explanation of communism's stability, collapse and continuing cultural influence. What is more, my cultural interpretation of communism's life, death and legacy in East Germany can help us understand political problems in other post-communist societies. Although the peoples of Eastern and Central Europe no doubt developed (on the basis of cultural traditions, social structural specificities, institutional particularities, creative innovations and historical accidents) a variety of adaptive strategies to life under communist rule, they all nonetheless had to come to some sort of cultural arrangement with largely similar political regimes of totalitarian ambition. Without calling into question the fundamentally repressive character of those regimes, it is necessary to acknowledge that the popular cultural arrangement with them incorporated some positive values. Specifically, the egalitarianism (albeit riddled with privilege), the social security (albeit paternalistic), and the stability (albeit 'a graveyard peace') that communist regimes generally proffered became positive cultural norms guiding individuals' behaviour and contributing to the political systems' survival. The politically relevant revival of these values in their East German form within the enlarged Federal Republic, where the cultural and structural conditions for post-communist citizens' adaptation to a new social, economic and political order are most favourable, suggests that the cultural legacy of communism will shape the transformation processes even more sharply in the other societies of Eastern and Central Europe. Indeed, more or less repentant and reformed communist parties have already won free elections in Lithuania and Poland precisely by appealing to voters' nostalgia for egalitarianism, social security, and stability. A better understanding of the present Eastern and Central European transformations will therefore require more study of the specific political cultures that developed in those societies under communism.

Finally, the kind of cultural analysis I have proposed for the East German case has an important normative justification. In this book, I have attacked structural arguments as inadequate for explaining communism's collapse because they assume either that human actors' motives closely reflect structural circumstances or, worse, that individuals' motives do not matter in the making of history. Instead, I adopted the interpretive method, according to which the explanation of social action depends on the identification of human motives. Taking as the point of departure for my qualitative and quantitative analysis the real life experiences and beliefs of the ordinary East Germans I surveyed, I have tried to show not only that motives matter but that the identification of shared values can explain more than the mere analysis of structural forces. To be sure, motives and culture do not exist independently of social structures. In fact, I have argued that cultural values are necessarily (but not exclusively) adaptive, functional strategies for living within a particular political system. Yet, as the Weberian tradition of interpretive social science has shown, sometimes heartfelt sentiments and freely chosen values do (for better or for worse) allow humans to break free from the straitjacket of structural determinism. Social scientific analysis owes this recognition of the human potential for subjective freedom especially to people who for up to 70 years lived under dictatorial rule based on an erroneous social scientific theory of historical determinism. If Eastern and Central Europeans are to find the courage and creativity to construct against all odds competitive economies, lively civil societies and democratic polities, they must believe in the force of freely chosen values.

Appendix: The Survey Questionnaire

In the following pages I reproduce an English translation of my survey questionnaire as I presented it to my 202 survey respondents in an interview format. For reasons of interviewing technique, the questions are not always in thematic order, and subjects can change abruptly. A question on gardening, for example, follows a series on the Stasi in order to relieve tension in the interview. I also provide the survey's raw statistical results. Because not all 202 respondents answered all questions, the total number of responses to each question may be less than 202. In other cases, where the question indicates the possibility for more than one response, the number of responses may exceed 202. Where appropriate, I provide the mean response value (indicated by a small *m* in parentheses). For the open-ended questions (indicated by an asterisk following the question number), I developed response categories over the course of the entire survey process. In the summary form presented here, these categories do not, of course, fully reflect the diversity and richness of the responses. For some of the closed-ended questions, the respondents had to identify among several pre-existing answer categories presented to them on a card the one or two that best described their opinion or experience. These questions include the words 'which of the following' or refer to a list or a text to be read. To illustrate the kinds of comments and responses my questions elicited, I have on occasion reproduced (in italics) some of the most typical or interesting remarks of individual respondents (cf. McFalls, 1992). Finally, I have annotated (in square brackets) some of the questions which posed methodological difficulties or whose meaning or context might require further explanation for non-East German readers.

QUESTIONNAIRE

Introduction

[After explaining to the respondent how I had randomly selected him or her (see Chapter 1), I read the following introduction. During the interview, I reminded the respondent as necessary of my introductory request to answer as much as possible as she or he would have before the revolution, or *Wende*.]

With this survey, I hope to gain an understanding of the daily life experiences of the so-called typical East German and in so doing would like to uncover the strengths and weaknesses of the social and political system of the former GDR. My main question, which I shall not ask directly but which I shall approach from different points of view, is: what led to the *Wende* in the GDR? I do not ask this question directly because I do not want you with hindsight to reinterpret the past in light of recent events. Instead, I would like to undertake a thought experiment with you. Imagine that we were speaking sometime before the *Wende*, say in early 1989, before anyone knew what the year would bring.

I would like to start with a few questions about your town and your life here in ————.

F1. Since what year have you lived in this town/city? 1960 (*m*)
F2a. Have you lived here your whole life?
    (0) 114 No (to F2c)
    (1) _88 Yes (to F2b)
  b. Are your parents from this area?
    (0) _23 No (to F2c)
    (1) _65 Yes
  c. Where did you (they) come from originally?
    (0) _25 from the same area (county or district)
    (1) __4 from the same Land
    (2) _63 from a different part of the GDR
    (3) _22 from East Prussia, Silesia, Pomerania
    (4) __2 from western Germany
    (5) __4 from non-German territory
F3.* Very briefly, since you've lived here, how has life changed? [A vague question designed to loosen respondents' tongues.]
    (0) _42 no big changes, stagnation, always the same
    (1) _10 constant rise in political pressure/repression
    (2) __3 modernisation of agricultural/rural life
    (3) _34 slow progress, general modernisation
    (4) _24 steady decline, degradation, discouragement
    (5) _46 progress until 1970s, then slow decline
    (6) __7 socialisation of industry with bad consequences
    (7) _13 rapid growth but service sector neglected
F4a. If you consider life in your town during the last five years before the *Wende*, would you say that the quality of life generally got better, stayed the same, or got worse?
    (0) _20 better
    (1) _62 about the same
    (2) 118 worse
  b.* Why?
    (0) __5 supply situation improved
    (1) __3 general liberalisation, more visits to West
    (2) __3 industry in good shape
    (3) __5 things always kept getting better
    (4) __1 community activities grew livelier
    (5) __2 isolated improvements in housing stock
    (6) __5 more political surveillance
    (7) _20 widespread dissatisfaction or resignation

(8) _9_ privileges/connections crucial during crisis
(9) _3_ factory shut down
(10) _65_ shortages, economic crisis
(11) _28_ physical decline of town `

F5a. In comparison to other towns/cities of the same size in the GDR, do you think that your town/city was relatively advantaged, average, or disadvantaged?
    (0) _76_ advantaged
    (1) _54_ average
    (2) _72_ disadvantaged

b.* Why?
    (0) _16_ favoured because of specific industry here
    (1) _15_ consumer goods supply better here
    (2) _10_ housing stock better here
    (3) _3_ town a centre for tourism
    (4) _4_ more goods available in countryside

    (5) _3_ environmental pollution bad here
    (6) _3_ few opportunities in villages
    (7) _14_ bad consumer goods supply
    (8) _6_ no subsidies for infrastructure/services here
    (9) _84_ all resources went to Berlin

    – *In Berlin they lived just like in the West.*
    – *We all hated the Berliners. They had trouble buying gas when they came to the provinces.*

F6a.* Did you ever do anything personally to improve or beautify your community, for example through complaints to officials or through participation in a citizens' initiative?
    (0) _66_ No (to F7)
    (1) _12_ through personal complaints to local authorities
    (2) _33_ through (written) complaints to higher authorities [including Honecker himself]
    (3) _4_ through participation in a citizens' initiative
    (4) _75_ through 'voluntary' neighbourhood work projects
    (5) _8_ as member of local government representation
    (6) _2_ as member of association for historic preservation

b. Was your action or your group's action effective/successful?
    (0) _53_ No
    (1) _48_ Yes

c.* Why (not)?
    (0) _3_ nothing possible without party connections
    (1) _31_ officials uncooperative
    (2) _1_ nothing possible without personal connections
    (3) _8_ after the 1970s nobody cared about community life

    (4) _30_ voluntary work projects successful
    (5) _7_ letter to higher official spurred action
    (6) _7_ constant complaining paid off

    – *I wrote to Erich Honecker when my kitchen sink was broken. I said that I was a single mother with five children. My sink was fixed within a week!*

F7a,b,c.* What kind of people in your community were the most important or most respected?

    (0) _38_ (question not asked before interview 39)
    (1) _58_ no one, everybody withdrew into private life
    (2) _22_ the party secretary
    (3) _19_ directors of enterprises
    (4) _9_ private artisans/entrepreneurs
    (5) _23_ artists
    (6) _32_ doctors, teachers, scientists (professionals)
    (7) _35_ mayor and/or city councillors
    (8) _23_ Stasi and SED officials feared
    (9) _10_ sports stars
    (10) _20_ pastors
    (11) _8_ people active in public life who didn't belong to a party
    (12) _2_ the National Front
    (13) _1_ the neighbourhood committee
    (14) _1_ anti-fascist resistance heroes
    (15) _1_ volunteer firemen
    (16) _1_ policemen

F8. Societal life in the GDR was apparently highly organised. I am going to give you a list of various societal organisations and commissions, and for each one of them, I would like to know if you were a member in early 1989, or in the case of the commissions if you were ever a member.

    a. _141_ Society for German–Soviet Friendship (DSF)
    b. _16_ Democratic Women's Federation (DFD)
    c. _3_ County or district court juror
    d. _14_ Conflict commission (workplace adjudication)
    e. _1_ Arbitration commission (neighbourhood court)
    f. _68_ PTA or school commission member
    g. _3_ Cooperative store council
    h. _8_ Workers-and-Peasants Inspectorate
    i. _29_ Cultural Federation
    j. _20_ Chamber of Technology
    k. _8_ Peasant Mutual Aid Association (VdgB)
    l. _28_ Small Gardeners' Association
    m. _36_ People's Solidarity (local social services)

F9a. Did you belong to the trade union (FDGB)?

    (0) _35_ No (to F10)
    (1) _167_ Yes

b.* What office, if any, did you hold in the FDGB?

    (0) _98_ none
    (1) _8_ Enterprise union council member
    (2) _14_ Work group treasurer
    (3) _12_ Departmental union council member
    (4) _1_ District vacation service commission

    (5) _1 District commission member
    (6) _6 Cultural activities coordinator
    (7) _14 Shop-steward
    (8) _2 Professional union functionary
    (9) _8 Social insurance coordinator
    (10) _3 Other commission member

F10a. Did you belong (in your youth) to the Free German Youth (FDJ)? (If not, why not?)
    (0)_152 Yes
    (1)_37 No, too old
    (2)_13 No, for religious or oppositional reasons

   b. Did you undergo the Youth Initiation (Jugendweihe)?
    (0)_102 No (to F10c)
    (1)_98 Yes (to F10d)

   c.* Why not?
    (0)_76 practically impossible, ceremony not yet available
    (1)_21 for religious reasons
    (2)_5 for explicit oppositional reasons

   d.* What did the Jugendweihe mean for you back then?
    (0)_32 not much, felt compelled to participate
    (1)_46 it was a normal part of growing up
    (2)_20 important experience, ideologically meaningful
    – *My first decent pair of shoes!*

F11a. Were you confirmed in a church?
    (0)_70 No
    (1)_132 Yes

   b. What is/was your family's religious/church background?
    (0)_137 Protestant
    (1)_15 Catholic
    (2)_4 other (non-conformist Protestant sect or Jewish)
    (3)_46 none, atheist

   c. What church/religion did you belong to or feel associated with in 1989?
    (0)_132 none (to F12)
    (1)_61 Protestant
    (2)_7 Catholic
    (3)_2 New Apostolic

   d. Which one of the following reasons would best explain your church membership/association?
    (0)_17 family tradition
    (1)_13 active faith
    (2)_26 opportunities for human contact
    (3)_14 alternative to state organisations

F12a. Were you a member of a political party in early 1989? If so, which one?
    (0)_134 none (to F13)
    (1)_60 SED
    (2)_3 CDU
    (3)_1 DBD

(4) _3_ LDPD
(5) _1_ NDPD
b. + c.* Tell me how you happened to join this party.
    (0) _25_ specific, positive ideological reasons
    (1) _9_ very general, vague ideological reasons
    (2) _12_ family tradition
    (3) _8_ no apparent reason, thoughtlessly joined
    (4) _9_ wanted political involvement, information
    (5) _23_ to get ahead in career
    (6) _15_ respondent uses word 'conviction'
    (7) _5_ SED was logical step after finishing FDJ
    (8) _4_ joined bloc party to avoid having to join SED
    (9) _1_ wanted to form an internal opposition
    (10) _3_ strongly pressured to join
    (11) _1_ needed membership to get hunting rifle permit
F13.* Did you belong to any other organisations? If so, which?
    (0) _109_ none
    (1) _58_ sports organisation/team
    (2) _15_ cultural organisation
    (3) _9_ professional association
    (4) _2_ entertainment club
    (5) _1_ hobby club (not incorporated in Kulturbund)
    (6) _1_ neighbourhood association
    (7) _1_ peace movement
    (8) _4_ volunteer fire department
    (9) _1_ animal protection society
    (10) _1_ volunteer police helper
F14. A well-known GDR-observer, Günter Gaus, described the GDR as a *Nischengesellschaft* [niche-society]. He meant that East Germans withdrew from public, politicised life into their private lives, i.e. into their circles of family and friends, into their hobbies, into their gardens, in a word, into their niches. Do you recognise yourself and your life-style in the expression *Nischengesellschaft*?
[As the FRG's first permanent representative in East Berlin, Gaus was very well known among my respondents, as was his famous term.]
    (0) _74_ No (follow-up to get answer for F15)
    (1) _128_ Yes
F15.* What was your niche?
    (0) _5_ respondent didn't understand Gaus's concept
    (1) _69_ refuse Gaus's label, personally engaged in public life
    (2) _54_ house and garden, family life
    (3) _32_ circle of friends
    (4) _11_ music or art
    (5) _2_ sports
    (6) _11_ other hobby
    (7) _8_ church
    (8) _9_ career, professional advancement
F16a. Inasfar as you had a private life or a niche, did you feel free of

state control, observation, or interference?

    (0) _69_ No
    (1) _36_ Yes, fairly free
    (2) _97_ Yes, entirely free

b.* Why was that?

    (0) _44_ one always felt observed
    (1) _25_ mail, telephone, West contacts controlled
    (2) _9_ family life taken into consideration for educational/
           professional opportunities
    (3) _16_ wasn't bothered by observation
    (4) _5_ considered observation normal/necessary
    (5) _61_ didn't notice any state interference
    (6) _18_ simply felt safe in niche

F17. Would you say that, in the last three or four years before 1989, the state interfered with private life more or less or no differently than before? That is, did you feel that there was an increase in observation (domestic spying)?

    (0) _84_ more state interference in private life
    (1)_110_ about the same, no perceptible change
    (2) _8_ less

F18a. What about in public life, at your place of work, for example, do you think that the state tried to control public life more or less or about the same during the last three or four years before 1989?

    (0) _99_ more
    (1) _88_ about the same (to F19)
    (2) _14_ less

b.* How was this change evident?

    (0) _9_ party loyalists got more advantages
    (1) _8_ applications for trips to West more scrutinised
    (2) _21_ less trust at work, more reports to submit
    (3) _17_ had to watch out more what you said in public
    (4) _17_ had to go to more political events
    (5) _17_ Stasi activities and buildings got bigger
    (6) _6_ Stasi agents got more clever in their techniques
    (7) _1_ even contacts in East restricted
    (8) _3_ demonstrations violently repressed [1987, 1988]
    (9) _13_ possible to complain more in public
    (10) _3_ easier to travel West
    (11) _1_ more private economic activity allowed

F19a. Did you always, sometimes, or almost never feel intimidated by state security organs?

    (0) _30_ always
    (1) _45_ sometimes
    (2)_127_ almost never

b.* Why (not)?

    (0) _15_ feared capricious penalties (e.g. visa denial)
    (1) _8_ tested for loyalty at work
    (2) _13_ telephone tapped, neighbours questioned about me
    (3) _36_ had to think about what you said or wrote

(4) _2_ job safe, could say what I thought
(5) _28_ simply don't let myself get intimidated
(6) _29_ no reason to be scared if you did nothing wrong
(7) _6_ knew and trusted everyone in village
(8) _11_ was up-standing citizen with good conscience

F20a. Did you ever have any personal problems/encounters with the state security organs?
    (0) _166_ No
    (1) _36_ Yes
  b.* Can you describe them for me?

     – *One day I got picked up by some men from the Stasi after work. They drove me out into the country, broke my glasses and left me there to get home alone. For months I was followed so that I couldn't tell anyone what happened. I still don't know what they wanted from me.*

F21. Were any of your closer acquaintances in any way active on behalf of the Stasi?
    (0) _111_ No
    (1) _11_ Yes, but found out after *Wende*
    (2) _80_ Yes, knew it before *Wende*
[No formal follow-up question. Most respondents explained spontaneously.]

     – *My art teacher at school was homosexual. The Stasi used that to blackmail him into being an informant.*

F22. Did you yourself consciously (or at the time unconsciously) provide information to the Stasi?
    (0) _184_ No
    (1) _18_ Yes
[All 18 respondents who admitted giving information to the Stasi said that they knew that a copy of every report they completed in exercising their normal work function went to the Stasi.]

F23a. Did you have a garden in 1989?
    (0) _74_ No (to F24)
    (1) _128_ Yes
  b. With a small garden house [*Laube*]?
    (0) _54_ No
    (1) _74_ Yes
  c. Did the fruit and vegetable production of your garden meet a significant proportion of your household's food consumption needs? That is, did you consider the fruit of your garden labour to be an important part of your household income?
    (0) _61_ No
    (1) _7_ Sometimes, partly, maybe
    (2) _60_ Yes

F24a. Did you live in a single-family house, a two- or three-family house, an older apartment [*Altbauwohnung*], or a new apartment block [*Neubaublock*]?
    (0) _46_ single-family house
    (1) _20_ two- or three-family house

(2) _57_ older apartment
(3) _79_ new apartment block
b. Did you own your home/apartment in 1989?
   (0)_151_ No (to F25)
   (1) _51_ Yes
c. Did you inherit your home (or buy it before 1945), buy it (after 1945), or build it yourself?
   (0) _29_ inherited
   (1) _14_ bought after 1945
   (2) _8_ built
F25a. If you owned your own car in 1989, what kind was it?
   (0) _77_ none
   (1) _64_ Trabant
   (2) _28_ Wartburg
   (3) _29_ Lada, Skoda (eastern import)
   (4) _4_ Western import (VW)
b. Have you bought yourself a new or used Western car since 1990?
   (0)_153_ No
   (1) _32_ Yes, used
   (2) _16_ Yes, new
F26a.* What was your occupation in 1989?
   [The sample included persons with 65 different occupations.]
b. Under which of the following categories would you place your occupation (or occupation before retirement)?
   (0) _6_ unskilled industrial worker
   (1) _19_ skilled industrial worker
   (2) _9_ industrial technician
   (3) _19_ industrial engineer
   (4) _13_ management or administration in industry
   (5) _1_ unskilled worker in other enterprise
   (6) _16_ skilled worker in other enterprise
   (7) _7_ unskilled worker in government services
   (8) _22_ skilled worker in government services
   (9) _11_ director or cadre in government services
   (10) _1_ artisan in cooperative
   (11) _5_ independent artisan or journeyman
   (12) _3_ private business person
   (13) _3_ independent professional (journalist)
   (14) _33_ 'intelligentsia' (school teachers)
   (15) _13_ doctor, architect, engineer, etc.
   (16) _4_ peasant in cooperative
   (17) _1_ agronomist or other skilled agricultural prof.
   (18) _4_ administration of societal organisation
   (19) _9_ student
   (20) _2_ church employee
   [The sample included one veritable capitalist, who after the expropriation of his factory continued textile production with a putting-out system.]
F27a. What is your current occupation [1990–91]?

(0) 124 same job
(1) _24 unemployed
(2) _32 new job
(3) _15 retired since 1989

b. Would you say that your personal professional situation has improved, deteriorated, or stayed the same since reunification?
(0) _39 improved
(1) _51 neither better nor worse even if different
(2) _75 deteriorated [unemployment anticipated]

F28. In which of the following categories would you place your gross monthly income in 1989?
(1) _12 less than 300 Marks
(2) _13 between 300 and 500 Marks
(3) _16 between 501 and 700 Marks
(4) _29 between 701 and 900 Marks
(5) _35 between 901 and 1100 Marks
(6) _30 between 1101 and 1300 Marks
(7) _22 between 1301 and 1500 Marks
(8) _27 between 1501 and 2000 Marks
(9) _15 over 2000 Marks

F29a. Did you also engage in moonlighting [*Feierabendarbeit*]?
(0) 163 No (to F30)
(1) _38 Yes

b. Did a significant part of your household income stem from your moonlighting?
(0) _23 No
(1) _15 Yes

F30a. What was approximately your average monthly net household income in 1989?
(1) _12 less than 500 Marks
(2) _16 between 500 and 800 Marks
(3) _40 between 801 and 1200 Marks
(4) _32 between 1201 and 1600 Marks
(5) _43 between 1601 and 2000 Marks
(6) _21 between 2001 and 2400 Marks
(7) _16 between 2401 and 2800 Marks
(8) _13 between 2801 and 3200 Marks
(9) _9 over 3200 Marks

b. How many persons were in your household in 1989? 2.66 (*m*)
c. How many of them were working or on pensions? 1.79 (*m*)
d. And now another very indiscreet question: how much money did your household have in its savings accounts on 2 July 1990, i.e. the day after monetary union?
(0) _37 4000 DM or less
(1) _23 between 4001 and 6000 DM
(2) _32 between 6001 and 10 000 DM
(3) _66 between 10 001 and 20 000 DM
(4) _21 between 20 001 and 30 000 DM
(5) _13 between 30 001 and 50 000 DM

(6) _5 between 50 001 and 100 000 DM
(7) _3 over 100 000 DM

F31. People say that connections were more important than money in the GDR because there wasn't much to buy with your money, but with good connections you could barter your way through life. Would you say they you were well connected or poorly connected?

(0) _67 well connected
(1) _30 neither well nor poorly, average
(2) _81 poorly connected
(3) _24 always against the use of connections

F32a. Would you say that your personal economic situation improved, stayed the same, or deteriorated during the last five years before the *Wende?*

(0) _70 improved
(1) _110 stayed the same (to F33)
(2) _22 deteriorated

b.* In what way did it improve/deteriorate?

(0) _58 earned more money
(1) _3 got own apartment, independent household
(2) _7 had more disposable income
(3) _7 had less disposable income
(4) _16 there was nothing to buy

F33a. Would you say that the general GDR economic situation improved, stayed the same, or deteriorated during the last five years before the *Wende?*

(0) _5 improved
(1) _21 stayed the same
(2) _176 deteriorated

b. + c.* And how was that evident?

(0) _93 nothing to buy but basic food stuffs
(1) _61 enterprises didn't get supplies/spare parts
(2) _8 plans not filled/unfulfillable
(3) _16 rising foreign debt
(4) _20 bad investments and bad planning
(5) _27 inflation
(6) _11 more corruption, connections more important
(7) _3 bureaucracy got more rigid
(8) _30 technology gap with West got bigger
(9) _13 workers unmotivated
(10) _15 cities and factories falling apart
(11) _5 social policies got too expensive
(12) _1 more goods available for purchase
(13) _6 slow growth, but things getting better

– *We knew that the economy was bad, but it had been bad before and we knew how to live with it. We didn't think this crisis would be the last.*

F34a–c.* As I said at the beginning of our interview, I'm trying to conduct a thought experiment with you. Imagine your life situation in early 1989. What were your hopes and expectations at that time?

(0) _44_ no hope, no change, pessimistic
(1) _37_ professionally and socially secure, satisfied
(2) _23_ buy house, get own apartment
(3) _16_ get a new car
(4) _65_ desire to travel (in East as well as West)
(5) _29_ don't ask for much, modest contentment
(6) _24_ improvement of the economic situation
(7) _37_ things get better, vague desire for change
(8) _54_ personal/professional advancement
(9) _16_ reunification and/or more political freedom
(10) _11_ reform of socialism
(11) _4_ emigration

[Despite people's tendency to claim in hindsight that they had anticipated an event, very few respondents retrospectively claimed to have expected the upheavals of 1989 early that year.]

F35a. Overall, leaving aside particular romantic or familial circumstances, would you say you were happy with your life in early 1989?

(0) _72_ No
(1) 126 Yes

b.* Why (not)?

(0) _11_ consumer frustration, drudgery of daily life
(1) _37_ felt psychologically stressed, under pressure
(2) _7_ opposed to the political system
(3) _13_ the whole system was in crisis
(4) _22_ happy with job/work life
(5) _7_ quiet, secure life
(6) _5_ satisfied in niche
(7) _25_ satisfied with existing social order
(8) _41_ modest desires all fulfilled
(9) _24_ knew nothing else, thus nothing to change

F36a. Because of the division of Germany, it was probably unavoidable that people in the GDR often compared their living conditions with those of people in the FRG. Before 1989 did you believe that you would have had more or fewer or the same chances for your personal and professional development if you had lived in the FRG?

(0) 101 more chances in FRG
(1) _46_ same chances
(2) _55_ fewer chances in FRG

b.* Why is that?

(0) _19_ friends/relatives there more successful
(1) _35_ higher standard of living with same job there
(2) _19_ better educational opportunities there
(3) _9_ more opportunities there for creativity, self-motivated activities
(4) _1_ profession more respected/prestigious there
(5) _7_ better work equipment/technology there
(6) _7_ politically persecuted/disadvantaged here
(7) _1_ bad work ethic here

(8) _17_ more social/job security here
(9) _6_ ordinary workers had same chances here/there
(10) _8_ more opportunities for women here
(11) _22_ better educational opportunities here
(12) _7_ more competition in my field there
(13) _4_ achieved all my goals here, what more to ask?
(14) _2_ less consumerist here

(15) _19_ can't compare, knew life chances only here
F37a. Did you ever think of emigrating to the FRG, or even apply for an emigration visa?
    (0) _141_ No
    (1) _57_ Yes, thought about it
    (2) _4_ Yes, applied to emigrate
b.* Why (not)?
    (0) _42_ my home [*Heimat*] was here
    (1) _28_ didn't want to give up what I had, too old to go
    (2) _22_ life was pleasant here
    (3) _34_ felt responsible for family/family property
    (4) _2_ didn't know anyone in West
    (5) _33_ GDR system/life-style better
    (6) _7_ felt responsible for, wanted to make best of GDR
    (7) _10_ too scared to leave
    (8) _4_ FRG system/life-style better
    (9) _3_ material conditions better in FRG
    (10) _1_ lots of relatives in West
    (11) _2_ had difficulties with party or Stasi
    (12) _3_ felt politically persecuted
F38a. Many scholars and others in the West as well as the East claimed that the different political, economic and social systems in the GDR and FRG had shaped the consciousness and even the national identity of the people in the two states differently. Do you think that the 40 years of Germany's partition led to the formation of two different national characters?
    (0) _36_ No
    (1) _164_ Yes
b.* Why (not)?
    (0) _23_ common German culture remained
    (1) _4_ only the communists believed in separate GDR
    (2) _4_ everybody dreamed of reunification

    (3) _30_ social orders very different
    (4) _21_ we were brought up to think like socialists
    (5) _38_ we always felt inferior, dependent
    (6) _12_ GDR relatively backward
    (7) _35_ we were more solidaristic and modest
    (8) _22_ they were always selfish and arrogant there
    (9) _5_ young here brought up to be lazy/indifferent
c. Do you think that if the GDR had continued to exist, it would have become a self-sufficient German-speaking nation (like Austria),

or do you think it already was one?
   (0) 135 No, never
   (1) _20 Yes, GDR would have become its own nation
   (2) _41 Yes, GDR was one already
d.* Why do you think that?
   (0) _66 independence economically impossible
   (1) _42 same culture/history as FRG; division unnatural
   (2) _7 people too dissatisfied here
   (3) _8 state/political system illegitimate
   (4) _12 GDR dependent on USSR; system imposed

   (5) _23 had distinct social/political system
   (6) _11 GDR politically/economically successful
   (7) _19 new culture created through *Abgrenzung*
   (8) _2 GDR treated as foreign by FRG
e. Which of the following expressions would best describe your feeling
   of national identity in early 1989?
   (1) _78 GDR-citizen [*DDR-Bürger*, official designation]
   (2) _78 German
   (3) _42 GDR-German
f.* Why did you feel that way?
   (0) _10 GDR was successful state
   (1) _47 born in GDR, knew nothing else
   (2) _23 treated as a GDR-citizen, second-class German
   (3) _5 didn't believe in/want reunification
   (4) _11 'German' sounds too much like Third Reich

   (5) _14 born/grew up before division
   (6) _2 had many relatives in West
   (7) _45 belong to German culture, division unnatural
   (8) _13 always opposed to regime, anti-communist

   (9) _28 GDR was my experience, German was my culture
F39a + b. This question is about your current feelings. I'm going to
   read six sentences with you. They describe the differences
   bewteen former GDR-citizens (the so-called Ossis) and the
   old FRG-citizens (the Wessis). I'd like to know which two of
   these sentences correspond best to your feelings about the
   differences between the two groups.
      (1) _4 The biggest differences between Ossis and Wessis
            are the ancient regional differences between areas
            such as Prussia and Bavaria, Saxony and Baden, etc.
      (2) _84 The Wessis distinguish themselves from the Ossis
            primarily in their well-being and by virtue of the
            life experiences that wealthier people can afford
            (e.g. travel).
      (3) _22 The Ossis have held on more than the Wessis to
            old German values and traditions because these were
            not destroyed by a consumerist economy and a
            mentality of social climbing.
      (4) 125 The Ossis and Wessis differ primarily in their

economic behaviour because 40 years of the social market economy and of state socialism motivated people differently.

(5) 125 The biggest difference between Ossis and Wessis lies in their relations with other people, and namely the Wessis are used to living in an [aggressive] 'elbow society'.

(6) 8 The differences between Ossis and Wessis are minimal or superficial and therefore not worthy of mention.

F40. Frankly speaking, if you've travelled to western Germany lately, did you feel a bit proud to come from the ex-GDR, or did you try not to stick out as an Ossi, or did you feel just like you do when you go to another part of the ex-GDR?

(0) 25 haven't been to the West

(1) 43 felt proud

(2) 56 tried not to stick out

(3) 47 felt no different

(4) 31 felt like in foreign country [answer offered spontaneously]

F41. Do you accept the Oder-Neisse line as the final, undisputed eastern border of Germany?

(0) 23 No

(1) 159 Yes

(2) 17 Yes, but with reservations

F42. The GDR has not existed politically since 3 October 1990, and economically not since 1 July 1990. But socially and mentally the GDR will continue to exist for some time. The GDR may have had some characteristics that you are glad to be rid of today but also surely some characteristics that you would like to see carried over into the united Germany. I am going to give you a list of some supposed positive characteristics of the GDR, and for each of these characteristics, I would like to know if you would like to keep it or would have liked to have kept it if it had been possible or whether you would (have) like(d) to get rid of it. [This question sought to identify which features of GDR life people found positive (coded 1) and which they found negative (coded 0). If the respondent spontaneously questioned whether the characteristic had ever been present, their response was coded −1. For the sake of simplicity, I here present only the mean score for each characteristic. Mean scores approaching 1 would thus show my respondents' positive appreciation of the characteristic.]

a. 0.72 women's independence through equal employment opportunities and special privileges for working mothers

b. 0.26 the promotion of world-class sports

c. 0.52 the cooperative farming system (LPGs)

d. 0.31 the Marxist critique of bourgeois society as a counterweight to capitalist thinking

e. 0.52 state control of large industry

f. 0.86 state subsidies for cultural facilities such as provincial theatres and orchestras

    g. <u>0.36</u> the anti-fascist tradition
    h.<u>-0.12</u> grassroots democracy, as in the neighbourhood committees
    i. <u>0.45</u> the promotion of mass amateur sports
    j. <u>0.75</u> the system of mid-career professional (re-)training
    k. <u>0.76</u> the right to work
    l. <u>0.76</u> guaranteed day-care for all children
    m. <u>0.53</u> the preservation of a representative number of socialist monuments and street names

F43. Since we've just mentioned monuments and are working with lists, I shall give you another list of names of famous people from German history and then another list of contemporary figures. But first I want to show you this thermometer. It runs from 0 to 6 degrees and measures your feelings towards other people. The more you like the person, the higher the temperature rises. Thus, six would, so to speak, be hot love and zero ice-cold hate. In the middle, at three, would be indifference:

6− +− hot/love/very good/positive, etc.
  |
5− +− warm
  |
4− +− lukewarm
  |
3− +− indifference/neither good nor bad/person unknown
  |
2− +− cool
  |
1− +− cold
  |
0− +− ice-cold/hate/very bad, etc.

So, for each of the following I'd like to know what kind of temperature he or she raised in you. Remember to try to answer as you would have in 1989. [Temperatures reported are means.]
    a. <u>3.33</u> Otto von Bismarck
    b. <u>3.44</u> Karl Marx
    c. <u>3.81</u> Rosa Luxemburg
    d. <u>3.60</u> Karl Liebknecht
    e. <u>0.40</u> Adolf Hitler
    f. <u>3.31</u> Ernst Thälmann
    g. <u>3.48</u> Wilhelm Pieck
    h. <u>2.97</u> Konrad Adenauer
    i. <u>2.95</u> Otto Grotewohl
    j. <u>1.78</u> Walter Ulbricht
    k. <u>4.37</u> Willy Brandt
    l. <u>3.39</u> Franz Beckenbauer
    m.<u>1.36</u> Erich Honecker

The next list of names includes people who played some role in the *Wende*. I'd like you to give them a score based on your sympathy for them today.

    n. 2.85 Hans Modrow
    o. 3.13 Wolf Biermann
    p. 4.73 Mikhail Gorbachev
    q. 2.02 Manfred Gerlach [LDPD leader]
    r. 2.65 Gregor Gysi
    s. 2.02 Peter-Michael Diestel
    t. 0.95 Egon Krenz
    u. 2.71 Helmut Kohl
    v. 2.51 Rainer Eppelmann
    w. 4.31 Kurt Masur
    x. 3.65 Bärbel Bohley
    y. 3.36 Oskar Lafontaine
    z. 2.12 Lothar de Maizière

F44. Here is another scale. It measures how much you agree with an opinion. It runs from 1 to 5 with the following values:

    (1) agree completely
    (2) tend to agree
    (3) indifferent, no opinion, not sure, etc.
    (4) tend to disagree
    (5) disagree completely
    [(.) indicates that respondent rejects premise of question, refuses to answer, doesn't understand question]

I am now going to read together with you sentences expressing various opinions about politics and society in the GDR. For each of these opinions, I'd like to know how much you agree with it. I ask once again that you answer as you would have before the *Wende*.

    a. The founders of the SED and of the GDR were entitled to a leading role because of their anti-fascist past.
      (1) 37 (2) 49 (3) 15 (4) 33 (5) 65 (.) 3 (m) 3.2
    b. Socialism could never develop itself successfully in the GDR primarily because simultaneous reconstruction and reparation payments to the USSR made it impossible to establish decent foundations for a socialist economy.
      (1) 45 (2) 51 (3) 13 (4) 55 (5) 33 (.) 5 (m) 2.9
    c. Real existing socialism tended to make people in the GDR morally worse rather than better.
      (1) 70 (2) 43 (3) 25 (4) 33 (5) 25 (.) 6 (m) 2.5
    d. GDR-citizens can be proud of the economic achievements of their country since they built up everything in this resource-poor country without a Marshall Plan or any other help (but rather after systematic Russian plundering).
      (1) 56 (2) 72 (3) 12 (4) 26 (5) 27 (.) 9 (m) 2.5
    e. The socialist economy got into difficulties because not enough competent experts were in responsible positions.
      (1) 119 (2) 39 (3) 4 (4) 22 (5) 15 (.) 3 (m) 1.9
    f. Socialism is inconsistent with human nature.
      (1) 47 (2) 25 (3) 25 (4) 46 (5) 53 (.) 6 (m) 3.2
    g. The state socialism we experienced in the GDR shouldn't be

confused with real socialism, which might still be possible.

(1)107 (2) 55 (3) 11 (4) 7 (5) 17 (.) 5 (*m*) 1.8

h. Only the Stasi's systematic intimidation of the population allowed the SED to rule for 40 years.

(1)100 (2) 33 (3) 15 (4) 32 (5) 20 (.) 2 (*m*) 2.2

i. The vast majority of all SED comrades were careerists who didn't care the least about the ideals of socialism.

(1) 68 (2) 48 (3) 19 (4) 38 (5) 26 (.) 3 (*m*) 2.5

j. In the last two decades, the Stasi was less intimidating than annoying.

(1) 31 (2) 22 (3) 28 (4) 36 (5) 76 (.) 9 (*m*) 3.5

F45. I'd like to work a bit more with this scale, from (1) agree fully to (5) disagree completely. I'm now going to read some hypothetical sentences together with you. They all have something to do with the *Wende*. I'd like to know how much you would have agreed with the opinions expressed in each sentence **before or during** the *Wende*.

a. If GDR-citizens had enjoyed greater freedom to travel, for example, four to six weeks in 'non-socialist foreign countries' with the possibility of buying hard currency, it would never have come to the emigration wave of summer 1989 nor to the mass opposition of the fall.

(1) 74 (2) 58 (3) 9 (4) 31 (5) 28 (.) 2 (*m*) 2.4

b. The SED could have reformed itself and maintained at least some of its power if it had adopted Gorbachev's programme of *perestroika* and *glasnost* in a timely manner.

(1) 57 (2) 67 (3) 9 (4) 30 (5) 36 (.) 3 (*m*) 2.6

c. Without the influence, if not agitation, of the Western media, it would never have come to the wave of emigration nor the massive opposition of autumn 1989.

(1) 21 (2) 35 (3) 10 (4) 48 (5) 86 (.) 2 (*m*) 3.7

d. If Erich Honecker had taken the occasion of the 40th anniversary of the GDR to step down and to present a younger, more pragmatic politburo, he would have taken the wind out of the opposition's sails.

(1) 25 (2) 42 (3) 10 (4) 49 (5) 75 (.) 1 (*m*) 3.5

e. If, after Honecker's resignation, Hans Modrow or Gregor Gysi instead of Egon Krenz had come to power, the SED might have been able to hold on to its leading role.

(1) 12 (2) 28 (3) 6 (4) 46 (5)109 (.) 1 (*m*) 4.1

f. If the Wall hadn't come down on 9 November 1989, the GDR demonstrators would never have raised the question of reunification.

(1) 30 (2) 27 (3) 9 (4) 43 (5) 89 (.) 4 (*m*) 3.7

g. If the *Wende* had not come, the SED would surely have introduced the necessary political and economic reforms at the 12th Party Congress [planned for 1991].

(1) 6 (2) 15 (3) 14 (4) 32 (5)132 (.) 3 (*m*) 4.4

F46a. And so, here we are at the *Wende*. It began with the massive wave of emigration in August–September 1989. Did anybody from your

family emigrate at that time?
(0)171 No
(1) 30 Yes
b. And from your friends and acquaintances?
(0)104 No
(1) 97 Yes
c. Was the emigration wave noticeable at your place of work?
(0)102 No (to F47)
(1) 64 Yes
[Question not asked to those who did not work in 1989.]
d. Did your enterprise get into production difficulties because of the emigration wave?
(0) 50 No
(1) 14 Yes
F47a. During the emigration wave, there was a joke: the last person who left the GDR should turn out the lights. If the emigration wave had continued on like that, would you have left too?
(0)162 No
(1) 37 Yes
b.* Why (not)?
(0) 24 you can't run away from problems
(1) 35 was happy here
(2) 46 personal/familial responsibilities here
(3) 51 future too uncertain there, too old to go
(4) 6 better professional opportunities there
(5) 5 had thought of emigrating before
(6) 27 would have gone if things here hadn't changed
F48a. The emigration wave introduced the first demonstrations about the time of the 40th anniversary celebrations. Which of the following sentences would best describe your attitude during the period of demonstrations preceding 9 November 1989, i.e. preceding the fall of the Wall?
(1) 6 I thought the demonstrations were stupid and wouldn't have gone under any circumstances.
(2) 52 I agreed with some of what the demonstrators wanted but wouldn't have gone myself.
(3) 54 I was completely in favour of the demonstrations but unfortunately couldn't go myself.
(4) 55 I participated in one or two demonstrations.
(5) 24 I regularly went to demonstrate.
(6) 8 I helped organise one or more demonstrations.
(7) 2 I gave a speech at one or more demonstrations.
b + c.* Why? (What was it like?)
(0) 52 wanted things to change (vague response)
(1) 17 went along with colleagues from work
(2) 18 wanted specific reforms
(3) 24 wanted to reform/improve socialism
(4) 22 wanted to see what was happening/be there
(5) 7 mobilised through church service

(6) _5 wanted reunification

(7) _4 out of solidarity for arrested demonstrators

(8) _19 every participant counted

(9) _27 too scared to participate

(10) _23 don't believe in street politics

(11) _9 couldn't go because of work responsibilities

(12) _23 age, illness, travel prevented participation

(13) _19 no opportunity to demonstrate in my region

(14) _15 against the demonstrators' demands

− *I overheard two old ladies talking at the demonstration. One asked the other if she wasn't afraid. She responded, 'Yes, but I've lived my life.'*

− *It was so exhilarating to be with so many people who wanted the same thing that I forgot to be scared.*

F49a. Did you sign the New Forum's petition of 10 September 1989?

(0) 138 No (to F50)

(1) _53 Yes

(2) _11 don't recall (to F50)

b.* How/where did you have access to the petition?

(0) _6 through friends

(1) _11 at a church service

(2) _18 at work

(3) _2 at theatre performance

(4) _12 on the street, signature collection

(5) _4 meeting at or after demonstration

F50a. Were you a member or participant in one of the following citizens' initiatives/movements in the fall of 1989?

(0) 191 none (to F51)

(1) _9 New Forum

(2) _1 Democracy Now

(3) _1 Democratic Awakening

(4) _0 Initiative for Peace and Human Rights

b.* How did you get involved?

(0) _2 through friends

(1) _7 through church (service)

(2) _1 through leaflet distribution

(3) _1 through door-to-door petitioners

F51a. Did you participate in any demonstrations after 9 November i.e. after the fall of the Wall?

(0) 162 No (to F52)

(1) _37 Yes

b.* Why?

(0) _26 against further rule by SED

(1) _1 against trade union corruption

(2) _4 for reunification

(3) _6 against reunification

F52a. If you could pick only one of the following slogans from the fall of 1989 that for you best expresses the sentiment and the causes of the *Wende*, which would it be?

(0) _55_ We're staying here!
(1) _56_ We are the people!
(2) _32_ Life punishes those who come too late.
(3) _41_ We are **one** people!
(4) _13_ We don't want to be guinea pigs!
b.* What did this slogan mean for you personally?
F53a. Were you in favour of a rapid reunification in the fall of 1989?
 (0) _143_ No
 (1) _59_ Yes
b. Do you believe today that the quick reunification was a good thing?
 (0) _110_ No
 (1) _27_ partly, yes and no
 (2) _65_ Yes
c.* Why (not)?
 (0) _20_ economic costs disappointing
 (1) _75_ everything here being inconsiderately destroyed
 (2) _5_ two societies too different
 (3) _17_ not everything was bad here
 (4) _10_ too much left uncertain, should have been faster or slower
 (5) _57_ couldn't happen any other way
 (6) _6_ happy about new freedoms
 (7) _4_ we'll all be better off in the end
F54a + b. Which two of the following are in your opinion the best explanations of why reunification became the main demand of East German demonstrators during late November and December 1989?
 (0) _34_ The long-repressed German national sentiment of the people finally had a chance to express itself.
 (1) _119_ After GDR-citizens had seen the level of material well-being in the FRG, they wanted to be included in it as soon as possible.
 (2) _34_ GDR-citizens recognised that only reunification could put an end to SED domination and Stasi spying.
 (3) _54_ The interference of West German politicians and parties into political events in the GDR raised the theme of reunification.
 (4) _94_ GDR-citizens recognised that only reunification could prevent a total economic and social breakdown in the territory of the GDR.
F55. The political *Wende* in the GDR surely had many deep causes. In fact, in hindsight we can probably find too many causes. There must be some way of assessing which causes were the real ones and which were less important. Perhaps you can help me weed out the decisive causes. I'm going to give you a list of some possible causes of the *Wende* and would like to know for each one whether you would consider it to have been:
 (1) ___ decisive (without it there would never have been a *Wende*);

(2)___ contributing (without it the *Wende* would not have come as quickly, easily, or successfully); or

(3)___ not very important (without it things would not have happened very differently).

[Reported answers are mean response values.]

a. 1.28 the economic crisis of state socialism
b. 1.67 the senility of the Politburo
c. 2.09 the electoral fraud of 7 May 1989
d. 1.62 the growing contradiction between the ideals and the reality of socialism
e. 1.81 the government's inaction in the face of the emigration wave of August–September
f. 2.07 the free societal space in the shelter of the church
g. 2.33 the example of reforms in Poland and Hungary
h. 1.91 the non-intervention of the armed (police) forces
i. 2.17 the dissemination by the Western media of important information critical of the regime
j. 2.28 the incapacity of the Stasi to dominate the citizens' movements
k. 1.93 Gorbachev's barely veiled critique of Honecker at the 40th anniversary celebrations
l. 2.47 growing awareness of an impending ecological catastrophe
m. 1.73 the encouragement of criticism through the example of *glasnost* and *perestroika* in the USSR

F56a. To conclude my interview, I'd like to ask a few questions about your current political opinions and behaviour. Once again, I remind you that your answers will remain strictly confidential.

Are you today a member of one of the following parties or do you strongly identify with one without being a member?

(0) 15 PDS
(1) 5 FDP
(2) 0 Republicans, NPD (or other far-right party)
(3) 3 CDU
(4) 2 Greens
(5) 17 SPD
(6) 9 Bündnis 90
(7) 3 DSU
(8) 148 no party

b.* And why (not)?

[Over 25 different response categories.]

F57a. For which party or list did you vote on 18 March 1990, for the Volkskammer election?

(0) 45 PDS
(1) 18 FDP
(2) 1 Democratic Awakening [allied with CDU]
(3) 45 CDU
(4) 11 Greens (including Independent Women's Fed.)
(5) 40 SPD
(6) 25 Bündnis 90

(7) _4_ DSU
(8) _2_ DBD
(9) _1_ NDPD
(10) _7_ did not vote
(.) _3_ answer refused
b.* And why for this party?

F58a. For which party or list did you vote on 14 October 1990, for the Landtag elections?
(0) _24_ PDS
(1) _19_ FDP
(2) _0_ NDP (or other far-right)
(3) _36_ CDU
(4) _7_ Greens
(5) _38_ SPD
(6) _19_ Bündnis 90
(7) _1_ DSU
(8) _16_ abstained
(.) _41_ Berliners did not vote for Senate in October
b.* And why?

F59a. And on 2 December 1990, for the Bundestag election?
(0) _34_ PDS
(1) _24_ FDP
(2) _0_ NDP
(3) _47_ CDU
(4) _4_ Greens (allied with Bündnis 90)
(5) _43_ SPD
(6) _26_ Bündnis 90
(7) _1_ DSU
(8) _1_ Grey Panthers
(9) _1_ extreme left
(10) _18_ abstained
(.) _3_ won't say
b.* Why?

F60a. Now I just have a few biographical questions. How old are you?
_44.25_ (m) years
b. (Respondent's gender:)
_109_ male   _93_ female

F61a. In which of the following categories would you place your father's principal practised profession?
(0) _19_ peasant/farmer
(1) _37_ worker
(2) _34_ artisan, craftsperson
(3) _17_ small businessperson
(4) _33_ civil servant
(5) _19_ engineer or technical employee
(6) _20_ managerial employee
(7) _16_ professional
(8) _1_ enterprise- or estate-owner
(9) _5_ military

b. What about your paternal grandfather?
(0) _38_ peasant/farmer
(1) _39_ worker
(2) _33_ artisan, craftsperson
(3) _23_ small businessperson
(4) _27_ civil servant
(5) _2_ engineer or technical employee
(6) _1_ managerial employee
(7) _3_ professional
(8) _2_ enterprise- or estate-owner
(9) _0_ military

c. Did your father belong to one of these parties?
(0) _97_ none
(1) _41_ SED
(2) _5_ KPD
(3) _11_ SPD
(4) _5_ CDU
(5) _3_ NDPD
(6) _1_ LDPD
(7) _5_ DBD
(8) _25_ NSDAP (Nazi)
(9) _0_ DVP
(10) _1_ DNVP
(11) _0_ Zentrum
(12) _1_ DDP

d. What about his father?
(.) _92_ don't know
(0) _85_ none
(1) _5_ SED
(2) _3_ KPD
(3) _7_ SPD
(4) _1_ CDU
(5) _0_ NDPD
(6) _0_ LDPD
(7) _1_ DBD
(8) _7_ NSDAP (Nazi)
(9) _0_ DVP
(10) _1_ DNVP
(11) _0_ Zentrum
(12) _0_ DDP

F62a.* If you had the time to read a newspaper before the *Wende,* which paper did you read primarily?
(0) _10_ none
(1) _124_ local/regional paper
(2) _1_ *Nationale* (NDPD newspaper)
(3) _25_ *Junge Welt*
(4) _32_ *Neues Deutschland* (official SED organ)
(5) _3_ *Neue Zeit* (CDU)
(6) _3_ *Tribune* (FDGB)

b. Would you say that you were generally well, poorly, or averagely informed about events in the GDR and the world?
   (0)_17_ poorly informed
   (1)_42_ averagely
   (2)140 well informed
c. Did you listen to or watch Western broadcast media exclusively, regularly (but not exclusively), occasionally, or hardly ever if at all?
   (1)_45_ exclusively
   (2)113 regularly
   (3)_32_ occasionally
   (4)_11_ hardly ever

F63a. In an election before the *Wende*, did you ever vote against the unitary list of the National Front or did you ever purposely not go to vote?
   (0)139 No
   (1)_39_ Yes, voted against list (or certain candidates)
   (2)_22_ Yes, purposely avoided voting
b.* Why (not)?
   (0)_65_ scared, didn't want trouble at work
   (1)_32_ conformist
   (2)_3_ knew candidates, liked electoral system
   (3)_23_ in favour of political system
   (4)_12_ voting is a citizen's duty
   (5)_6_ wanted to reform the system
   (6)_46_ was opposed to system
   (7)_2_ protest, wanted something specific from state
   (8)_1_ didn't like certain candidate personally
   – *Once I didn't vote because I had moved and wasn't on the electoral list. I was very proud of that.*

F64a. What is the highest level of education you have achieved?
   (0)_23_ elementary
   (1)_14_ secondary
   (2)_40_ secondary and apprenticeship
   (3)_6_ 'Abitur'
   (4)_74_ post-secondary technical or vocational
   (5)_44_ university or equivalent
b. Were you able to complete the level of education you wanted to reach?
   (0)160 Yes (to F65)
   (1)_39_ No
c. Why not?
   (0)_11_ insufficient financial means, had to work
   (1)_2_ parents didn't want me to continue
   (2)_8_ not enough slots available
   (3)_4_ got children
   (4)_1_ got sent to jail
   (5)_2_ not allowed because of relations in West
   (6)_3_ not allowed because of bourgeois origins
   (7)_3_ not allowed because not member of FDJ

(8) _1_ didn't want to serve longer in military
(9) _1_ quit teacher training because I didn't want to have to lie to children

F65a. Did you perform military service in the National People's Army (NVA)?
    (0)_133_ No (to F65b)
    (1) _68_ Yes (to F65c)
  b.* Why not? (and on to F65e)
    (0)_110_ too old, too young, or female
    (1) _7_ health exemption
    (2) _3_ conscientious objector
    (3) _1_ in police
    (4) _1_ exempted as construction worker
    (5) _2_ exempted because of large age cohort
  c. Did you perform an extended service (beyond mandatory 18 months)?
    (0) _50_ No (to F65e)
    (1) _18_ Yes (to F65d)
  d.* Why?
    (0) _7_ professional soldier
    (1) _1_ for job training
    (2) _6_ to get a place in university
    (3) _3_ wanted to serve in specific service
    (4) _1_ thought it was fun
    – *I did extra service because I wanted to be in the border troops. At least there I knew everybody would be serious and I wouldn't have to live with a bunch of morons.*
  e. Did you belong to a Fighting Group [Kampfgruppe, militia] or (in the case of women) to the Civil Defence force?
    (0)_174_ No (to F66)
    (1) _27_ Yes
  f.* Why?
    (0) _6_ out of conviction/loyalty to party
    (1) _2_ required to at school
    (2) _2_ wanted extra pension
    (3) _2_ thought it was fun
    (4) _5_ didn't want to have to do army reserve service
    (5) _8_ job requirement
    (6) _1_ wanted training
    (7) _1_ somebody from my work brigade had to go

F66a. What is the approximate population of your city/town?
    (0) _9_ less than 300
    (1)_13_ 301 to 1000
    (2) _8_ 1001 to 2000
    (3)_20_ 2000 to 5000
    (4) _3_ 5000 to 10 000
    (5) _8_ 10 000 to 20 000
    (6)_22_ 20 000 to 50 000
    (7)_25_ 25 000 to 100 000

(8) _94_ over 100 000

b. (Economic character of town):
   (1) _30_ agricultural
   (2) _50_ light industry
   (3) _48_ heavy industry
   (4) _69_ tertiary
   (5) _5_ mixed

c. (Region):
   (1) _65_ south-central industrial region
   (2) _27_ Leipzig
   (3) _15_ southern Thuringia
   (4) _46_ Berlin and suburban Brandenburg
   (5) _46_ Inner Pomerania
   (6) _3_ other

F67. Did you have a private phone at home in 1989?
   (0) _95_ No
   (1)_107_ Yes

F68a. Did you have occasional or regular (and if regular, frequent) contact with friends or relatives in the FRG before the *Wende*?
   (0) _45_ No
   (1) _46_ Yes, occasionally
   (2) _42_ Yes, regularly
   (3) _68_ Yes, regularly and often

b. Which of the following was your closest or most important contact or relation in the FRG?
   (0) _24_ none
   (1) _24_ only distant relatives or friends
   (2) _19_ cousins, great uncles or great aunts
   (3) _34_ good friends
   (4) _60_ uncles, aunts, grandparents, grandchildren
   (5) _40_ siblings, parents, children
   (6) _0_ spouse, partners

F69.* How do you see your future now? What are your hopes and expectations?
   (0) _60_ negative, pessimistic response
   (1) _44_ mixed feelings
   (2) _86_ optimistic, positive

F70. For a last time, I'm going to ask you to pretend that our conversation was occurring two years ago, well before the *Wende*. Which of the following sentences would best describe your personal attitude towards socialism in the GDR?
   (1) _24_ I believed in socialism and contributed to its construction.
   (2) _14_ I would have been happier to live under socialism if the SED had brought in more democratic freedoms.
   (3) _64_ I accepted socialism as given and tried to make the best of it.
   (4) _39_ I was opposed to socialism but conformed with the system to avoid dangers for my family and myself.

(5) _2_ I hated the GDR and would have done almost anything to get out.

(6) _13_ I was fundamentally opposed to socialism and criticised it as much as possible.

(7) _6_ I was not interested in politics and lived my life without thinking about politics.

(8) _18_ I criticised real existing socialism as much as possible so that true socialism could develop in the GDR.

(9) _20_ [spontaneously offered response:] I initially believed in socialism and helped build it up (response 1) and then criticised the system so that true socialism might develop in the GDR (response 8).

F71. And as a last question: did you regret the disappearance of the GDR at all?

(0)_119_ No

(1) _83_ Yes

– *It was like emigrating without packing your bags.*

F72.* [Supplementary question posed to about a quarter of the respondents:] I am supposed to give a talk about my research to some American students next week [actually true when I first started asking the question]. If these students should learn only one thing about the GDR from my talk, what one thing would you like them to know?

– *It wasn't a nightmare.*

Notes

1 WHO OVERTHREW HONECKER

1. George Kennan (1951: 120–5), the father of American containment policy, actually did foresee the Soviet Union's collapse from within, though in a shorter period than 40 years. Problems of uneven economic development, political succession, and societal disorganisation meant that 'Soviet power, like the capitalist world of its conception, bears within it the seeds of its own decay, and that the sprouting of these seeds is well advanced.'

2. I experimented with offering potential respondents a 20 D-Mark cash incentive for participation but found that the mention of money only awakened suspicion among people who were just beginning to be bombarded with direct-mail advertising, sweepstakes and 'free' samples. Favourable response rates varied by time (with a low of 10 per cent during the Gulf War) and by region (with a high of 50 per cent in Greifswald) for an average participation rate of about 20 per cent.

3. I have often heard the following critique of my methodology and the generalisations it generated: 'Well, the East Germans I know don't think and act the way you say.' This objection is no doubt valid; the East Germans in my sample contradicted each other in many ways. Nonetheless, the generalisations I make in this book, though illustrated with individual anecdotes, are based on a systematic (and ongoing) dialogue with over 200 not atypical East Germans. I am of course happy to consider counter-arguments and examples based on comparable or better samples. A more egregious critique I have had to suffer has been: 'You didn't need to interview 200 people to draw that (banal) conclusion.' While many of my findings are indeed not always entirely original or counter-intuitive, I have never known the empirical confirmation of longstanding or previously unsubstantiable assumptions to be a scientific vice.

2 BEHIND THE WALL: THE EAST GERMAN *SONDERFALLE*

1. For good general histories of the GDR see Dennis (1988) and McCauley (1983) in English and Weber (1990) in German. Leonhard (1990) provides an interesting overview of GDR history in the form of an anthology of personal commentaries and reports, while Neumann (1991) recounts GDR history from the perspective of the party and its progressive perversion of Marxist idealism. The opening of archives in Berlin and Moscow has of course allowed and necessitated a re-examination of GDR history, though for the present overview the general histories cited here are adequate and I draw on them for basic factual information.

3 POPULAR EXPLANATIONS OF THE POPULAR REVOLUTION

1. See Appendix for an English translation of the survey questionnaire, including results.
2. In a regression model including the variables F68a, F37a, and F62c, all three independent variables had significant *t*-values, but the corrected *r*-squared for the model was only 0.13. See Chapter 5 for a more complete statistical analysis of survey results.
3. Interview with Dr Bernd Lindner, sociologist at the former Zentralinstitut für Jugendforschung (Leipzig), 27 May 1991.
4. In a survey conducted in early March 1990 and reported in the *Frankfurter Allgemeine Zeitung* of 23 March 1990, Elizabeth Noelle-Neumann found that 60 per cent of East Germans believed that socialism had not failed but rather that incompetent politicians had ruined it.
5. In a cross-tabulation, gamma = 0.52 and *p* = 0.0004.
6. Förster and Roski (1990: 161) estimate that the initial core of demonstration participants in Leipzig were workers and employees aged 25 to 55. Students were not an important mobilising force as in Czechoslovakia (cf. Urban, 1990), and teenagers and children, according to one study, experienced the *Wende* as objects and not subjects of history (cf. Lindner, 1992).
7. In a cross-tabulation, 63 per cent of those Berlin respondents whose economic situation had improved went to demonstrate as compared to 34 per cent whose situation was stable or had deteriorated (gamma = 0.54, *p* = 0.08, *n* = 46).
8. Finding presented by Karl-Dieter Opp during a guest lecture at the Université de Montréal, 2 April 1992.
9. In a cross-tabulation, 62 per cent of those who had a friend emigrate participated in demonstrations as compared to only 28 per cent who had not (gamma = 0.61, *p* = 0.000003, *n* = 200).

4 THE MODEST GERMANS: THE CULTURAL CONTEXT OF MASS MOBILISATION

1. The particularly paranoid character of East German élite political culture that Leonhard (1955) revealed has received confirmation with the recent publication of various leaders' memoirs and of studies of the Politburo (cf. Krenz, 1990; Andert and Herzberg, 1990; Schabowski, 1990; Kirschey, 1990; Przybylski, 1991).
2. When I write here of 'the East Germans', I do not of course wish to imply a uniformity of behaviour and attitudes among GDR citizens but am referring to common traits or tendencies that emerged from my survey interviews.
3. Writing in the early 1980s, Gaus naturally stressed historical continuity since at that time the East German state was seeking popular legitimacy through a revival of the Prussian heritage. In fact, throughout its history the GDR – from its creation of a goose-stepping National People's Army in 1955 to its celebration of Luther in 1983 – drew

on Prussian authoritarian traditions (cf. Chapter 2).

4. A few of the *Neues Deutschland* subscribers in my survey sample said they read it avidly in order to know which slogans they should utter the next time they had to speak at some mandatory political meeting.

5. The East German author Landolf Scherzer (1989: 107), in his book-length study of the daily routine and functions of a county first party secretary offers an insight into the relatively minor level of material corruption that offended East German egalitarianism. When he visits the party secretary's standard prefabricated apartment, Scherzer is surprised not to discover any Western toiletry products in the bathroom and uses this incident to build up his portrait of the secretary as a particularly honest, praiseworthy politician.

5 DIFFERENT STROKES FOR DIFFERENT *VOLKS*

1. Numerous commentators have of course identified this contradiction as the source of the psychological energy behind the Eastern European revolutions (cf. Kuran, 1991; Di Palma, 1991; Bunce and Chong, 1990). Most base themselves on Havel's classic formulation 'living in [public] lies' vs 'living in [private] truth' in 'The Power of the Powerless' (1978).

2. The respondents were asked to pick the one sentence among the following that best expressed their posture towards the anti-government protests leading up to the fall of the Wall:

   (1) I thought the demonstrations were stupid and wouldn't have gone (joined them) under any circumstances.

   (2) I agreed with some of what the demonstrators wanted but wouldn't have gone myself.

   (3) I was completely in favour of the demonstrations but unfortunately couldn't go myself.

   (4) I participated in one or two demonstrations.

   (5) I regularly went to demonstrate.

   (6) I helped organise one or more demonstrations.

   (7) I gave a speech at one or more demonstrations.

6 THE CULTURAL LEGACY OF COMMUNISM

1. The term *Wende* had several immediate origins in the autumn of 1989. Egon Krenz used the expression to describe and to legitimate his breaking with Honecker's policies after 18 October. Some East Germans also embraced the ideologically less-charged term *Wende* in conversation because they did not know what their interlocutors' opinion of the revolutionary events were. Whatever the precise origins of the term, its nearly universal adoption signalled a retreat from the revolutionary aspirations of the early autumn of 1989.

Select Bibliography

Almond, Gabriel and Sidney Verba (1963). *The Civic Culture: Political Attitudes and Democracy in Five Nations* (Princeton, NJ: Princeton University Press).

——(eds) (1980). *The Civic Culture Revisited* (Boston: Little, Brown).

·Andert, Reinhold and Wolfgang Herzberg (1990). *Der Sturz* (Berlin: Aufbau-Verlag).

Arendt, Hannah (1951). *The Origins of Totalitarianism* (New York: Harcourt, Brace).

Asmus, Roland (1984). 'The GDR and Martin Luther,' *Survey*, v. 28, no. 3 (Autumn).

Bajohr, Walter (ed.) (1992). *Das Erbe der Diktatur* (Bonn: Bouvier).

Bauer-Kaase, Petra (1993). 'A Political System after the Shock: The Impact of Unification on the Fabric of Political Orientations in Germany.' Paper presented to American Political Science Association Annual Meeting, Washington, DC, 2–5 September.

Bensing, Manfred (1984). 'Erbe und Tradition in der Geschichte der Deutschen Demokratischen Republik,' *Zeitschrift für Geschichtswissenschaft*, v. 32, no. 10.

Blanke, Thomas and Rainer Erd (eds) (1990). *DDR – Ein Staat Vergeht* (Frankfurt/M.: Fischer Taschenbuch Verlag).

Böhme, Irene (1982). *Die da druben: Sieben Kapitel DDR* (Berlin: Rotbuch Verlag).

Borchers, Andreas (1992). *Neue Nazis im Osten: Hintergründe und Fakten* (Weinheim: Beltz Verlag).

Brie, Michael and Dieter Klein (eds) (1991). *Umbruch zur Moderne?* (Hamburg: VSA-Verlag).

Brzezinski, Zbigniew and Samuel P. Huntington (1964). *Political Power: U.S.A./U.S.S.R.* (London: Chatto & Windus).

Brown, Archie (1984). *Political Culture and Communist Studies* (London: Macmillan).

—— and Jack Gray, (eds) (1977). *Political Culture and Political Change in Communist States* (London: Macmillan).

Brubaker, Rogers (1990). 'Frontier Theses: Exit, Voice, and Loyalty in East Germany,' *Migration World Magazine*, v. 18, no. 3–4.

Bunce, Valerie and Dennis Chong (1990). 'The Party's Over: Mass Protest and the End of Communist Rule in Eastern Europe.' Paper presented to American Political Science Association Annual Meeting, San Francisco, 30 August – 2 September.

Bürgerkomitee Leipzig (1991). *Stasi Intern: Macht und Banalität* (Leipzig: Forum Verlag).

Bussiek, Hendrik (1979). *Notizen aus der DDR: Erlebnisse, Erfahrungen, Erkentnisse in der unbekannten deutschen Republik* (Frankfurt/M.: Fischer Taschenbuch Verlag).

Dahrendorf, Ralf (1967). *Society and Democracy in Germany* (New York: W.W. Norton).

Davies, James C. (1962). 'Toward a Theory of Revolution', *American Sociological Review*, v. 27.

Dennis, Mike (1988). *German Democratic Republic: Politics, Economy and Society* (London: Pinter).

——(1984). 'The Red Robots are Here,' *GDR Monitor*, no. 12 (Winter).

Di Palma, Giuseppe (1991). 'Legitimation from the Top to Civil Society: Politico-Cultural Change in Eastern Europe,' *World Politics*, v. 44, no. 1 (October).

Dittrich, Gottfried (1982). 'Zur Geschichte der DDR als Nationalgeschichte,' *Zeitschrift für Geschichtswissenschaft*, v. 30, no. 8.

Dönhoff, Marion Gräfin, Rudolf Leonhardt and Theo Sommer (1964). *Reise in ein fernes Land: Bericht über Kultur, Wirtschaft, und Politik in der DDR* (Hamburg: Nannen-Verlag).

Drach, Marcel (1990). *La crise dans les pays de l'Est* (Paris: La Découverte).

Drieschner, Frank (1993). 'Gestiefelte Schwäche,' *Die Zeit*, no. 32 (13 August).

Durkheim, Emile (1930). *Le Suicide.* (Paris: Presses Universitaires de France).

Eckart, Gabriele (1984). *So sehe ick die Sache: Protokolle aus der DDR* (Cologne: Kiepenheuer & Witsch).

Ekiert, Grzegorz (1990). 'Transitions from State-Socialism in Eastern Europe,' *States and Social Structures Newsletter*, no. 12 (Winter).

—— (1991). 'Democratization Processes in East Central Europe: A Theoretical Reconsideration,' *British Journal of Political Science*, no. 21 (July).

Ernst, Anna-Sabine (1989). 'Von der Bekleidungskultur zur Mode,' in Wehling (1989).

Falter, Jürgen and Siegfried Schumann (1993). 'The Mass Basis of the Extreme Right in Europe in a Comparative Perspective.' Paper presented to American Political Science Association Annual Meeting, Washington, DC, 2–5 September.

Ferree, Myra Marx and Brigitte Young (1993). 'Three Steps Back for Women: German Unification, Gender, and University "Reform",' *PS: Political Science and Politics*, v. 26, no. 1 (June).

Filmer, Werner and Heribert Schwan (1985). *Das andere Deutschland: Alltag in der DDR* (Düsseldorf: Goldman).

Förster, Peter and Günter Roski (1990). *DDR zwischen Wende und Wahl: Meinungsforscher analysieren den Umbruch* (Berlin: Links Druck).

Friedrich, Carl J. and Zbigniew Brzezinski (1956). *Totalitarian Dictatorship and Autocracy* (Cambridge, MA: Harvard University Press).

——, Michael Curtis, and Benjamin R. Barber (1969). *Totalitarianism in Perspective: Three Views* (New York: Praeger Publishers).

Garton Ash, Timothy (1990). *We the People* (London: Granta Books).

Gati, Charles (1990). *The Bloc that Failed* (Indianapolis: Indiana University Press).

Gauck, Joachim (1991). *Die Stasi-Akten: Das unheimliche Erbe der DDR* (Reinbek: Rowohlt).

Gaus, Günter (1983). *Wo Deutschland liegt* (Hamburg: Hoffmann und Campe).

Gedmin, Jeffrey (1992). *The Hidden Hand: Gorbachev and the Collapse of East Germany* (Washington, DC: The AEI Press).

Gensicke, Thomas (1992). 'Mentalitätsentwicklungen im Osten Deutschlands seit den 70er Jahren,' *Speyerer Forschungsberichte* No. 109 (Speyer: Forschungsinstitut für Öffentliche Verwaltung).

—— (1991). 'Sind die Ostdeutschen konservativer als die Westdeutschen?' in Reßig and Glaeßner (1991).

Geertz, Clifford (1973). *The Interpretation of Cultures* (New York: Basic Books).

Gibowski, Wolfgang and Matthias Jung (1993). 'System Support and Economic Change.' Paper presented to American Political Science Association Annual Meeting, Washington, DC, 2–5 September.

Goeckel, Fobert F. (1990). *The Lutheran Church and the East German State* (Ithaca, NY: Cornell University Press).

Gräbner, Wolf-Jürgen, Christiane Heinze, Detleff Pollack, (eds) (1990). *Leipzig im Oktober: Kirchen und alternative Gruppen im Umbruch der DDR* (Berlin: Wichern).

Green, Donald and Ian Shapiro (1994). *Pathologies of Rational Choice Theory: A Critique of Applications in Political Science* (New Haven, CT: Yale University Press).

Grew, Raymond (1962). 'How Success Spoiled the Risorgimento,' *Journal of Modern History*, v. 34, no. 3 (September).

Grunenberg, Antonia (1990a). *Aufbruch der Inneren Mauer: Politik und Kultur in der DDR, 1971–1990* (Bremen: Edition Temmen).

——. (1990b) "Ich finde mich überhaupt nicht mehr zurecht": Thesen zur Krise in der DDR-Gesellschaft' in Blanke and Erd (1990).

Gurr, Ted Robert (1970). *Why Men Rebel* (Princeton, NJ: Princeton University Press).

Habermas, Jürgen (1990). *Die nachholende Revolution* (Frankfurt/M: Suhrkamp Verlag).

—— (1992). 'Die zweite Lebenslüge der Bundesrepublik: Wir sind wieder "normal" geworden,' *Die Zeit*, no. 51 (18 December).

Hahn, Reinhardt (1990). *Ausgedient: Ein Stasi-Major Erzählt* (Halle: Mitteldeutscher Verlag).

Häuser, Iris (1989). "Wir wollen immer artig sein, denn nur so hat man uns gern": Jugendpolitik und das Verhältnis Jugendlicher zu Politik und Gesellschaft,' in Wehling (1989).

Havel, Vaclav (1978). 'Le pouvoir des sans-pouvoir,' in Havel (1989).

—— (1989). *Essais politiques* (Paris: Seuil).

Henkys, Reinhard (1990). 'Die Kirchen im Umbruch der DDR,' in Gräbner *et al.* (1990).

Henrich, Rolf (1989). *Der Vormundschaftliche Staat* (Reinbek: Rowohlt).

Hirsch, Kurt and Peter Heim (1991). *Von links nach rechts: Rechtsradikale Aktivitäten in den neuen Bundesländern* (Munich: Goldmann Verlag).

Hirschmann, Albert O. (1993). 'Exit, Voice, and the Fate of the German Democratic Republic: An Essay in Conceptual History,' *World Politics*, v. 45, no. 2 (January).

—— (1970). *Exit, Voice, and Loyalty* (Cambridge, MA: Harvard University Press).

Huntington, Samuel P. (1968). *Political Order in Changing Societies* (New Haven, CT: Yale University Press).
—— (1984). 'Will More Countries Become Democratic?' *Political Science Quarterly*, v. 99, no. 2 (Summer).
Israel, Jürgen (1991). *Zur Freiheit Berufen: Die Kirche in der DDR als Schutzraum der Opposition* (Berlin: Aufbau Taschenbuch Verlag).
Janos, Andrew C. (1991). 'Social Science, Communism, and the Dynamics of Political Change,' *World Politics*, v. 44, no. 1 (October).
Johnson, Chalmers (1966). *Revolutionary Change* (Boston: Little, Brown).
Jowitt, Kenneth (1983). 'Soviet Neo-Traditionalism: The Political Concept of a Leninist Regime,' *Soviet Studies*, v. 35 (July).
—— (1992). *The New World Disorder* (Berkeley: University of California Press).
Keane, John (ed.) (1988). *Civil Society and the State* (London: Verso, 1988).
Kennan, George (1951). *American Diplomacy, 1900–1950* (Chicago: University of Chicago Press).
Kirschey, Peter (1990). *Wandlitz Waldsiedlung: Die geschlossene Gesellschaft* (Berlin: Dietz).
Klier, Freya (1990). *Lüg Vaterland: Erziehung in der DDR* (München: Kindler Verlag).
Koch, Thomas (1992). '"Hier ändert sich nie was!" Kontinuitäten, Krisen und Brüche ostdeutscher Identität(en) im Spannungsfeld zwischen "schöpferischen Zerstörung" und nationaler Re-Integration,' in Thomas (1992).
—— (1993). 'Die Ostdeutschen zwischen Einheitsschock und "doppeltem Zukunftshorizont",' in Reißig (1993).
Krenz, Egon (1990). *Wenn Mauern Fallen* (Vienna: Neff Verlag).
Krieger, Leonard (1957). *The German Idea of Freedom* (Boston: Beacon Press).
Krisch, Henry (1993). 'Constitutions as Reflections of Political Change: Eastern and All-German Constitutional Debates'. Paper presented to the American Political Science Association Annual Meeting, Washington, DC, 2–5 September.
—— (1978). 'Official Nationalism,' in Legters (1978).
—— (1988). *Politics and Culture in the German Democratic Republic* (Ann Arbor: University of Michigan Press).
Kroh, Ferdinand (ed.) (1988). *»Freiheit ist immer nur Freiheit...«: Die Andersdenkenden in der DDR* (Frankfurt/M.: Ullstein).
Kuechler, Manfred (1993). 'The Germans and 'Others': Racism, Xenophobia, or Self-Defense?' Paper presented to American Political Science Association Annual Meeting, Washington, DC, 2–5 September.
Kuran, Timur (1991). 'Now Out of Never: The Element of Surprise in the East European Revolution of 1989,' *World Politics*, v. 44, no. 1 (October).
Labelle, Jean-François (1992). 'Culture politique en RDA: duplicité du système de valeurs et appartenance à la civilisation occidentale,' master's thesis, Université de Montréal.
Le Gloannec, Anne-Marie (1989). *La nation orpheline* (Paris: Calmann-Lévy).
—— (1991). 'L'Allemagne: reconstruction d'une nation,' *Pouvoirs*, no. 57.

—— (1993). 'Y a-t-il un nationalisme allemand,' *Hérodote*, no. 68 (January–March).

Lemke, Christiane (1991). *Die Ursachen des Umbruchs 1989: Politische Sozialisation in der ehemaligen DDR* (Opladen: Westdeutscher Verlag).

—— (1989). 'Eine politische Doppelkultur,' in Wehling (1989).

Legters, Lyman H. (ed.) (1978). *The German Democratic Republic: A Developed Socialist Society* (Boulder, CO: Westview).

—— (1978). 'Introduction: The GDR in Perspective,' in Legters (ed.) (1978).

Leonhard, Wolfgang (1955). *Die Revolution Entläßt ihre Kinder* (Cologne: Kiepenheuer & Witsch).

—— (1990). *Das kurze Leben der DDR* (Stuttgart: Deutsche Verlags-Anstalt).

Lewis, P. G. (ed.) (1984). *Eastern Europe: Political Crisis and Legitimation* (London: Croom Helm).

Liebsch, Heike (1991). *Dresdner Stundenbuch: Protokoll einer Beteiligten im Herbst 1989* (Wuppertal: Peter Hammer Verlag).

Lindner, Bernd (1992). 'Kulturelle Dimensionen biographischer Wenden: Leipzig – Herbst 89,' *Kultursoziologie*, no. 3.

Loest, Erich (1991). *Die Stasi war mein Eckermann* (Göttingen: Steidl Verlag).

Ludz, Peter (1970). *The German Democratic Republic from the Sixties to the Seventies* (Cambridge: Harvard University Center for International Affairs).

—— (1977). *Die DDR zwischen Ost und West.* (Munich: C. H. Beck).

—— (1968). *Parteielite im Wandel* (Opladen: Westdeutscher Verlag).

Maier, Charles (1988). *The Unmasterable Past: History, Holocaust, and German National Identity* (Cambridge, MA: Harvard University Press).

——(1991). 'Why did Communism Collapse in 1989?' Program on Central and Eastern Europe Working Paper Series #7 (Cambridge, MA: Harvard University Center for European Studies).

Maaz, Hans-Joachim (1990). *Der Gefühlsstau: Ein Psychogramm der DDR.* (Berlin: Argon).

—— (1991). *Das Gestürzte Volk.* (Berlin: Argon).

Marcuse, Peter (1990). *A German Way of Revolution* (Berlin: Dietz).

Marx, Karl and Friedrich Engels (1848). *The Communist Manifesto.*

McCauley, Martin (1983). *The German Democratic Republic since 1945* (London: Macmillan).

McFalls, Laurence (1992). *Revolution und Alltag: Ein ostdeutscher Fragebogen,* manuscript awaiting publication.

—— (1992b). 'The Modest Germans: Towards an Understanding of the East German Revolution', *German Politics and Society*, no. 26 (Summer).

—— (1993). 'Une Allemagne, deux sociétés distinctes: les causes et conséquences culturelles de la réunification', *Revue canadienne de science politique*, v. 26, no. 4 (December).

Menge, Marlies (1990). *»Ohne uns läuft nichts mehr«: Die Revolution in der DDR* (Stuttgart: Deutsche Verlags-Anstalt).

Meyer, Gerd (1989). 'Der versorgte Mensch: Sozialistischer Paternalismus: bürokratische Bevormundung und soziale Sicherheit,' in Wehling (1989).

Minkenberg, Michael (1993). 'The Far Right in Unified Germany.' Paper presented to American Political Science Association Annual

Meeting, Washington, DC, 2–5 September.

Moore, Barrington, Jr. (1966). *Social Origins of Dictatorship and Democracy.* (Boston: Beacon).

Naumann, Gerhard and Eckhard Trümpler (1991). *Der Flop mit der DDR-Nation 1971* (Berlin: Dietz).

Neuhäußer-Wespy, Ulrich (1983). 'Von der Urgesellschaft bis zur SED: Anmerkungen zur "Nationalgeschichte der DDR"', *Deutschland Archiv,* v. 16, no. 2 (February).

Neumann, Thomas (1991). *Die Maßnahme: Eine Herrschaftsgeschichte der SED* (Reinbek: Rowohlt).

Niethamer, Lutz (1991). *Die volkseigene Erfahrung: Eine Archäologie des Lebens in der Inudstrierprovinz der DDR* (Berlin: Rowohlt).

Noelle-Neumann, Elisabeth (1991). *Demoskopische Geschichtsstunde: Vom Wartesaal der Geschichte zur Deutschen Einheit.* (Zürich: Edition Interfrom).

Offe, Claus (1983). 'Competitive Party Democracy and the Keynesian Welfare State: Factors of Stability and Disorganization,' *Policy Sciences,* no. 15.

Opp, Karl-Dieter (1991). 'DDR '89: Zu den Ursachen einer spontanen Revolution,' *Kölner Zeitschrift für Soziologie und Sozialpsychologie,* v. 43, no. 2 (April).

—— and Christiane Gern (1992). 'Dissident Groups, Personal Networks, and Spontaneous Cooperation: The East German Revolution of 1989,' unpublished manuscript.

—— and Peter Voß (1993). *Die volkseigene Revolution* (Stuttgart: Klett-Cotta).

Opp de Hipt, Manfred (1989). 'Deutsche Lust am Staat? Marxistisch-leninistisches Staatsverständnis und realsozialistische Wirklichkeit in der DDR,' in Wehling (1989).

Pakulski, Jan (1986). 'Bureaucracy and the Soviet System,' *Studies in Comparative Communism,* v. 19 (Spring).

—— (1990). 'Eastern Europe and "Legitimacy Crisis",' *Australian Journal of Political Science,* v. 25.

Philipsen, Dirk (1993). *We Were the People: Voices from East Germany's Revolutionary Autumn of 1989* (Durham, NC: Duke University Press).

Pickel, Andreas (1992). *The Survival and Revival of Entrepreneurship in the GDR* (Boulder, CO: Westview Press).

Polanyi, Karl (1944). *The Great Transformation* (Boston: Beacon Press).

Pollack, Detleff (1990). 'Ursachen des gesellschaftlichen Umbruchs in der DDR aus systemtheoretischer Perspektive,' in Gräbner *et al.* (1990).

Porsch, B. and M. Abraham (1991). 'Die Revolution in der DDR: Eine strukturell-individualistische Erklärungsskizze,' *Kölner Zeitschrift für Soziologie und Sozialpsychologie,* v. 43, no. 2 (April).

Poznanski, Kazimierz (1991). 'The Decline of Communism, Rise of Capitalism, and Transformation of East European and Soviet Political Economics,' Program on Central and Eastern Europe Working Paper Series #15, Center for European Studies, Harvard University.

Prins, Gwyn (ed.) (1990). *Spring in Winter: The 1989 Revolutions* (Manchester: Manchester University Press).

Przybylski, Peter (1991). *Tatort Politbüro: Die Akte Honecker* (Berlin: Rowohlt).

Rein, Gerhard (1990). *Die Protestantische Revolution* (Berlin: Wichern Verlag).

Reißig, Rolf (1991). 'Der Umbruch in der DDR und das Scheitern des "realen Sozialismus"' in Reißig and Glaeßner (1991).

—— and Gert-Joachim Glaeßner (1991). *Das Ende eines Experiments* (Berlin: Dietz Verlag).

Riecker, Ariane, Annet Schwarz, and Dirk Schneider (1990). *Stasi Intim: Gespräche mit ehemaligen MfS-Angehörigen* (Leipzig: Forum Verlag).

Rigby, T. H., A. Brown and P. Reddaway, (eds) (1980). *Authority, Power and Policy in the USSR* (London: Macmillan).

Rigby, T. H. and Ferenc Feher (eds) (1982). *Political Legitimation in Communist States* (London: Macmillan).

Roegele, Otto B. (1992). 'Jugendweihe – Ein Ritus in alter Regie – die Jugendweihe überlebt', in Bajohr (1992).

Roth, Dieter K. (1993). 'Wandel der Politischen Einstellungen seit der Bundestagswahl 1990,' *German Studies Review,* v. 16, no. 2 (May).

Rupnik, Jacques (1990). *L'autre Europe* (Paris: Éditions Odile Jacob).

Schabowski, Günter (1990). *Das Politburo* (Reinbek bei Hamburg: Rowohlt).

Scherzer, Landolf (1989). *Der Erste: Eine Reportage aus der DDR* (Cologne: Kiepenheuer & Witsch).

Schmidt, Hartwig (1991). 'Wertewandel in einheimischen und westlichen Lebenswelten: Sozialphilosophische Nachforschungen' in Reißig and Glaeßner (1991).

Schüddekopf, Charles (ed.) (1990). *Wir Sind Das Volk: Flugschriften, Aufrufe und Texte einer Deutschen Revolution* (Reinbek bei Hamburg: Rowohlt).

Schulz, Eberhard (1982). 'Die deutsche Nation in Europa,' *Deutschland Archiv,* v. 15, no. 5 (May).

Schweigler, Gebhard (1975). *National Consciousness in Divided Germany* (London: Sage Publications).

Shils, E. A. and H. Finch (eds) (1949) *The Methodology of the Social Sciences* (New York: Free Press).

Skocpol, Theda (1979). *States and Social Revolutions* (Cambridge: Cambridge University Press).

Smith, Gordon (1991). 'The German Constitution: A Changing National and European Context' in Wildenmann (1991).

Smith, Jean E. (1967). *Germany Beyond the Wall: People, Politics . . . and Prosperity* (Boston: Little, Brown).

Sontheimer, Kurt (1990). *Deutschlands Politische Kultur* (Munich: R. Piper).

Spengler, Oswald (1967). *Selected Essays* (New York: Henry Regnery Co.).

Starrels, John M. and Anita M. Mallinkrodt (1975). *Politics in the German Democratic Republic* (New York: Praeger).

Stassen, Manfred (1993). 'Ost-West-deutsche Befindlichkeiten: Identitätsmythos und die Zukunft der deutschen Teilung,' paper presented to 'Die Nation: Zwischen Traum und Trauma,' Interdisciplinary Symposium, Université de Montréal, 22–25 April.

Steele, Jonathan (1977). *Socialism with a German Face: The State that Came in from the Cold* (London: Jonathan Cape).

Stock, Ulrich (1992). 'Knüppel gegen Krüppel,' *Die Zeit,* no. 49 (4 December).

Strassel, Christophe (1993). 'Bonn-Berlin: une capitale pour quelle nation?' *Hérodote,* no. 68 (January–March).

Sur, Etienne (1993). 'A propos de l'extrême droite en Allemagne: de la conception ethnique de la nation allemande,' *Hérodote*, no. 68 (January–March).

Süß, Walter (1993). 'Wahrnehmung und Interpretation des Rechtsextremismus in der DDR durch das MfS,' *Deutschland Archiv*, v. 26, no. 4 (April).

Thaa, Winfried (1992). 'The Implosion of a Goal-Rational System: Causes and Consequences'. Paper presented to GDRSA Triennial Conference, Washington, DC, 12–15 November.

Thaysen, Uwe (1993). 'A New Constitution for Germany?', *German Studies Review*, v. 16, no. 2 (May).

Thibaud, Paul (1989). 'Comment se décomposent les communismes?' *Esprit*, no. 155 (October).

Thomaneck, J. K. A. and James Mellis (eds) (1989). *Politics, Society and Government in the German Democratic Republic: Basic Documents* (Oxford: Berg Publishers).

Thomas, Michael (1992). *Abbruch und Aufbruch: Sozialwissenschaften im Transformationsprozess* (Berlin: Akademie Verlag).

Tilly, Charles (1984). *Big Structures, Large Processes, Huge Comparisons* (Beverly Hills, CA: Russell Sage Foundation).

Touraine, Alain, François Dubet, Zsuzsa Hegdus, and Michel Wieviorka (1981). *Le pays contre l'état: luttes occitanes* (Paris: Editions du Seuil).

—— (1983). *Solidarity: The Analysis of a Social Movement.* (New York: Cambridge University Press).

Tournadre, Jean-François (1993). 'Extrême droite, nationalisme et problèmes d'identité dans l'ex-RDA,' *Hérodote*, no. 68 (January–March).

Urban, Jan (1990). 'Czechoslovakia: The Power and Politics of Humiliation,' in Prins (1990).

Veen, Hans-Joachim (1993). 'Political Priorities and Elements of National Identity in East and West.' Paper presented to American Political Science Association Annual Meeting, Washington, DC, 2–5 September.

Voigt, Dieter, Hannelore Belitz-Demeriz, and Sabine Meck (1990). 'Die innnerdeutsche Wanderung und der Vereinigungsprozess: Soziodemographische Struktur und Einstellungen von Flüchtlingen/Übersiedlern aus der DDR vor und nach der Grenzöffnung,' *Deutschland Archiv*, v. 23, no. 5 (May).

Volkmer, Werner (1984). 'Political Culture and the Nation in the GDR,' *GDR Monitor*, no. 11 (Summer).

Wawrzyn, Lienhard (1990). *Der Blaue: Das Spitzelsystem der DDR* (Berlin: Wagenbach).

Weber, Hermann (1990). *DDR: Grundriß der Geschichte, 1945–90* (Hannover: Fackelträger).

Weber, Max (1949 [1904]). '"Objectivity" in Social Science' in Shils and Finch (1949).

—— (1958 [1920]). *The Protestant Ethic and the Spirit of Capitalism* (New York: Scribner's).

—— (1947). *The Theory of Social and Economic Organisation* (London: Hodge).

Wehling, Hans-Georg (ed.) (1989). *Politische Kultur in der DDR* (Stuttgart: W. Kohlhammer).

Weidenfeld, Werner (1992). 'Identität,' in Weidenfeld and Korte (1992).

Weidenfeld, Werner and Karl-Rudolf Korte (1991). *Die Deutschen – Profil einer Nation* (Stuttgart: Klett-Cotta).

—— (eds) (1992). *Handbuch der Deutschen Einheit* (Bonn: Bundeszentrale für politische Bildung).

Welsh, Helga A. (1993). 'Germany: A Multicultural Society, Issues of Assimilation and Integration.' Paper presented to American Political Science Association Annual Meeting, Washington, DC, 2–5 September.

Wildenmann, Rudolf (ed.) (1991). *Nation und Demokratie: Politischstrukturelle Gestaltungs probleme im neuen Deutschland* (Baden-Baden: Nomos Verlagsgesellschaft).

Wilkening, Christina (1990). *Staat im Staate: Auskünfte ehemaliger Stasi-Mitarbeiter* (Berlin: Aufbau Verlag).

Winkler, Gunnar (ed.) (1990). *Sozialreport '90: Daten und Fakten zur sozialen Lage in der DDR* (Berlin: Verlag Die Wirtschaft).

Woderich, Rudolf (1992). 'Mentalitäten zwischen Anpassung und Eigensinn,' *Deutschland Archiv*, v. 25, no. 1 (January).

Yoder, Jennifer (1993). 'The Renewed Salience of East German Identity after Unification.' Paper presented to American Political Science Association Annual Meeting, Washington, DC, 2–5 September.

Index